Owen

Planning Theory for Practitioners

Michael P. Brooks, AICP

D0904352

PLANNERS PRESS
AMERICAN PLANNING ASSOCIATION
Chicago, Illinois
Washington, D.C.

Contents

Preface 5

Part 1 Introduction

1. **Planning Practice and Political Power**   9
    Public Planning 9
    Planning and Political Power 13

2. **Planning Practice and Planning Theory**   21
    The Uses of Theory in Planning 21
    Is There a Theory-Practice Gap? 25
    Planning Theory Today 28

Part 2 Foundations of Public Planning

3. **Running the Gauntlet of Planning Critics**   35
    Planning Is Perilous 36
    Planning Is Impossible 37
    Planning Is Impotent 39
    Planning Is Malevolent 42
    Planning Is Unconstitutional 43
    Planning Is... Alive and Well 47

4. **Rationales for Public Planning**   50
    The Search for Planning's Bedrock 50
    The Public Interest: Real or Illusory? 53
    Conclusions 58

5. **The Critical Role of Values and Ethics**   62
    Values 62
    Ethics 67
    Conclusions 75

Part 3 Alternative Paradigms for Public Planning Introduction

6. **Centralized Rationality: The Planner as Applied Scientist** 81
    The Nature of Rationality 81
    Rationality-Based Planning Strategies 87
    The Latest Contender: Strategic Planning 89
    Current Status of the Rationality Concept 91

7. **Centralized Non-Rationality: The Planner Confronts Politics** 97

Simon Says "Satisfice" 97

Incrementalism 99

Current Status of Incrementalism 101

8. **Decentralized Rationality: The Planner as Political Activist** 107

Advocacy Planning 107

Current Status of Advocacy Planning 114

9. **Decentralized Non-Rationality: The Planner as Communicator** 119

Postmodernism 119

Planning as Communicative Action 121

Implications for Practice 123

Current Status of the Communicative Action Concept 125

Part 4 Toward a More Practical Strategy
Introduction

10. **Setting the Stage: Ideas, Feedback, Goals—and Trial Balloons** 139

Where Do Planning Ideas Come From? 139

The Critical Role of Feedback 144

Formulating Workable Goals: Easier Said Than Done 145

The Benefits of Creative Trial Ballooning 153

11. **The Feedback Strategy of Public Planning** 158

Planning as Social Experimentation 158

The Habits of Effective Planners 160

The Feedback Strategy 161

How the Feedback Strategy Relates to Other Paradigms 176

Potential Shortcomings of the Feedback Strategy 178

Part 5 Effective Planning in a Political Milieu

12. **The Politically Savvy Planner** 185

The Nature of Political Savvy 185

The Elements of Political Savvy 188

13. **Vision** 196

The Importance of Vision 196

How to Be a Visionary—and Keep Your Job 201

References 205

Index 213

Preface

This book is intended primarily for two audiences: those who currently practice in the planning profession, and those who intend to do so in the future—that is, students in planning degree programs. The book deals with two topics that tend to be viewed with trepidation by those two audiences: theory and politics. (If several readers should reach this point in the book simultaneously, the collective shudder would probably be audible.)

The book is first and foremost about the relationship between planning practice and planning theory. The take on theory, however, is decidedly applied—that is, the book deals with a number of issues central to the planning theory literature, but focuses on the ways in which those issues affect the role performance of professional planners. Planning theory, I will argue, is extremely important to the profession's sense of identity and purpose, and thus should not be ignored. If it is to engage the attention of practitioners, however, it must speak to the issues and challenges they encounter on a daily basis—and that, too, is a major purpose of this book.

The book is also about the relationship between planning and politics. I will argue that planners need not be fearful of, or dismayed by, the political processes that they frequently encounter—that in fact there are ways in which these processes can be harnessed to planning's benefit.

Having become firmly ensconced in the last few years of my career, I am keenly aware of the extent to which my thoughts about the planning profession have been influenced by hundreds—in fact, probably thousands—of encounters with others, both in person and through their writings. It is therefore difficult to know where to begin in acknowledging my substantial intellectual debts. I'll resolve the matter by mentioning the people who probably had the greatest impact on my professional development: Arnold Sio, Colgate University sociologist and teacher *extraordinaire*, who first exposed me to a host of urban issues—and to the existence of a profession bent on addressing those issues; Martin Meyerson, an early and compelling role model; Jack Parker, who knew better than anyone else how to build a community among the students and alumni of a university planning program; Larry Mann, who challenged me to think more clearly about planning theory; and Paul Davidoff, who was my only professional hero. There have been many others whose ideas have mattered a great deal to me, of course, but these five make up my all-star team.

The book probably would have remained forever in the idea stage without the semester's leave of absence granted to me by Virginia Commonwealth University (VCU). I am grateful, as well, to my colleagues in VCU's Department of Urban Studies and Planning, who covered for me during my absence and have provided support in countless other ways.

Finally, I thank my family—present and past—for their patience and cooperation during periods of intense professional activity. Most of all I am deeply grateful to my wife, Ann, who has made dozens of contributions, both tangible and intangible, to this book—not the least of them being her frequent prod: "Mike, you're never going to write that book!" I think it worked.

PART

1

Introduction

1

Planning Practice and Political Power

PUBLIC PLANNING

This book is about planning—which I define, quite simply, as the process by which we attempt to shape the future. The future, in this definition, refers to anything beyond the present; the purpose of planned action may be as short-run as one's projected activities for the rest of the day or as long-run as the conservation of an important natural resource for the benefit of future generations. Defined in this manner, planning is clearly a pervasive human activity. Each day of our lives features a sequence of locations, actions, and outcomes that have been, at least in some measure, planned in advance. It is undoubtedly true, of course, that our lives are also enriched by those occurrences that are entirely unplanned. A totally planned life is rather dreadful to contemplate, as would be a totally planned community or a totally planned society. Fortunately, history suggests that there is little risk of encountering such phenomena.

Just as each of us must do at least some planning in order to function on a daily basis, so must the institutions and organizations of which we are a part. Any organization that has a purpose or mission, along with some resources to expend, must plan how it will use its resources to achieve that purpose or mission. The opposite of planning is aimless drift, and few individuals or organizations would want to entrust their futures to such a process when other options are available.

This book does not deal, however, with the plans made by individuals and organizations in the course of their daily activities. Rather, it focuses on the planning that is done in the public sector by those who are responsible for helping to guide the future development of particular jurisdictions—typically cities or towns, counties, metropolitan areas, or other substate regions. While many of the principles discussed in this book are potentially relevant to planning at higher levels (the state or nation) as well, it is primarily at the local and metropolitan levels that a profession has emerged to carry out the planning process—a profession variously referred to as urban planning, city planning, community planning, regional planning, or some combination of these terms (for example, urban and regional planning).[1] The book's focus, then, is on the planning processes carried out by the members of this profession.

Many, though not all, planners who engage in public sector planning are employees of local governments. Others operate as private consultants, working for firms that provide professional services to jurisdictions on a contractual basis. Still others—an increasing percentage of the profession, if anecdotal accounts from planning school professors are indeed accurate—work for private nonprofit organizations focused on housing, economic development, environmental quality, and other community issues. Regardless of where they are employed, however, most of these planners are engaged in public planning as the term is used in this book—that is, they are dealing with matters of public concern and relevance.[2]

I have referred here to planning as a profession, but does it really deserve that label? This question was vigorously debated in previous decades, but—blessedly—appears today to have been consigned to the trash heap of irrelevant issues. To be sure, if one defines a profession in terms of required training, tightly controlled membership criteria, and the restriction of practice to those who have earned that membership (as is the case, for example, with attorneys and their state bar associations), then planning hardly qualifies. On the other hand, many other characteristics commonly associated with professions—discipline-specific graduate degree programs, national organizations, journals, conferences—are indeed in place. Thousands of people work for planning agencies, organizations, or firms; carry out planning tasks; and interact with their peers in a community of planning activity. Whether we refer to that community as a profession, or simply as a discipline or field, is of little consequence. I have chosen to use the term *profession* throughout this book.

Numerous efforts have been made, through the years, to define the central purposes and themes of the planning profession.[3] Should planners restrict their efforts to matters of land use and the physical environment, or should their purview include a broader array of social and economic concerns? Most planners subscribe intellectually to the latter view even while dealing primarily, on a day-to-day basis, with land use matters. Are planners distinguished by the processes they employ or by the phenomena to which those processes are applied? "Yes" is a reasonable answer to both. Should the planner possess in-depth expertise in a particular area—know a great deal about transportation or economic development, for example—or a comprehensive grasp of the relationships among many such issues? Again, both alternatives merit a "yes," though individual planners are apt to identify with only one or the other of these approaches; that is, the profession includes, to its benefit, both specialists and generalists.

In 1997, the Strategic Marketing Committee of the Association of Collegiate Schools of Planning issued a discussion paper listing the "generic themes" that have characterized planning thought and practice in the second half of the twentieth century.[4] The committee suggested that the field had focused on (1) the "improvement of human settlements"; (2) "interconnections" among the various facets of the community (again, the "comprehensiveness" theme); (3) "pathways of change over time," referring to the processes of goal formulation, forecasting, and plan-making for the future; (4) "the diversity of needs and distributional consequences in human settlements," reflecting concerns about social and economic equity; (5) "open participation in decisionmaking," involving concerns for citizen participation and representation, negotiation and dispute resolution, and clear communication; and (6) "linking knowledge and collective action," which refers to recognition of the interdependence between the practice and academic branches of the profession, and the importance of the knowledge generated by both. I consider this a useful list.

In more applied terms, of course, planners today confront a variety of pressing issues—the proper use of land, downtown survival, neighborhood revitalization, suburban sprawl, growth management, inadequate transportation systems, a shortage of affordable housing (and outright homelessness for some), air and water quality, decaying infrastructure (roads, bridges, sewerage systems, public buildings, and so on), and inadequate or outmoded parks and recreation facilities, to name just a few. Other planners roam farther afield, depending on their organizational affiliations, and find themselves addressing issues related to crime, public health, hunger, economic development, the location and quality of public schools, and other matters of broad societal concern. Quite simply, the scope of the planning profession is as broad as the array of problems confronting today's cities and regions.

It would be delightful, of course, if we were able to claim that such problems are regularly and routinely resolved once they have been subjected to planners' ministrations. Alas, this is not the case. One reason stems from the nature of the problems themselves. Horst Rittel and Melvin Webber proposed the term *wicked* to describe the problems typically addressed by planners. Wicked problems, they suggest, are ill- and variously defined; often feature a lack of consensus regarding their causes; lack obvious solutions— or even agreement on criteria for determining when a solution has been achieved; and have numerous and often unfathomable links to other problems.[5] Why have we been unable, thus far, to solve the problems of homelessness, or crime, or inadequate schools? The simple answer is that these are indeed wicked problems, as are most of those within the planner's purview. Rarely do planners complain of professional boredom![6]

In addressing such issues, planners do not operate in a vacuum; on the contrary, they are subject, at any given time, to a number of external forces beyond their control. The political economy of the nation—capitalist democracy, in our case—does much to shape the planner's sphere of action. Location matters; planning for an inner-city neighborhood is a different experience from planning for a rural county. The regions of the nation are characterized by differing political cultures, which in turn generate unique orientations toward the role of planning; it does indeed matter whether one is doing planning in Phoenix or Birmingham or Buffalo or Minneapolis. Economic cycles have a great impact on development trends, which in turn affect the planner's role, as does the local jurisdiction's current rate of growth or decline.[7] The locality's power configuration matters a great deal; Francine Rabinovitz's classic study of planning in several New Jersey cities illuminated the different planning styles most likely to succeed in communities with identifiable "power elites" versus those with more diffuse systems of political power.[8] These and other factors comprise a bundle of characteristics often referred to as the "culture of planning" in a particular city or region, and they are characteristics that job-seeking planners should take seriously in making their employment decisions. (See Chapter 12 for further discussion of this point.)

Planners address the most important, and often most visible, issues confronting their communities; these issues tend to be wicked problems for which definitions, causes, and solutions remain elusive; and planners are subject to numerous external influences that assist in shaping their roles and responsibilities. Another way of saying all this, of course, is simply to note that planning is a highly political undertaking—a matter to which I shall now turn.

PLANNING AND POLITICAL POWER

Spend fifteen minutes with a planner, inquire about the project on which she or he is currently spending the most time, and you will very shortly be hearing about the politics of the situation. Recent issues addressed by planners in my own region, for example, include these:

• One city's planning staff has tried for several years to update the city's comprehensive plan but has been thwarted by a ward-based political system that renders difficult the task of acquiring consensus on citywide issues. Extensive citizen participation has highlighted widespread differences of opinion on major issues. The update will eventually be accomplished, but it has taken far longer than anyone anticipated at the outset. Politics.

• County planners undertook the task of developing a corridor plan for a busy street that connects two major commercial thoroughfares. The street is now largely residential (at points, even rural)—but, because of the heavy traffic volume, there are strong pressures to "go commercial." Property owners along the street, anticipating major windfall profits, strongly support such development; the residents of adjacent neighborhoods are opposed, however, and have formed a citizens' organization to do battle. The planners propose a compromise: permitting nodes of commercial development at key intersections while retaining the residential character of the remaining land. The result: no one is happy (except for landowners at the intersections), and the battle intensifies. Politics.

• A regional planning organization spearheads a highly participatory "goals for the region" project. On a pleasant day in March, over six hundred people, representing all walks of life, convene on a local university campus to listen to speakers, participate in focus groups, and identify key issues for inclusion in the project. The day is considered a rousing success, and soon the second step is initiated: a round of neighborhood-based meetings throughout the region. Along the way, however, an unanticipated phenomenon begins to emerge—namely, the people who opt to participate at the neighborhood level tend to be those most interested in significant change. Many are impatient with talk of regional cooperation; instead, they want changes in the region's governmental structure. Not surprisingly, this approach does not sit well with the commissioners of the regional agency, who are elected officials of the constituent jurisdictions. As a result, the project simply fades into oblivion over time. Politics.

• In the face of severe budgetary pressures, the president of a state university decides to initiate the preparation of a strategic plan for the school. The plan is to focus on programs rather than on facilities, for which other planning mechanisms already exist. A small staff is created, as is a twenty-three-member Commission on the Future of the University (in effect, the planning board for this project), which consists of faculty members, students, and administrators. At first the members of the university community are skeptical about the project and pay it little heed; they've "been through this before," and "nothing ever comes of it." This attitude changes, however, when a first draft of the plan is given wide circulation. At the heart of the plan is a list of programs to be given additional resources, the "enhancement list," and another list of programs scheduled for reduction or termination, the "diminution list"—which quickly comes to be known as the "hit list." Suddenly the campus is a hotbed of frenetic activity, with projected winners supporting the plan and projected losers devising numerous strategies (enlisting the involvement of prominent alumni and donors, for example) to have it altered. The plan is eventually approved and adopted, but only after many changes have been made to the first draft. Politics.

• A major entertainment corporation attempts to locate a history-based theme park in a wealthy residential county to the west of the nation's capital. The state's governor, the county's business community, and most of the county's elected officials are strong supporters of the project; a number of citizen, environmental, and historical interest groups, however, are opposed. Both sides pull out all the stops in furthering their positions; expert studies, the media, nationally prominent organizations and individuals, and vast sums of money are brought into play. Meanwhile, the county's planners have a challenging assignment. Given the support of local elected officials, opposing the project is not an option, but the planners are allowed—even encouraged—to work with the corporation to ensure that the project does minimal damage to other aspects of life in the county. As time passes, however, the battles between supporters and opponents become increasingly intense—until, to nearly everyone's surprise, the corporation announces its withdrawal from the project.[9] Politics.

Other examples could be cited—zoning battles pitting developers against residents, churches that want to provide food for the homeless encountering opposition from the residents of the surrounding middle-income neighborhoods, "adult" book and video stores wanting to operate anywhere they can, and so on. Any reader of this book could undoubtedly provide a similar list of recent planning issues in his or her own jurisdiction. Virtually all of them would have a significant political component.

Earlier in the profession's history, the prevalent view of planning held it to be a technical endeavor and the planning process an exercise in applied science, with rationality as the key operating principle for practice (see Chapter 6 for a detailed discussion of this concept). By the 1970s, however, it had become impossible to ignore the intensely political nature of the planning process.[10] In Nigel Taylor's words, "planning action can significantly affect the lives of large numbers of people, and since different individuals and groups may hold different views about how the environment should be planned, based on different values and interests, it is therefore also a *political* activity."[11] The essential requirement of political support for the acceptance and implementation of plans had also become obvious. As Alexander Garvin observes:

> By themselves, urban planners cannot accomplish very much. Improving cities requires the active participation of property owners, bankers, developers, architects, lawyers, contractors, and all sorts of people involved with real estate. It also requires the sanction of community groups, civic organizations, elected and appointed public officials, and municipal employees. Together they provide the financial and political means of bringing plans to fruition. Without them even the best plans will remain irrelevant dreams.[12]

While the political nature of planning is indeed widely recognized today, many planners continue to display ambivalence on this matter.[13] Acceptance is one thing; acting upon that acceptance is quite another. Too often, planners are ill-prepared to act upon the political content of their work; they may lack understanding of the political system (ignorance), or lack knowledge of the techniques needed to function effectively within it (inadequate education), or feel overwhelmed by political forces (despair), or even reject the notion that they—in their particular roles—are subject to the play of political power (denial). It is clear, of course, that planners differ in their affinity for the hurly-burly of the political arena. Some thrive on it ("politicals," as Elizabeth Howe and Jerome Kaufman have referred to them); others prefer careers spent primarily at the computer or the drafting table ("technicals"); and still others combine both roles ("hybrids").[14]

One reason for planners' ambivalence toward their political role is their inherent vulnerability. As Charles Hoch has noted,

> official public planning holds a subordinate organizational position at the local level. Planners are pushed to the margins of civic life and public culture in the United States. This lack of institutional authority handicaps professional planners when they offer advice from their governmental offices. When planners expose the conflicts between private purposes and the public good, they receive little institutional support. Planners are left to cope on their own with the conflicts that public planning engenders when it tackles some of the paradoxical problems of a liberal, capitalist society.[15]

Given the widely recognized political constraints on planning, then, coupled with the planner's vulnerability in the political system, why would anyone choose a career in this field? Indeed, there is reason to be concerned that the political nature of the profession might be discouraging some young planners from entering public sector employment.

In 1997 I taught Virginia Commonwealth University's Planning Internship Seminar, in which students in the Master of Urban and Regional Planning program were encouraged to reflect on their internships and to relate them to their future career aspirations. Based on some of their comments about public service, I conducted an informal poll of the students in the class. Of the twelve present on that day, nine said that they intended to make their careers in the private practice of planning (that is, with planning consulting firms, private nonprofit organizations, or architectural or engineering firms that take on planning assignments); three said that they were not yet sure. None expressed a preference for a job in the public sector. Surprised by these results, I initiated an ongoing (and admittedly not very systematic) conversation about the reasons behind their views. Included among the issues they raised were these:

• Our planning program frequently invites practitioners to serve as guest speakers in our various courses and special programs. The students said that they were hearing too many tales of frustration and failure: projects that didn't pan out, plans that didn't get adopted or implemented, unsuccessful efforts to hold off ill-conceived developments, compromises that undermined a project's basic purpose, and so forth. Only rarely, the students complained, did they hear success stories. (One irreverent wag suggested that I could solve this problem by no longer inviting practitioners to the classroom. I did not consider that a good solution.)

• A second, and closely related, problem cited was the high degree of controversy that seemed to characterize most major planning issues—and the frequency with which such controversy tended to turn genuinely nasty. This was daunting to the students, leading them to conclude that the political process is too frustrating; some noted that they would rather do their technical work for clients, and let those clients worry about the politics of the situation.

• The students were concerned that public planning seems to lack clout. Plans, zoning ordinances, and other planning mechanisms appeared to be too fragile, too easily circumvented by those with sufficient resources or political power. Planning commissions and city councils that are based on ward or district representation, they observed, seem to function primarily as vehicles for the protection of constituents' interests at the expense of the larger city, county, or region.

In sum, the students seemed to be saying, "Give me the tools I need to do a good job of rational analysis and plan-making, then point me in the direction of a private firm that wants to hire someone with those tools." I have no basis as yet for determining how representative that particular group might have been; indeed, several members of that graduating class are now working for public planning agencies. I wondered, of course, whether other planning schools were observing similar student aspirations; informal conversations with colleagues elsewhere suggested that many of them are. A faculty member at one of the nation's most highly visible planning schools, for example, reported that many of his program's graduates now go to work for private nonprofit organizations, viewing these as the best vehicles for creative and value-based planning of the sort that first attracted them to the profession.

Public sector planning practice might be less daunting, however, if students were given more instruction and hands-on experience designed to familiarize them with the nature of such practice. Howell Baum argues that planning students in graduate programs have a natural tendency to internalize the roles modeled by their professors rather than those played by the practitioners with whom most of them will soon be interacting:

> New planners often expect their work to involve more or less rational analysis to solve relatively well-defined problems. Instead, they find complex relationships with other professionals, bureaucratic managers, elected officials, and community groups. Many have difficulty making or affecting decisions under political conditions; many wish for securely technical roles. Apparently, such planners expect to conduct research, but are not prepared for interaction and intervention.[16]

Clearly, this situation needs some attention; planners do indeed need to be prepared for that interaction and intervention. One step toward doing so is to stop thinking of the political system as a dysfunctional external disturbance—something that keeps us from being effective—and to identify and employ planning strategies that are integrated with, and make creative use of, that political system.

That is a major theme of this book. I suggest that there are indeed strategies available to planners for enhancing the likelihood of effectiveness in the face of political power. Parts 4 and 5 of this volume describe the strategies and attitudes that are most likely to prove effective. First, however, we will examine, in Part 2, some of the fundamental issues involved in the relationship between planning and politics. Part 3 features an examination of a number of other strategies that have been proposed for planners in the course of the profession's history; these will be evaluated through the filter of their relevance to, and feasibility for, planning practice in a political environment.

By now it should be clear to the reader that the focus of this book is on the process of planning rather than on the substance of specific planning issues. This is not the place to learn more about the New Urbanism, or suburban sprawl, or Smart Growth, or sustainable cities, or any other topic related to what it is that planners—yesterday's, today's, or tomorrow's—are attempting to accomplish. Instead, this book addresses the very nature of planning as a distinct form of professional activity. Other professions deal with many of the same substantive issues and problems that planners confront; what sets us apart from those professions, I suggest, is our focus on the processes by which we endeavor to resolve those issues and shape a more desirable future—that is, our focus on *planning*.

Many of the matters discussed in this chapter are central to the body of issues and scholarship that constitute the planning theory enterprise. The next chapter examines the role of planning theory in offering insights and guidance to the practitioner.

NOTES

1. Since urban planners—present and future—are the primary intended audience for this book, I make no effort here to provide a history of the planning profession or to define it more precisely. Readers interested in such matters might want to consult Mel Scott, *American City Planning Since 1890* (Berkeley: University of California Press, 1971); Donald A. Krueckeberg, ed., *Introduction to Planning History in the United States* (New Brunswick, N.J.: Center for Urban Policy Research, Rutgers University, 1983); Krueckeberg, ed., *The American Planner: Biographies and Recollections*, 2nd ed. (New Brunswick, N.J.: Center for Urban Policy Research, Rutgers University, 1994); and Edward J. Kaiser and David R. Godschalk, "Twentieth Century Land Use Planning: A Stalwart Family Tree," *Journal of the American Planning Association*, Vol. 61, No. 3 (Summer 1995), pp. 365–385.

2. Since private organizations also plan, they too have employees who carry out this function, though usually without the word *planning* in their titles. Sound planning capabilities are considered, in fact, to be among the most important attributes of upper-level managers in the private sector. I will be gratified if any of the points made in this book are deemed useful to private planners, but they are not the book's primary audience.

3. A major vehicle for this discussion has been the accreditation program operated by the Planning Accreditation Board, a joint undertaking of the American Institute of Certified Planners and the Association of Collegiate Schools of Planning. Early efforts to identify a definitive set of knowledge and skills, mandated to be taught by every accredited planning program, have softened through the years in the face of the diversity that characterizes these programs. The current approach is more a matter of asking each school to explicate its specific educational goals, then assessing the extent to which those goals are being achieved.

4. See Dowell Myers et al., "Anchor Points for Planning's Identification," *Journal of Planning Education and Research*, Vol. 16, No. 3 (Spring 1997), pp. 223–224. For a related discussion of this issue, see Michael P. Brooks, "A Plethora of Paradigms?" *Journal of the American Planning Association*, Vol. 59, No. 2 (Spring 1993), pp. 142–145.

5. Horst W. J. Rittel and Melvin M. Webber, "Dilemmas in a General Theory of Planning," *Policy Sciences*, Vol. 4 (1973), pp. 155–169. For an interesting discussion of the "wicked problem" concept, see Hilda Blanco, *How to Think about Social Problems: American Pragmatism and the Idea of Planning* (Westport, Conn.: Greenwood Press, 1994), pp. 21–22.

6. For a useful—and, under the circumstances, reasonably upbeat—discussion of planners' effectiveness as problem solvers, see Jill Grant, *The Drama of Democracy: Contention and Dispute in Community Planning* (Toronto: University of Toronto Press, 1994).

7. For a related discussion, see Nigel Taylor, *Urban Planning Theory Since 1945* (London: Sage Publications, 1998), p. 108.

8. Francine Rabinovitz, *City Politics and Planning* (New York: Atherton Press, 1969).

9. See Michael P. Brooks, "Getting Goofy in Virginia: The Politics of Disneyfication," in *Planning 1997: Contrasts and Transitions*, proceedings of the American Planning Association National Planning Conference, San Diego, Calif., April 5–9, 1997, ed. Bill Pable and Bruce McClendon, pp. 691–722.

10. Early arguments for a more political view of planning included those made in Dennis A. Rondinelli, "Urban Planning as Policy Analysis: Manage-ment of Urban Change," *Journal of the American Institute of Planners*, Vol. 39, No. 1 (January 1973), pp. 13–22; and Anthony James Catanese, *Planners and Local Politics: Impossible Dreams* (Beverly Hills: Sage Publications, 1974).

11. Taylor, *Urban Planning Theory*, p. 83.

12. Alexander Garvin, *The American City: What Works, What Doesn't* (New York: McGraw-Hill, 1996), p. 2.

13. For perceptive discussions of this ambivalence, see Howell S. Baum, "Politics in Planners' Practice," in *Strategic Perspectives on Planning Practice*, ed. Barry Checkoway (Lexington, Mass.: Lexington Books, 1986), pp. 25–42; and Karen S. Christensen, "Teaching Savvy," *Journal of Planning Education and Research*, Vol. 12, No. 3 (Spring 1993), pp. 202–212.

14. See Elizabeth Howe and Jerry Kaufman, "The Ethics of Contemporary American Planners," *Journal of the American Planning Association*, Vol. 45, No. 3 (July 1979), pp. 243–255; and Elizabeth Howe, "Role Choices for Planners," *Journal of the American Planning Association*, Vol. 46, No. 4 (October 1980), pp. 398–410.

15. Charles Hoch, *What Planners Do: Power, Politics, and Persuasion* (Chicago: Planners Press, 1994), p. 9.

16. Howell S. Baum, "Social Science, Social Work, and Surgery: Teaching What Students Need to Practice Planning," *Journal of the American Planning Association*, Vol. 63, No. 2 (Spring 1997), p. 182.

2

Planning Practice and Planning Theory

THE USES OF THEORY IN PLANNING

Planning theory, I have written elsewhere, "is a term that strikes terror in the hearts of many planners; it conjures up images of esoteric word games played by planning educators who have little knowledge of what practicing planners actually do."[1] Robert Beauregard paints an even bleaker picture, observing that planning theory "is generally held in low esteem. Practitioners have little use for it, students (for the most part) find it a diversion from learning how to do planning and a requirement to be endured, and planning academics, on average, tolerate it. Within academia, planning theory is marginalized; within practice, it is virtually ignored."[2]

This state of affairs is unfortunate, to say the least. I will attempt to demonstrate in this book that, on the contrary, a sound body of theory is an essential component of the planning profession—both fundamental to an understanding of what planning is and helpful to those who practice it. John Forester expresses a similar viewpoint when he suggests that planning theory "is what planners need when they get stuck; another way to formulate a problem, a way to anticipate outcomes, a source of reminders about what is important, a way of paying attention that provides direction, strategy, and coherence."[3]

More generally, I view planning theory as the *process* component of our profession; it guides us through a continuous self-examination of what it is we are doing, how we are doing it, why, for whom, and with what results. In short, it is a vehicle for professional introspection about our roles as planners. Without theory, we would have little justification for doing what we do. Theory places our feet firmly on the ground; properly conceived, it provides ethical and behavioral frameworks for the definition of professional planning practice. "Far from being an irrelevant exercise in academic game playing, then, planning theory is absolutely indispensable to our sense of identity and our ongoing development."[4]

Theory has, of course, been defined in a number of ways. It will suffice here to note a basic distinction between two types of theories. (1) *Positive* (sometimes called empirical or descriptive) theories attempt to explain the relationship between two or more variables—concepts, actions, objects, events, qualities, and so forth—in order to generate predictions about phenomena not yet observed. Once the hypotheses derived from such theories have been tested, the theories may be verified, refuted, or modified. This is the stuff of scientific investigation—of carefully designed, conducted, and controlled research projects. (2) *Normative* theories, on the other hand, prescribe what the relationship between the variables in question should be in order to produce results that are deemed desirable. In short, positive theories attempt to explain *how* things operate, while normative theories tell us how they *should* operate.

Normative theories can be further divided into two subtypes. (a) An *ethical* normative theory prescribes a given relationship because of its "rightness" in view of some external principle; one should undertake action X because it will produce outcome Y, which is the desired outcome from the perspective of principle Z. The principle, Z, may be a value (equity, justice, fairness), or simply a decision criterion in current use (increase employment opportunities, control sprawl, reduce automobile congestion). (b) A *functional* normative theory, on the other hand, is complete in itself and thus requires no external principle. A particular way of doing things is prescribed simply because it is deemed a good way (more workable, more productive, more efficient) to proceed; one should do X because it is a good way to achieve any Y, regardless of the reasons for wanting to get to Y.[5]

The planning profession has provided numerous examples of these various types of theories. Positive theory-building is at play, for example, in researchers' attempts to create urban development models that can predict the impact of alternative transportation patterns on a range of other variables (such as population density, residential and commercial development, and land values). Planning research has become increasingly sophisticated during the past several decades, and planners have formulated and tested numerous positive theories in an effort to heighten our understanding of the processes by which cities and regions develop and function. Such theories relate, of course, to the *subject matter* or *content* of planning; these are differentiated from theories pertaining to the *process* of planning, here referred to as normative theories.

Ethical normative theories have often been troublesome for the planning profession. One problem has been the unfortunate durability of many so-called sound planning principles that turn out to be based on little more than tradition ("Everyone knows this is right," or "This has always been a basic tenet of planning"). For example, planners long held to the principle that land uses should be rigidly separated so as to protect property values and ensure the efficient performance of urban functions (movement of traffic, conduct of commerce and industry, and so forth). Thus, in the terms introduced earlier, the planner might prepare a zoning ordinance (X) that achieves a strict separation of land uses (Y) so that the "separation of land uses" principle (Z) can be satisfied. In more recent years, the validity of this "sound planning principle"—as well as that of many others—has been scrutinized and challenged.

In reality, most "sound planning principles" are quite amenable to empirical testing, and thus belong more appropriately to the realm of positive theory. Indeed, whether a particular proposition reflects positive or normative theory will often depend on how that proposition is conceptualized and presented. For example, the statement that citizens should be involved in the planning process (X) because this will give them a voice in decision-making (Y), which is an essential feature of a democracy (Z), is not an empirical proposition. Given a commitment to democratic participation, there is nothing to be tested; the statement simply reflects allegiance to a particular value. If, on the other hand, it is asserted that citizens should be involved in the planning process (X) because this will give them a voice in decision-making (Y), which is essential to the successful implementation of a project (Z), then the proposition can be tested—for example, by comparing the rates of successful implementation in high-participation versus low-participation projects—

and we find ourselves in the realm of positive theory. The "separation of land uses" example mentioned earlier is also open to empirical testing; in fact, research on this issue through the years has contributed to the principle's demise.

The critical point is simply that we should take care, in our professional lives, to distinguish between those propositions that are essentially expressions of our values or ethics, on the one hand, and those that are subject to empirical testing, on the other. In short, we should maintain clear distinctions between our positive theories and our normative theories.

There is a second way in which ethical normative theories have been problematic for the planning profession. Much of the work being done by today's planning theorists is strongly "ethical normative" in character, reflecting and building upon particular social and political values. Planners reading the resulting literature are typically urged to carry out their professional activities in a manner that manifests those values. Regardless of how one feels about a particular set of values, however, some important questions are thereby suggested: *Is* there a set of values that are fundamental to the planning profession and that should therefore be held by all planners? If so, what are those values, and how is their possession to be enforced? If not, how do we decide which values should prevail in any given instance? These and other value-related questions will be discussed in Chapter 5.

The other type of normative theory, the functional, has also been prominent in the planning profession, though perhaps somewhat less so in recent years. The so-called rational model of planning (see Chapter 6), at one time the dominant paradigm in planning theory and practice, serves as a good example; it was typically presented as the best X for achieving any Y. No external value or principle was at issue; one behaved rationally simply because it was the best way to plan. Our entry into the postmodern era (discussed later in this chapter), however, has been accompanied by serious questions about the utility of that approach. Values are indeed central to all planning—and it is not surprising, therefore, that most current planning theories are of the ethical normative variety.

Approaches to planning theory can also be differentiated on the basis of their intent. Here I distinguish between (1) theories *about* planning, which focus on its role in a particular milieu—the community, nation, society, or political economy; (2) theories *of* planning, which seek to explicate characteristics of planning practice (for example its communicative effects, discussed in Chapter 9), and are sometimes—but not always—accompanied by suggestions for improving that practice; and (3) theories *for* planning, which propose models or strategies for consideration by practitioners.[6]

The second of these three approaches is most closely aligned with ethical normative theorizing, and is the most prevalent today. The other two approaches remain potentially useful, however, and should not be ignored. Indeed, the strategy proposed in Part 4 of this book incorporates both the second and third approaches.

IS THERE A THEORY-PRACTICE GAP?

Whether a gap exists between theory and practice depends on how the issue is conceptualized. On the one hand, it is true that much contemporary planning theory focuses on what planners do; in that sense, then, there are indeed bridges between theory and practice. On the other hand, however, there is relatively little traffic on those bridges. For the most part, planning practice and planning theory constitute two distinct communities of interest, each with its own membership, forums for interaction, modes of communication, and other internal dynamics.[7] There is, in fact, little incentive at present for genuine communication between the two realms.[8]

Part of the problem, of course, has to do with the often-described historical transition in the nature of the planning professoriate. The early university planning programs were staffed largely by "master practitioners" who taught planning practice as they had experienced it. In time, however, it became apparent that such programs would enjoy little status or success unless they became more academically respectable—that is, hired faculty members with "proper academic credentials" (Ph.D.'s), developed high-quality programs of research and theory building, and generated admirable publication records. It was inevitable, then, that the primary "reference group" for most planning educators would come to be their fellow academics rather than those who practice in the field.[9]

Another source of difficulty is the differing languages employed by the two groups. Nigel Taylor traces the theory-practice gap to the 1960s, attributing it to the "abstract, highly technical (and frankly abstruse) language of systems theory, with its talk of mathematical modelling, 'optimisation' and so on.... Planning theory concerned with much broader systemic considerations tended to be seen as irrelevant by the everyday local planner with a heavy case-load."[10] Indeed, drop your local planning director into one of the planning theory sessions at the annual conference of the Association of Collegiate Schools of Planning (the largest annual gathering of planning educators), and he or she is apt to feel that an alien tongue is being spoken.

Nor, ironically, do theorists and practitioners necessarily focus on the same set of issues. Writing from his perspective as a theorist, Beauregard perceptively observes: "My ideal practitioner would consider the epistemological underpinnings of action, the broad sweep of history, the tensions within a capitalist democracy, the elusive qualities of space, and unresolvable societal conflicts. I expect, however, that most practitioners would be satisfied with making one aspect of the community work better."[11]

The theory-practice gap is hardly unique to the planning profession; I suspect, in fact, that most disciplines experience tension between their practice and theory-building wings. Beauregard's point is echoed, for example, in a 1988 *New York Times Magazine* article by novelist and attorney Scott Turow. Law school, Turow complains, is not "lawyer school"; except for clinical programs focusing on practice skills, there is little emphasis on what it means to practice law. Instead, he charges, law school is "about training legal scholars," about teaching students to "think like law professors."[12]

> Practicing lawyers rarely think first about the grand sweep of the law and its rational development. They think about the needs of their clients and how the law can be applied or shaped to accomplish certain aims.... [M]ost law professors don't practice, some never have practiced and don't ever want to. Their focus is on scholarship: cutting-edge changes in the law, law-review articles, complex analyses of vexing legal problems. And law school is a world made in their image.[13]

Turow concludes that what "can and should be commonly instilled" in law school is "a sense of mutual enterprise, a vision of the worthy, if complicated, ambitions of the profession, and the freedom to take pride in this difficult and venerable calling."[14] Many practicing planners would have no difficulty substituting planning school for Turow's law school.

Other causes and/or effects of the theory-practice gap can be posited. Throughout the 1970s, the Association of Collegiate Schools of Planning (ACSP) held its annual conference in conjunction with (usually on the weekend preceding) the annual conference of the American Institute of Planners (AIP), at that time the nation's principal organization for professional planners. The ACSP conferences were attended primarily by the administrators of university planning programs; a turnout of twenty to forty of them was considered successful. Early in the 1980s, however, the ACSP developed its own conference, widening its format to include all faculty members and transforming it into a major forum for the presentation of scholarly papers (often publications in progress) by academics to other academics. By the turn of the century, the conference was being attended by as many as eight hundred people, and registration in excess of one thousand planning educators was deemed to be just around the corner. The ACSP's divorce from the AIP conference, then, was a strong contributing factor in the organization's growth and maturation. On the other hand, there has also been a price to pay—namely, reinforcement of the inevitable distance between educators and practitioners, who no longer meet together. Few would advocate a return to the arrangements of the 1970s—the conferences of both the ACSP and the American Planning Association (APA), the AIP's successor organization, are far too successful to "need" the other group—but the separation of the conferences stands as yet another symbol of the theory-practice gap. To be sure, a fair number of planning educators do attend the annual APA conference, though I suspect that the ranks of planning theory specialists are rather thin at these gatherings. Very few practitioners attend the ACSP conference unless they have been invited to participate in a particular panel, program, or committee meeting.

The two wings of the profession tend to rely on separate vehicles for the communication of their interests and ideas. One of my tasks in preparing to write this book was to review the content of the profession's major journals and periodicals over the past fifteen years—a process that gave me some rather strong impressions about authors and audiences. *Planning,* a monthly publication of the APA, is written largely by practitioners (or professional writers who are strongly oriented toward planning practice) for practitioners; its articles are practical and accessible. Both the *Journal of Planning Education and Research* (published by the ACSP) and the *Journal of*

Planning Literature are written, for the most part, by and for academics. The *Journal of the American Planning Association (JAPA)* is, in some ways, the closest to a hybrid; while most (but not all) of its articles are written by academics, the topics tend to be somewhat more applied, and many of the authors make an effort to communicate across the theory-practice divide. Occasional complaints by practitioners that *JAPA* is too theoretical or esoteric continue to be heard, however.

Not all of the complaints are directed by practitioners toward academics. Planning theorists occasionally complain that practitioners lack appropriate values, or technical and political skills, or analytical depth, or thoughtful introspection, or proper appreciation for the fruits of academic research and theory building. Indeed, one contemporary school of planning theory—the (aptly named) critical theorists—is devoted to a systematic critique of planning practice in capitalist societies (see Chapter 3).

However wide the gap between theory and practice sometimes appears to be, it would be highly erroneous to conclude that planning theory and planning practice are ultimately irrelevant to one another. On the contrary, as noted earlier, theory provides the essential foundation on which the profession is built. Much of today's theory, moreover, is indeed focused on practice. At the same time, it is clear that the ideas of planning theory have not always been articulated in a way that *engages* practitioners constructively, in terms that have comprehensible and practical meaning for them. Much planning theory talk occurs within the theory community—that is, among theorists who are communicating their ideas to others who share their interests. Certainly there is nothing wrong with this process; it is, in fact, a crucial element in the ongoing development of a sound body of theory. More ways should be found, however, to widen the conversation on occasion so that those whose work is being analyzed can actively participate, rather than serve merely as the objects of research and publication.

PLANNING THEORY TODAY

What are the major characteristics of current planning theory? For one thing, it is less concerned than it has been in the past with presenting models and strategies that prescribe how planning should be carried out—that is, with functional normative theories. The rational model, in its many forms, was clearly such a theory.

But rationality has been discredited (at least in the theory literature) as a workable paradigm, and nothing has emerged to take its place. Attention has shifted, instead, to theories *about* and *of* planning. The authors of a recent planning theory reader, for example, view the

> central question of planning theory as the following: *What role can planning play in developing the city and region within the constraints of a capitalist political economy and a democratic political system?* The emphasis is not on developing a model planning process but rather on finding an explanation for planning practice based on analyses of the respective political economies of the United States and Great Britain. Our effort is to determine the historical and contextual influences and strategic opportunities that shape the capacity of planners to affect the urban and regional environment.[15]

Practitioners may or may not find this "central question" meaningful. Judith Innes argues, however, that they should. Despite having become—in her view—more "grounded in the realities of practice" in recent years, planning theory ironically "less often purports to say how planning ought to be done and more often tells us in a nuanced way how practice of various kinds has worked, permitting readers to draw their own lessons for their own situations. Planning theory is now much more about helping planners to see themselves and what they do than it is about providing prescriptions."[16] To which one must respond by asking: how often are those lessons being drawn, and are planners indeed feeling helped by such planning theory?

A second characteristic of contemporary planning theory is its grounding in an explicitly "postmodern" world view. Definitions of this term vary widely (as do its applications in various professions), but the central ideas are reasonably clear with regard to their relevance to planning. The modernist era was one of order, comprehensibility, rationality, and predictability; it was characterized by the optimistic notion that science and technology could readily be harnessed to solve our major problems, and it was the heyday of rational planning. With the 1970s and 1980s, however, came the growing recognition that our communities (as well as other societal levels) simply did not function in accordance with the precepts of the rational planning model. Instead, planning problems were proving to be "wicked," characterized by unpredictability, irreconcilable differences between interested parties, a lack of discernible solutions, and a general sense of chaos. Meanwhile, new forms of social, economic, and political organization were emerging, featuring new voices, skepticism toward expertise, new demands for meaningful participation, and increased expectations regarding the results of governmental action.[17] Much of today's planning theory, then, deals with the implications of postmodernism for the planner's role.

One major theme of postmodern planning theory has been its emphasis on the communicative effects of the planner's words and actions; this approach will be discussed in Chapter 9. Another theme has been the purported ills—ineffectiveness, injustice, and so on—of the planning profession, this from the above-mentioned critical theorists who focus on the "dark side" of planning (see Chapter 3). Still another theme has been a desire to infuse planning theory with new voices, particularly those of women and people of color.[18]

Are the dominant themes of today's planning theory relevant to planning practitioners? Yes and no. Yes, because these themes embody issues of genuine relevance to the nature and quality of planning practice, and its role in improving the quality of life in our communities. No, because most planning theorists—despite their focus on planning practice—tend, in the final analysis, to be talking primarily to one another. As noted earlier, the theorist must more effectively engage the practitioner in a two-way flow of communication if the benefits of theory are to be shared by those outside the academy. Jill Grant states it well:

> In building a theory of practice, we will need to articulate an understanding of what happens in community planning. Explanations should be clear both to practitioners and to academics. Theory must make sense of practice. A theory of practice should account for the role of the planner, the citizen, and the politician in community planning. It should clarify the nature of decision-making and illuminate the values and meanings transacted through planning activities. It should reveal the context in which planning occurs.[19]

This book is intended to satisfy Grant's criteria. Its purpose is to bridge the theory-practice gap—an ambitious undertaking to be sure, and one, as we shall see, in which others are participating as well. Because planning theory is fundamental to our professional purpose and identity, the chapters that follow examine a great deal of theoretical material. This material is viewed, however, through the filter of practice. When considering a particular body of theory, the critical question will be: to what extent does this approach assist the practicing planner in carrying out his or her role in the intensely political environment of the local community?

NOTES

1. Michael P. Brooks, "A Plethora of Paradigms?" *Journal of the American Planning Association*, Vol. 59, No. 2 (Spring 1993), p. 143.

2. Robert A. Beauregard, "Edge Critics," *Journal of Planning Education and Research*, Vol. 14, No. 3 (Spring 1995), p. 163.

3. John Forester, *Planning in the Face of Power* (Berkeley: University of California Press, 1989), p. 137.

4. Brooks, "Plethora of Paradigms," p. 143.

5. It might be argued that efficiency, say, can be viewed as an "external principle" in the light of which a given Y is judged, thus rendering my distinction invalid. Note, however, that I have used efficiency as a criterion for assessing the quality of the way in which we move from X to Y, not for assessing the quality or value of Y itself. Functional normative theories care little about the nature of Y; it is the means of getting to Y that counts. Ethical normative theories focus on the end result; often, alternative means are evaluated solely in terms of their ability to produce the result desired.

6. Numerous other categorizations of planning theory have been suggested; see, for example, Leonie Sandercock and Ann Forsyth, "A Gender Agenda: New Directions for Planning Theory," *Journal of the American Planning Association*, Vol. 58, No. 1 (Winter 1992), pp. 49–50; and Ernest R. Alexander, *Approaches to Planning: Introducing Current Planning Theories, Concepts, and Issues*, 2nd ed. (Philadelphia: Gordon and Breach, 1992), p. 7.

7. Many planning educators belong to an electronic mail network called PLANET, which serves as a useful vehicle for the exchange of information and views. A recent request for assistance, issued by an assistant professor in a major planning program, was worded as follows: "Can anyone recommend to me a source of planning case studies? I am trying to identify cases that can introduce to students the types of problems planners face." The objective here is commendable, but it does illustrate the gap that I am describing.

8. An early and perceptive treatment of this issue is found in Judith Innes de Neufville, "Planning Theory and Practice: Bridging the Gap," *Journal of Planning Education and Research*, Vol. 3, No. 1 (Summer 1983), pp. 36–45.

9. Sociologists use the term *reference groups* to indicate those groups to which we look for acceptance and approval— and, conversely, whose disapproval or rejection would concern us most deeply.

10. Nigel Taylor, *Urban Planning Theory Since 1945* (London: Sage Publications, 1998), p. 64.

11. Beauregard, "Edge Critics," p. 164.

12. Scott Turow, "Law School v. Reality," *New York Times Magazine*, September 18, 1988, p. 71.

13. Ibid. Howell Baum makes similar points in "Social Science, Social Work, and Surgery: Teaching What Students Need to Practice Planning," *Journal of the American Planning Association*, Vol. 63, No. 2 (Spring 1997), pp. 179–188.

14. Turow, "Law School," p. 74.

15. Scott Campbell and Susan S. Fainstein, eds., *Readings in Planning Theory* (Cambridge, Mass.: Blackwell

Publishers, 1996), pp. 1–2. Emphasis in the original.

16. Judith E. Innes, "Challenge and Creativity in Postmodern Planning," *Town Planning Review*, Vol. 69, No. 2 (April 1998), pp. viii–ix.

17. For discussions of postmodernism and planning, see Innes, "Challenge and Creativity," pp. v–ix; Allan Irving, "The Modern/Postmodern Divide and Urban Planning," *University of Toronto Quarterly*, Vol. 62, No. 4 (Summer 1993), pp. 474–487; Robert A. Beauregard, "Between Modernity and Postmodernity: The Ambiguous Position of U.S. Planning," in Campbell and Fainstein, *Readings in Planning Theory*, 213–233; and George Hemmens, "The Postmodernists Are Coming, the Postmodernists Are Coming," *Planning*, Vol. 58, No. 7 (July 1992), pp. 20–21.

18. See, for example, Leonie Sandercock, "Voices from the Borderlands: A Meditation on a Metaphor," *Journal of Planning Education and Research*, Vol. 14, No. 2 (Winter 1995), pp. 77–88.

19. Jill Grant, *The Drama of Democracy: Contention and Dispute in Community Planning* (Toronto: University of Toronto Press, 1994), p. 219.

Foundations of Public Planning

3

Running the Gauntlet of Planning Critics

In Chapter 4, several of the concepts that have been proposed to justify the validity of, and need for, public planning will be reviewed, with particular emphasis on the public interest. That discussion will lead, in turn, to an examination of the important role played by values and ethics in the planning process. First, however, I will review the arguments raised by those who are critical or skeptical of public planning. I find this a useful device for examining the role of planning in our society. If it is impossible to counter these arguments, then all planners should seek other lines of work forthwith, and this book should go no further. Needless to say, none of these arguments are sufficiently compelling, in my view, to necessitate reworking our resumes.

If planning is indeed a pervasive human activity, as suggested earlier, then why would anyone oppose it? The criticisms are not aimed, of course, at the planning that we all undertake daily, but rather at the planning that is carried out by governments as they attempt to shape the future of their jurisdictions. The nature of such planning—dealing, as it so often does, with highly visible and controversial issues—virtually ensures that it will generate concern and even hostility in some quarters. I have organized the resulting arguments according to their basic charges—respectively, that planning is perilous, impossible, impotent, malevolent, or unconstitutional. These charges may well overlap at points, but their central ideas are sufficiently distinct to allow them to be discussed separately.

PLANNING IS PERILOUS

There is much in the history and traditions of the United States—the Protestant ethic, the spirit of "rugged individualism," the development in the nineteenth century of a dynamic system of capitalism stressing the importance of individual entrepreneurship—that is potentially antithetical to the notion of planning as a valid governmental function. Private planning is not a problem; no one questions the planning done by corporations, for example, as they develop new products, determine appropriate marketing strategies, and identify tactics for competing successfully with rival firms. Public planning, on the other hand, is a different matter. A preference for as little government as possible is not just a contemporary phenomenon but has been a part of the nation's ethos since its founding.

Indeed, it was not until the Great Depression of the 1930s that widespread doubt began to emerge about the ability of the "unseen hand" of laissez-faire capitalism to move American society ever onward and upward. While the state of the nation's economy in that decade suggested to many the need for at least a modest amount of central planning and direction, events taking place in other parts of the world led others to fear planning. The sizable body of anti-planning literature that emerged during the 1940s and 1950s can perhaps best be understood as a reaction to the emergence of totalitarianism in Europe; central planning, after all, seemed to be closely associated with the Nazi, Fascist, and Communist movements developing, respectively, in Germany, Italy, and the Soviet Union.[1]

In broad outline, the argument of those who saw planning as dangerous was as follows. First, there is little reason to plan unless it is going to be effective. Effectiveness requires, however, a concentration of central power, which inevitably leads to a loss of individual freedom. There is simply no way to guarantee that those in charge of central planning mechanisms will be benevolent; too often, in fact, they have proven to be tyrants. By and large, then, government should leave planning to private individuals who, in seeking to maximize their own well-being, thereby contribute to the best interests of the society as a whole.

This position has ebbed and flowed in the world of scholarly writing about the role of planning, reflecting the era and the political orientation of the writer. For the most part, however, planning is no longer feared as a prelude to totalitarianism in the United States (though a small number of those concerned about the constitutionality of local planning might choose to add this argument to their arsenals). The questions today are not so much about *whether* planning should occur, but about *how* it should be carried out and *who* should be involved, and in what capacities.

American experience with planning since the Great Depression has probably eased concerns about its potential perils. While much local government activity has been carried out under the banner of planning, the dire consequences predicted by the anti-planners have simply not come about—at least not to the extent that was feared. Freedom is always a matter of degree, of course, and a certain amount of individual freedom must be sacrificed in order for any society to govern itself. The critical question is: how much freedom can we afford to sacrifice to allow a governmental planning function to operate? Given the general absence of public debate on this question, it would appear that planning in the United States—particularly at the local level—has not exceeded the limits considered tolerable by the majority of our citizens. Some, however, have argued that planning has proven so acceptable precisely because it is ineffective or has been co-opted, and therefore threatens no one. Let us turn now to these views.

PLANNING IS IMPOSSIBLE

In 1973, Aaron Wildavsky, then dean of the Graduate School of Public Policy at the University of California at Berkeley, took aim at planning in a scathing article entitled "If Planning Is Everything, Maybe It's Nothing."[2] His argument, in brief, was as follows. To be valid, planning must guide governmental decisions—that is, it must govern; otherwise there is no reason to do it. In reality, however, planning never governs, and thus is rarely successful or even accurate in its projections for the future. Instead of shaping reality, plans are constantly adjusted to reflect the reality that has occurred despite the plans. Planning fails, then, to carry out its basic purpose. The favorite concepts of planners—such as rationality, coordination, and efficiency—are all platitudes; none of them truly fall within the planners' range of control. A review of several so-called planned economies produces not a single example of successful national economic planning. Overall, planners never seem to get things right, in large part because their professed role is simply impossible. Nor would it be desirable even if it *were* possible. Ultimately, those who continue to support planning do so as an expression of faith, not reason; accordingly, planning "is not so much a subject for the social scientist as for the theologian."[3]

Shortly after the article's publication, Wildavsky was invited to give a lecture at the University of Illinois at Urbana-Champaign, where I was serving as head of the Department of Urban and Regional Planning. He was to elaborate on the theme of the article, and I was asked to be a respondent (something akin, in this case, to a sacrificial lamb) to his talk. I raised what I considered to be three telling rebuttals. First, I suggested that he had depicted planning in all-or-nothing terms; if a given plan was not totally successful, totally governing, then in his view it was completely unsuccessful. This ignored, I said, the vast majority of situations, in which planning contributes significantly to outcomes while not necessarily "governing" them. Planners provide information, generate ideas and plans, participate in (and sometimes even manage) processes in which decisions do get made; in short, they are useful in many ways that fall short of total control—something most planners would not want even if they could have it. What Wildavsky had done, I argued, was to create a straw man that was all too easy to destroy.

Second, I pointed out that his analysis had focused almost entirely on the national level. In the United States, however, national planning has never been a popular concept (with the possible exception of the 1930s and 1940s), even though every federal department, agency, and program must engage in planning in order to carry out its basic mission. At the local level, on the other hand, planning has been far more acceptable and has accomplished a great deal.

This led to my third point, which was that Wildavsky had ignored the fact that planning is a pervasive activity, and that virtually every organization and institution must plan continuously in order to fulfill its mission and remain in existence. If planning is indeed nothing, then how did he propose that the important operating decisions of any organization should be made?

A skilled and aggressive debater, Wildavsky conceded none of these points. Instead of planning, he said, we should simply rely on existing administrative and political processes (as though these entail no planning!).[4]

Few readers of this book will need to be persuaded that planning is possible, and in fact necessary. Our work yields results that are sometimes very successful, sometimes out-and-out failures, and most often somewhere in between. To claim that planning is impossible, however, is to ignore the fact that thousands of people are doing it in a professional capacity, and that documentable results of their efforts abound. Planning may not rule, but it is certainly alive and kicking.

PLANNING IS IMPOTENT

While critiques of planning in the 1940s and 1950s tended to emanate from the political right, in subsequent decades the debate shifted leftward. The failures of highly visible federal programs, such as urban renewal; the social unrest associated with the Vietnam War and the Civil Rights movement; the emergence of grass-roots organizations determined to participate in political decision-making activities from which they had long been excluded—these and other processes produced radical changes in American life. (Some authors, as previously noted, have described this as the dawning of the postmodern era.) Along with these changes came growing skepticism about public planning.

In general terms, the argument from the political left was that planning had become acceptable because it had sold out, thereby becoming a highly useful instrument for those who had previously feared it. In this view, planning now rested firmly in the hands of governmental and business elites that used it to impose their own values, manipulate the public, and control resources (and the wealth that those resources generated). At the local level, this viewpoint translated into the charge that planning had fallen under the thumb of the chamber of commerce, downtown business interests, and other forces of economic development—in short, the economic power structure. Why should they oppose planning when it was serving their interests so well? According to this critique, planning had been transformed into a conservative process, serving the interests of those already in power and preserving the status quo rather than seeking institutional change and societal improvement.

For many years, beginning in the 1960s, planning theory was dominated by this perspective, and a vast and rich body of literature was produced. Its authors were referred to variously as progressives, radicals, critical theorists, political economy theorists, or simply Marxists; there were subtle differences among these designations, of course, but the subtleties frequently eluded their readers.

This literature's central themes may be briefly summarized as follows. First, planning does not occur in a vacuum, but in a social, political, and economic context. Planning cannot be analyzed in a meaningful way without considering the larger system of which it is a part. For the progressives (the term I will use here), the critical context is the capitalist state: *"the specific interventionist sphere of urban planning emerges, like all State intervention, out of a web of concrete, historically-determinate conflicts and problems embedded in the social and property relations of capitalist society generally, and out of capitalist urbanization in particular."*[5] Neither the city nor planning is an independent variable; both are products of capitalism. Accordingly, "planning does not, and cannot, transcend the social and property relations of capitalist society, but is contained within and is a reflection of those same relations."[6]

From this it is but a short step to the conclusion that planning, as practiced in capitalist societies, is fundamentally an instrument for maintaining the stability of the system and the power of the state. "The role of the planner," wrote David Harvey, "ultimately derives its justification and legitimacy from intervening to restore that balance which perpetuates the existing social order."[7] Planners work to protect the system, to preserve the domination of capital over labor.

If this were indeed the role of planning in a capitalist society, what might planners do to improve the situation? Norman and Susan Fainstein identified three possibilities.[8] First, work within the state to make it more humane. Find out what can be defended, and do so; open up repressive bureaucratic structures; share knowledge and expertise; de-professionalize; fight secrecy.[9] This may entail functioning, for example, as "a watchdog, a whistle-blower, a guerrilla in the bureaucracy, or as a monitor of communication flows who guards against the dissemination of false information."[10] Second, work outside the state, attempting to affect governmental policy as a social critic and activist. Third, develop alternative systems of production and distribution—symbolized in the 1970s, perhaps, by communes, and today by food cooperatives. Other authors were more inclined toward a fourth role: planning for the "reconstruction of society,"[11] including "the replacement of existing social institutions benefiting capital by new ones serving the interests of society at large."[12] How does one do this? Well...revolution comes to mind.

In practice, according to John Friedmann, most progressive planners tended to align themselves with "groups of citizens arrayed in opposition to the state"; as a result, "theorists of radical planning are principally concerned with community organization, urban social movements, and issues of empowerment. Most of them argue for a redistribution of power to (or sharing in power by) the marginalized and excluded sectors of society."[13]

What can be made of all this? For one thing, it seems clear that this literature did little to bridge the theory-practice gap discussed in the previous chapter. Most of its authors were safely ensconced in universities; as I have written elsewhere, "the progressive spirit thrives far more readily in the halls of academe—where there is virtually no risk attached to its espousal—than it does in the nation's city halls."[14] I consider naive the notion that "planners everywhere can somehow take up the cudgel of progressivism and thereby play a significant part in changing the nature of urban political discourse—all of this without altering the organizational structure of planning in our cities, or indeed without threatening the very basis upon which most planners are currently employed."[15] Adds Richard Foglesong: "Planners are unlikely to mount a progressive assault from within the state; it would amount to professional suicide."[16]

On the other hand, there is an uncomfortable element of validity in the progressives' analysis of today's planning scene. Any planner who has ever shelved a good idea because of concern about the potential reaction of local power figures—and who among us has not?—has experienced the co-optation described by the progressives. Nevertheless we plug away, looking for ways to improve the quality of life in the jurisdiction that we serve and succeeding often enough to make the effort worthwhile.

It is useful to distinguish between social reform, which takes for granted the existence of a particular system and looks for ways to improve it, and radical reform, which calls for a fundamental change in (or of) the system itself.[17] Most reform-oriented practicing planners, I suggest, necessarily operate in the spirit of social reform. Unless one is independently wealthy, there are compelling practical reasons for doing so. Nor is it necessary for such a planner to feel that he or she has sold out. The central theme of this book is that planners can be effective, can indeed make significant contributions to community well-being, as along as they understand, and know how to use, the workings of the local political system.

PLANNING IS MALEVOLENT

The planner portrayed by the progressive theorists may be co-opted and impotent, but nevertheless comes across as a naïve innocent; planners may well enter the planning profession with strong social reform motives, but the fact that planning is inevitably embedded in the "capitalist web of property relations" means, for the progressives, that little of genuine significance can be accomplished.

For an emerging group of critical or "dark side" theorists, on the other hand, the planner is anything but an unwitting victim of capitalism. Oren Yiftachel, for example, writes that

> planning is conceived by both planners and the public as a rational professional activity that produces a public good of one kind or another. Planning's theoretical and professional discourse therefore tends to concentrate on its contribution to well-established societal goals such as residential amenity, economic efficiency, social equity, or environmental sustainability. Far less attention is devoted to planning's advancement of regressive goals such as social oppression, economic inefficiency, male domination, or ethnic marginalization.[18]

These things happen too, he argues—and he doesn't want to let planners off the hook. They are willing participants in the "state mechanisms of social control and oppression."[19]

Yiftachel examines four "dimensions of planning control": the territorial dimension, "expressed in the pattern of intergroup land control that results from plans and policies"; the procedural dimension, encompassing the ways in which plans and policies are formulated and implemented; the socioeconomic dimension, which involves planning's impact on social and economic relations; and the cultural dimension, which embraces "planning's impact on the various cultures and collective identities that exist within city and state."[20] On the basis of his examination of these four dimensions, Yiftachel concludes that planning "facilitates elite domination and control of four key societal resources: space, power, wealth, and identity."[21] Planning theorists have avoided attention to the "dark side" of planning, he argues, because of their close functional relationship to planning practice.[22]

Those who take this "dark side" view of planning have no words of advice to share with practitioners; they position themselves primarily as external observers and critics, not as fellow planners who want to work closely with practitioners to improve the quality of their practice. Like the progressives, the "dark side" theorists tend to view planning behavior as a logical and necessary outcome of capitalist property relations. The only significant difference is the question of intent: to the progressives, the planner is basically an unwitting dupe; to the current group of critical theorists, the planner is a conscious and willing participant in oppressive government practices. The only solution, apparently, would be to shift from capitalism to another form of political economy.

Based more on political ideology than on rigorous empirical analysis, this perspective offers little of value to one interested in improving the quality of planning practice. The planner portrayed by the "dark side" theorists does not possess the values and aspirations of the vast majority of the planners with whom I have interacted over the past several decades. Far from helping to bridge the theory-practice gap, these theorists seem intent on burning any bridges that might already exist.

Critical reviews and analyses of specific planning practices or programs have been published in abundance throughout the profession's history, of course, and have often been highly effective vehicles for improving practice. Like those in other professions, we learn from our mistakes. On occasion, these critiques have characterized planners as politically naive, or overly cautious, or inadequately informed, or technologically unsophisticated, or even socially insensitive. It is a major (and, in my view, untenable) leap, however, to the notion that planners are purposeful and malevolent oppressors.

PLANNING IS UNCONSTITUTIONAL

Views on the constitutionality of planning generally reflect one's place in the system. If I own waterfront property that I want to sell to a prospective hotel developer but am told that an array of zoning and environmental regulations render the project impossible, I may decide that "those planners" are a significant part of my problem. If I am a farmer nearing retirement whose land is eagerly being sought by developers who want to convert it to suburban housing and shopping centers, I will be furious with a governmental body that refuses to let my land be developed for such purposes and thereby deprives me of financial comfort in my retirement years. Indeed, if I am a developer active on the outskirts of virtually any major metropolitan area in the nation, the chances are good that my opinion of planners is not particularly charitable. In these and countless similar situations, the issue boils down to one of property rights: I paid for this land, it's mine, and who do these people think they are, telling me how I can—or, more frequently, cannot—use it? Isn't that unconstitutional?

Because this critique emerges from practice rather than from theory, it is one with which most practitioners are quite familiar—and many have the battle scars to prove it. What follows is a brief overview of the legal issues at stake.

The logical beginning point is the so-called takings clause of the Fifth Amendment of the United States Constitution, which states that private property may not be "taken" for public use without "just compensation." Elaboration on this basic idea is found in the Fourteenth Amendment, which states that no person shall be deprived of "life, liberty, or property without due process of law," thus establishing the requirement for a judicial procedure in the event that voluntary agreement cannot be reached; and in the Fourth Amendment, which guarantees "the right of the people to be secure in their persons, houses, papers and effects against unreasonable searches and seizures," thus preventing the courts from supporting a taking for a trivial purpose.[23]

The power of eminent domain, under which a government indeed has the right to take private property for public purposes, such as roads and utilities, is built upon the takings clause of the Fifth Amendment. The government must, however, compensate the owner for the value of the land that has been taken. If the owner and the government cannot agree on a fair market price, the matter goes to court, where the size of the so-called condemnation award is determined.

But what about those circumstances in which the land is not actually taken, but is simply controlled or regulated with regard to the ways in which it can be used? In the United States, public control of the use of private property has historically been based on an entirely different set of concepts and body of law. As John Levy notes, "The evolution, over several decades, of the right of government to exercise some control over the use of privately owned property is one of the central stories in the history of modern planning."[24]

The legitimacy of zoning, for example, is predicated on the legal concept of the police power, the term used to describe the community's right to regulate the activities of private citizens in order to safeguard the interests of the public as a whole. The police power is most often justified by reference to the "health, safety, and public welfare" of the community. For example,

> a law that limited the height of buildings so that they not cast the street below into a permanent shadow might be justified as an exercise in the police power. So, too, might a law that prevented certain industrial or commercial operations in a residential neighborhood. So, too, might laws that prevented property owners from developing their lands so intensively that undue congestion resulted in nearby streets.[25]

Laws of this sort may indeed impose uncompensated losses on property owners, insofar as their use of the land is restricted to something less than its full economic potential. Zoning ordinances, for example, have been enforced with no need for compensation and no required judicial procedure; the jurisdiction's zoning law stands unless the property owner brings a successful lawsuit against the jurisdiction.

The U.S. Supreme Court affirmed the constitutionality of zoning in 1926, in the famous *Village of Euclid v. Ambler Realty Co.* case. In sustaining a village zoning ordinance that prevented Ambler Realty from building a commercial structure in a residential zone, the Court firmly established the idea that a municipality could exercise its police power to impose an uncompensated loss upon a private property owner. The Court determined, in effect, that such control did not constitute a taking, an interpretation that faced little serious challenge for many years. Indeed, for most of the twentieth century the Supreme Court supported the notion that government has "the constitutional authority to restrict activities that damage the environment, harm neighboring property owners, or adversely affect the public interest."[26]

This is not to suggest, however, that these matters have been free of contention. On the contrary, the courts frequently hear cases pitting the rights of a jurisdiction, operating under the police power, against the constitutionally based rights of property owners. In the 1990s, property-rights activists became more vocal and organized than ever before, arguing that the Fifth Amendment "requires government to pay landowners when it 'takes' their property—not only when it condemns land for a public purpose, but when it imposes regulations that, in owners' eyes, forbid them full economic use of their property."[27] The combined efforts of these activists came to be called the "wise use movement"—surely a strange designation from the perspectives of planners, environmentalists, and others concerned with the protection of community interests. Collectively, these "wise use" groups have attempted to "challenge the use of federal, state, and local regulations to implement land use plans and protect environmental resources when the result is any reduction in the economic value of affected private property."[28] John Tibbetts cites "wetlands laws, endangered species regulations, regional growth management rules, and local land-use ordinances" as the most common targets of "wise use" groups.[29] At both the state and federal levels, numerous bills have been introduced to expand the definition of takings and enforce compensation in many situations now covered by the police power; some of these bills have become law, while others have disappeared in the wake of newly invigorated public concern about environmental and land use issues.

Writing in 1993, John Echeverria and Sharon Dennis concluded pessimistically that the property-rights movement was leading to "a notion of rights divorced from responsibility" that, in their view, had the potential to "destroy not only precious natural resources but the fabric of U. S. society."[30] Certainly the diminution or disappearance of governments' abilities to control land use and impose environmental regulations would deal a serious blow to the public planning enterprise. In the years since 1993, however, the "wise use" movement has not become as dominant as many had feared (perhaps genuine wisdom exists in greater abundance than was realized), and the constitutionality of land use planning, while continuously being fine-tuned and even reshaped, has remained intact. The delicate balance between public interests and private property rights, crafted from nearly a century of careful judicial oversight, has not been seriously damaged. All of this could change, of course, in the twinkling of a public mood swing or with a spate of damaging legislation. In this as in countless other ways, planners operate in a precarious political environment—and must therefore possess the knowledge and skills that will enable them to strengthen the chances of success in that environment.

PLANNING IS...ALIVE AND WELL

As this chapter illustrates, opposition to public planning has come from many sources and has reflected a variety of political stances, values, and personal experiences. None of the arguments reviewed, however, are sufficiently compelling to necessitate abandonment of the planning ship. On the contrary, planning has persisted and remains a robust, if challenging, profession.

I suspect that planning has thrived, in part, because planners are good at adapting to changes in the national mood (witness, for example, the social planning specialization that emerged in response to the Civil Rights and anti-poverty movements of the 1960s and 1970s, and the emphasis on economic development and public-private partnerships in the business-dominated 1980s and 1990s). More fundamentally, however, planning continues to prosper because planners carry out essential activities that are performed by no other profession or group. Jurisdictions need to know where they are headed. Accordingly, studies must be carried out, alternative possibilities must be explored, decisions must be made, plans for the implementation of those decisions must be crafted, and the public must be involved in meaningful ways at every step. Public planning is not a luxury but an indispensable component of the process by which jurisdictions move from the present to the future. As noted earlier, the question is not whether planning should exist but how it should be done and who should be involved, and in what capacities.

Before dealing with that set of questions, however, it is necessary to examine more closely *why* we plan. This question is basic to an understanding of the role of politics in planning practice.

NOTES

1. See, for example, F. A. Hayek, *The Counter-Revolution of Science: Studies on the Abuse of Reason* (New York: The Free Press of Glencoe, 1955); Chester I. Barnard, *Organization and Management* (Cambridge, Mass.: Harvard University

Press, 1948), pp. 176–193; and Ludwig
von Mises, *Omnipotent Government* (New
Haven, Conn.: Yale University Press,
1944).

2. Aaron Wildavsky, "If Planning Is
Everything, Maybe It's Nothing," *Policy
Sciences*, Vol. 4 (1973), pp. 127–153.

3. Ibid., p. 153.

4. A more systematic and thorough
rebuttal of Wildavsky's article is found
in Ernest R. Alexander, "If Planning Isn't
Everything, Maybe It's Something,"
Town Planning Review, Vol. 52, No. 2
(April 1981), pp. 131–142.

5. A. J. Scott and S. T. Roweis, "Urban
Planning in Theory and Practice: A
Reappraisal," *Environment and Planning
A*, Vol. 9, No. 10 (1977), p. 1103.
Emphasis in the original.

6. Ibid., pp. 1118–1119.

7. David Harvey, "On Planning the
Ideology of Planning," in *Planning
Theory in the 1980s: A Search for Future
Directions*, ed. Robert W. Burchell and
George Sternlieb (New Brunswick, N.J.:
Center for Urban Policy Research,
Rutgers University, 1978), p. 224.

8. Norman I. Fainstein and Susan S.
Fainstein, "New Debates in Urban Planning: The Impact of Marxist Theory
within the United States," in *Critical
Readings in Planning Theory*, ed. Chris
Paris (Oxford: Pergamon Press, 1982),
p. 155.

9. Several of these suggestions are
discussed in Glen McDougall, "Theory
and Practice: A Critique of the Political
Economy Approach to Planning," in
Planning Theory: Prospects for the 1980s,
ed. Patsy Healey, Glen McDougall, and
Michael J. Thomas (Oxford: Pergamon
Press, 1982), pp. 267–270.

10. Michael P. Brooks, "A Plethora of
Paradigms?" *Journal of the American Planning Association*, Vol. 59, No. 2 (Spring
1993), p. 143.

11. Harvey, "Ideology of Planning,"
p. 231.

12. Richard E. Klosterman, "Arguments for and against Planning," in
Readings in Planning Theory, ed. Scott
Campbell and Susan S. Fainstein (Cambridge, Mass.: Blackwell Publishers,
1996), p. 160.

13. John Friedmann, "Teaching Plan-
ning Theory," *Journal of Planning
Education and Research*, Vol. 14, No. 3
(Spring 1995), p. 160.

14. Michael P. Brooks, "The City May
Be Back In, But Where Is the Planner?"
*Journal of the American Planning Associa-
tion*, Vol. 56, No. 2 (Spring 1990), p. 219.

15. Ibid., pp. 219–220.

16. Richard Foglesong, "Planning for
Social Democracy," *Journal of the Ameri-
can Planning Association*, Vol. 56, No. 2
(Spring 1990), p. 215.

17. For a discussion of this distinction, see Robert Kraushaar, "Outside the
Whale: Progressive Planning and the
Dilemmas of Radical Reform," *Journal of
the American Planning Association*, Vol.
54, No. 1 (Winter 1988), pp. 91–100.

18. Oren Yiftachel, "Planning and
Social Control: Exploring the Dark Side,"
Journal of Planning Literature, Vol. 12, No.
4 (May 1998), p. 395.

19. Ibid.

20. Ibid., pp. 401–402.

21. Ibid., p. 403.

22. Similar perspectives on the planning process emerge from Bent
Flyvbjerg's case study of center-city
planning in Aalborg, Denmark. His conclusions will be discussed in Chapter 6.
See Flyvbjerg, *Rationality and Power:
Democracy in Practice* (Chicago: University of Chicago Press, 1998).

23. U.S. Constitution, amend. 4.

24. John M. Levy, *Contemporary Urban
Planning*, 4th ed. (Upper Saddle River,
N.J.: Prentice-Hall, 1997), p. 65.

25. Ibid., p. 66.

26. John Tibbetts, "Everybody's
Taking the Fifth," *Planning*, Vol. 61, No. 1
(January 1995), p. 5.

27. Ibid., p. 6.

28. Edward J. Kaiser and David R.
Godschalk, "Twentieth Century Land
Use Planning: A Stalwart Family Tree,"
*Journal of the American Planning Associa-
tion*, Vol. 61, No. 3 (Summer 1995), p.
382. For an excellent review of the tak-
ings issue, see Ann Louise Strong,
Daniel R. Mandelker, and Eric Damian
Kelly, "Property Rights and Takings,"
*Journal of the American Planning
Association*, Vol. 62, No. 1 (Winter 1996),
pp. 5–16.

29. Tibbetts, "Taking the Fifth," p. 5.

30. John Echeverria and Sharon Dennis, "Takings Policy: Property Rights and Wrongs," *Issues in Science and Technology* (Fall 1993), p. 28.

4

Rationales for Public Planning

THE SEARCH FOR PLANNING'S BEDROCK

It is all very well, of course, to suggest that planners perform their professional role because it is important to the community and because no other professional group is doing these things. But what is the rationale, the justification, for asserting the importance of that role in the first place? Physicians practice because illness is a reality of the human condition, and we consider it important that people be aided in their quest for good health. Attorneys practice because we operate under a body of law that is critical to virtually all aspects of our lives, is highly complex, and is widely variable in interpretation; we consider it important to have access to expertise, far beyond that which most of us could provide for ourselves, to assist us in hacking our way through the legal jungle. In the same spirit, it is reasonable to ask why planners plan.

The literature on this topic is too vast and diverse to be summarized here; suffice it to say that numerous authors (myself included) have published their conceptions of the essence of planning—what it is all about. If all the pages from the papers and books written on this topic were placed end to end, they would stretch...well, at least around the block.

A good overview of the topic is provided in "Arguments for and against Planning," a classic article written in 1985 by Richard Klosterman.[1] The article illustrates the difficulty of attempting to identify rationales for planning on which we can all agree. As part of his "for" presentation, for example, Klosterman suggests four "vital social functions" that are performed by public planning. Liberally paraphrased, they are as follows:

(1) Planning provides the data needed for effective public and private decision-making. Planners' studies, analyses, projections, social and economic indicators, maps, and other forms of information, according to this argument, are particularly important elements in facilitating smooth market operations at the local level.[2] How one feels about this function depends in part, of course, on one's perspective on market operations in a capitalist society.[3]

Also worthy of note is the impact of the computer-based information explosion that has occurred since Klosterman wrote his article. Data are now so widely available, from so many sources, that planning organizations no longer enjoy any exclusivity whatsoever in their roles as central data repositories. Many years ago, the planning director of a large city told me that the data that his department controlled was its major—indeed, perhaps its only—resource for the exercise of clout in the local political system; people had to come to the planning department for critical information regarding land matters, and this interaction provided the department with opportunities to influence key development decisions. One hopes the department has been able to identify other mechanisms for influence since that time.

(2) Planning promotes the common or collective interests of the community, particularly with respect to the provision of public goods. Klosterman offers transportation, environmental, and economic development planning as examples of planning that is done under this rationale.[4] The rationale relies on two concepts that have proven difficult to pin down, however. First, the phrase "common or collective interests of the community"[5] evokes the concept of the public interest, which will be examined later in this chapter. For now it will suffice to ask whether we have sound, and widely agreed upon, mechanisms for defining those "common or collective interests." The answer, as we shall see later, is not very encouraging.

The second troublesome concept is that of public goods, which are generally defined in terms of two characteristics. First, "it is either difficult or costly to exclude people from access to public goods. Unlike private goods, the property rights for public goods are not specified clearly."[6] Terry Moore (whose definitions are used here, and who has argued for the provision of public goods as *the* fundamental rationale for public planning) offers the following examples:

All persons using highways benefit from the provision of traffic signals whether they are residents of the jurisdiction providing them or not. The zoning practices of one jurisdiction may enhance the property values in other jurisdictions. In these and similar cases, it usually is argued that the costs of excluding people from these goods exceed the benefits to be gained from their exclusion.[7]

Of course, herein lies one of the problems associated with public goods: "If people cannot be excluded from the benefits of public goods, they will have little incentive to contribute for their provision. Hence, it is likely that in a market economy people will underallocate resources to the production of public goods."[8] The budgetary problems of most public schools stand as a telling example.

The second characteristic of public goods is their "nonrivalrous" nature; that is, "the consumption of a public good by one person does not preclude anyone else from consuming it."[9] Indeed, public goods "can be enjoyed simultaneously by more than one person"[10]—or, more to the point for our purposes here, by all those residing in the jurisdiction providing the good.

As Moore notes in his article, public goods are not definable in absolute terms; rather, they occupy one end of a continuum, with private goods (those allocated by market mechanisms) at the other end.[11] Determining precisely where a particular good belongs on that continuum has become increasingly difficult; the privatization of many functions once considered almost entirely public has certainly served to confuse the issue. Defense, public education, the postal service, highways, and even clean water and air are examples of functions that have been privatized to some extent, and thus subjected to market forces. Indeed, to restrict planning solely to matters involving the production and distribution of public goods would rule out much of what today's planners do.

(3) Planning attempts to remedy the negative effects of market actions. The market tends to produce unintended externalities, or spillover effects, that create problems for a community; industrial pollution, clogged traffic arteries, and suburban sprawl are examples. Some argue, in fact, that much of the planning enterprise in America consists of cleaning up after the problems that accompany market behavior—a sort of "pooper-scooper" theory of planning. By itself, however, this view does not present a particularly compelling

rationale for public planning. If remedying the negative effects of market actions were the sole function of planning, we would want to do a much better job of shifting the costs to those whose external effects require public action. Moreover, planning based on this rationale is largely reactive; it focuses on smoothing out existing problems rather than on helping to define and achieve a more desirable future.

(4) *Planning considers the distributional effects of public and private action, and attempts to resolve inequities in the distribution of basic goods and services.* This is a theme to which we shall return at several points in this book. For now, it will suffice to note that this is a value-based assertion regarding what planning *should* do, rather than an empirical description of what it does. Certainly Norman Krumholz's equity planning in Cleveland was consistent with this description (see Chapter 9). On the other hand, the "dark side" theorists encountered in the previous chapter would argue that resolving distributional inequities is precisely what planning does *not* generally do. Overall, I suspect that many planners attempt to abide by the spirit of Klosterman's fourth rationale in their work, but often find it all too easy to let their good intentions slip in the face of other, more pressing imperatives.

Clearly, all four of Klosterman's "vital social functions" of planning are open to debate. Some present conceptual complications, while others seem inconsistent with the dynamics of contemporary planning practice. As answers to the question "Why do planners plan?" they are only partially satisfying—for some kinds of planning, some of the time, under certain circumstances.

Another answer offered far more frequently, however, is implicit in Klosterman's second point about "the common or collective interests of the community." That answer asserts that planners plan in service to the public interest—that the public interest is, in fact, the very bedrock of planning. Let us turn, then, to an examination of that concept.

THE PUBLIC INTEREST: REAL OR ILLUSORY?

In in-depth interviews with ninety-six public agency planners, Elizabeth Howe found that most of them claimed to use the concept of the public interest in their work. There was no uniformity, however, in how they defined it. "All their definitions had at their core the obligation to serve the public, but, not surprisingly, how knowledge of the 'interest' or the 'good' of the public might be arrived at was open to different interpretations."[12] Significantly, Howe notes that when her interviewees "introduced the idea of the public interest or raised ethical issues in which it figured, they were primarily talking about their own ideas about the public interest."[13]

Few planning terms are simultaneously so widely invoked and so ill-defined. On the one hand, it is eminently reasonable to say that public planners should plan in (or for) the public interest; we would hardly want them to do otherwise. The problem, however, is in attempting to render the concept operational—that is, to give it a definition that is concrete, unambiguous, widely accepted, and applicable to real-world situations. Ideally, a planner confronted with a difficult professional decision should be able to consult the public interest concept for guidance, using it as a template to differentiate the more public-serving outcomes from those that are less so. Alas, such a template does not exist.

Scholars have long struggled with the notion of the public interest, and the work of welfare economists has been particularly instructive. A central tenet of their approach to the public interest (sometimes called the general welfare or the common good) has been the judgment that "it is ethically wrong to evaluate social states on a basis other than that of the welfare of individuals, and this primary value should be the base for any policy maker's set of objectives."[14] Ideally, then, the public interest of a particular society should somehow comprise the individual interests of all those who make up that society. The question is, how do we move from the individual level to the societal? That is, how do we take the preferences of all individuals in the society and transform them into a single societal preference? Of the considerable scholarship that has been devoted to this question, only a few highlights will be mentioned here.

Writing early in the twentieth century, Vilfredo Pareto proposed a criterion for determining whether a given policy proposal is consistent with the principle that social decisions should reflect the welfare of all individuals who make up the society. As paraphrased by William Baumol, Pareto's criterion stated that "any change which harms no one and which makes some people better off (in their own estimation) must be considered to be an improvement."[15] If I introduce a policy that will result in considerable profits for some individuals while imposing absolutely no perceived costs on anyone else, then this policy is "in the public interest" by Pareto's standard. This formulation sounds perfectly reasonable, but it is of little use in assessing any proposal that, as is usually the case, will benefit some while imposing expenses on others. Virtually any planning issue of any significance involves the potential for unequal distribution of costs and benefits; some people win while others lose. Moreover, a loss is no less real if it is merely by comparison rather than actual; if the neighborhood next to mine receives a large infusion of public funds, I may be resentful even if my taxes are not being raised to make it happen and even if my neighborhood has no immediate need for additional funds. Overall, it is safe to conclude that the opportunities for planners to define the public interest by applying the Pareto principle are so rare (and would generally involve problems so trivial) as to be of no significance.

Nicholas Kaldor suggested a refinement of Pareto's criterion. Again as paraphrased by Baumol, Kaldor held that "a change is an improvement if those who gain evaluate their gains at a higher figure than the value which the losers set upon their losses."[16] Potentially, then, the losers could be compensated for their losses and there would still be a net gain for the society. (I gained $100 from this policy while it cost you $40; in theory, I can compensate you for your loss and the net gain for our two-person society will still be $60. Sounds good to me!) An interesting wrinkle in Kaldor's criterion, however, is that in order for it to apply, compensation of the losers must remain potential *only*; if compensation actually occurs, then we are back to the situation covered by the Pareto criterion. In short, Kaldor's definition sounds fine in theory, but in practice it encounters the usual glitches.

Yet a third criterion was proposed by Abram Bergson, who asserted that the only way out of the problem is to formulate a set of explicit value judgments regarding the appropriate procedure to employ in passing from individual preferences to social policies. These judgments would reflect one or another view as to what constitutes justice, efficiency, or some other virtue in the distribution of the society's resources.[17] The problems here are obvious: who is to make these value judgments, and how? All we have to do, Bergson seemed to say, is achieve societal consensus on the way in which our resources will be distributed. Unfortunately, Bergson's criterion did not come equipped with a set of instructions for achieving that consensus, so the difficult part of the task remains unaddressed.

A more general problem was raised by Kenneth Arrow, who argued convincingly that the attempt to pass from individual to social preferences is impossible in most situations.[18] Figure 4-1 illustrates this point.

Preferences

		First choice	Second choice	Third choice
	1	A	B	C
Individuals	2	B	C	A
	3	C	A	B

Figure 4-1. Arrow's impossibility theorem illustrated.

In the figure's hypothetical decision-making situation, a majority of the individuals (1 and 3) prefer alternative *A* to alternative *B*. A majority (1 and 2) also prefer alternative *B* to alternative *C*. If the ranking of these alternatives were linear (or "transitive," to use Arrow's terminology), we would expect that a majority would therefore prefer *A* to *C* as well. This is not the case, however; a majority (2 and 3) prefer *C* to *A*. In this situation, then, no collective decision can be made that is based on the personal preferences of the individuals involved.[19]

It is possible, of course, to argue with Arrow's point (and numerous scholars have done so, their chief weapons being the equations of symbolic logic). For example, his theorem does not take into account the differing intensities with which individual preferences are held, a matter that is frequently of some import in public planning issues. Overall, however, Arrow's theorem does a fine job of illustrating a reality with which any practicing planner is all too familiar: namely, that it is virtually impossible to generate a course of action that will be equally satisfactory to all of one's constituents. Indeed, public opinion on planning matters is generally ill-defined, diverse, contentious, confusing—and decidedly nonlinear. If the welfare economists are correct in their assertion that a legitimate conception of the public interest must be based upon the preferences of each of the society's individual members, then we appear to be out of luck; this conception of the public interest simply isn't workable in the real world.

Other authors have attempted to define the public interest somewhat less rigorously, without concern for the problem of passage from individual to societal preferences. For example, Israel Stollman has written that

> Planners serve the public interest primarily…and must fit the client-employer's interest to the public interest or else not serve that client. This guide is needed most when the public interest is hardest to identify. It is needed most, then, when its guidance is least clear.
>
> The public interest is an amalgam of many specific interests. These include serving the interests of democratic majorities; improving the conditions of the weak, poor, or handicapped; protecting resources in the long run; economizing in the use of public funds; living up to our laws; protecting health and safety; preserving human rights—in short, doing all the things that pursue our abiding values.[20]

This is a good list—but it is one person's. Asked to make a list of our society's abiding values, each of us would put our own unique spin on the task, reflecting the values we consider most important.[21] Much as we may concur with Stollman's list of abiding values at this level of abstraction, moreover, our consensus rapidly evaporates as soon as we begin developing specific plans and strategies for achieving these things. One person's action to preserve natural resources is another person's taking; one person's idea for reforming the health-care system is another person's sure-fire method for destroying that system; and so on. Overall, attempts to define the public interest in this manner—by equating it with one or more values of importance to the definer—tend not to be very fruitful (except, of course, for the definer!).

In an article defending the utility of the public interest concept, Klosterman described it as the "collective interest of all" and argued that it is possible to assess this collective interest in an objective and scientific manner—as long as there is agreement on the criterion to be employed.[22] He offers as an example the proposed construction of an urban expressway linking the central city to an affluent suburb. Should the decisive criterion be economic? Environmental? Distributive? Political? It is possible, he argues, to assess the potential impact of the highway along each of these dimensions, and to make a decision accordingly—as long as there is agreement on the weights to be assigned to the various criteria.[23] His argument is similar to Bergson's, and encounters the same problems. Yes, it would be relatively easy to pursue the public interest if we could achieve consensus on the criteria to be employed. But the selection of a criterion is itself highly subjective, and strongly influenced by the values—and personal stakes—of those who are doing the selecting.[24]

CONCLUSIONS

Where does this leave us, then, with regard to the public interest concept? Does it have a legitimate claim to status as the bedrock of public planning?

Certainly planners continue to use the concept—and to struggle with it. From her interviews with practicing planners, Howe reports that some of them equate the public interest with "environmental, safety, and health regulations and to equal opportunity in housing and employment."[25] Others relate it to social and economic equity. However, "the most common way that planners articulate their idea of the public interest is to say that it is concerned with the long-term good of the entire community."[26]

Linda Davis, a Portland, Oregon, planning consultant with considerable public agency experience as well, provides an illustration of this position:

> What is the "public interest"? Admittedly, this is hard to define, and the longer you are engaged in the profession the more you see that the world is not black and white, but shades of gray.... Today I like to think of public interest more in terms of "community interest." This is because the "public" is indefinite geographically and increasingly diverse socially. There is no way we can know all the values and beliefs of this public. However, we can come to know and understand the values and beliefs of our community, our "local public." Thus, when faced with a difficult situation, ask yourself, "What is good for the community?" This will be an effective guide that will serve you well.[27]

Again, this sounds eminently reasonable, and I suspect that many planners would readily endorse this statement. But wait a moment.

Can the planner really "know and understand the values and beliefs" of everyone in the community? What if some of those values and beliefs are in conflict with one another? If that is the case, whose values and beliefs should prevail? Have planners indeed been authorized to decide what is good for the community? For that matter, can we be certain that we always *know* what is good for the community?

Most people, whether professional planners or not, have ideas about the changes and improvements they would like to see in their community—and many, if pushed on the point, would likely argue that their preferences are indeed in the public interest. But if conceptions of the public interest vary from one person to the next, does the concept really have anything useful to offer as a guide for public action? I suggest that it does not, other than as a rationalization that is sometimes used to justify recommendations for which we can generate no better argument. "Why are you making that particular recommendation?" "Because of all the possibilities that I considered, this one best serves the public interest." "Oh well, then…" Sometimes this works for us, sometimes it doesn't—and when it does, it probably shouldn't.

A municipality introduces major revisions to its zoning ordinance; inevitably, some citizens will benefit while others will be inconvenienced (or worse). A city government fosters major new development on its downtown waterfront; again, there will be winners and losers—the latter including, for example, property owners in other parts of downtown. A revised master plan, a plan for conserving wetlands, plans for a new downtown convention center or performing arts center—each of these, as well as any other significant public initiative, will inevitably distribute its costs and benefits in an unequal manner. Virtually any planning initiative is apt to generate responses from *many* publics, each with its own set of interests—and these varying interests often conflict. Which citizens, then, make up the public whose interests we want to serve? How many people must be benefited before an action is in the public interest? How many must be harmed before we decide to the contrary? These are the sorts of questions that confound the public interest idea and ultimately deprive it of substance and utility.

A community is not a single, monolithic entity. Rather, it is a collectivity of subcommunities (some spatial, some based on shared interests), each with its own special characteristics, values, and aspirations. Each subcommunity, moreover, is itself a collectivity of individuals, often equally diverse. Since virtually anything we do as planners will benefit some (individuals, organizations, communities, institutions) more than others, we are confronted with two basic questions in any planning situation. First, who should benefit? And second, who should *decide* who benefits? The second question occurs at the intersection of planning and politics, and will be discussed at greater length in later chapters. The first question—who should benefit?—places us squarely in the realm of values, the topic of the next chapter.

I suggest, in fact, that values—those of the planner, and those of the diverse individuals and communities whom the planner serves—constitute the real bedrock of planning. Planners plan, ultimately, because they hold values that impel them to do so. Those values will not always prevail, of course. Virtually everything that is done under the aegis of planning involves a body of divergent values that must ultimately be reconciled sufficiently to justify an action.

Yes, Virginia, there is a public interest—but each of us defines it in our own unique manner, reflecting our own values and interests. A conception of what constitutes the public interest may, then, guide an individual's decisions, but it is not a valid basis for justifying those decisions to others. We would do better to explain our decisions in terms of the values—both ours and those of others—that we are attempting to serve.

NOTES

1. Richard E. Klosterman, "Arguments for and against Planning," in *Readings in Planning Theory*, ed. Scott Campbell and Susan S. Fainstein (Cambridge, Mass.: Blackwell Publishers, 1996), pp. 150–168.

2. An early and well-argued case for the provision of information as the primary justification for public planning is made in Stephen S. Skjei, "Urban Problems and the Theoretical Justification of Urban Planning," *Urban Affairs Quarterly*, Vol. 11, No. 3 (March 1976), pp. 323–344.

3. For discussion of this point, see Scott Campbell and Susan S. Fainstein, "Introduction: The Structure and Debates of Planning Theory," in Campbell and Fainstein, *Readings in Planning Theory*, pp. 6–7.

4. Klosterman, "Arguments," p. 155.

5 The wording is Klosterman's; see "Arguments," p. 162.

6. Terry Moore, "Why Allow Planners to Do What They Do? A Justification from Economic Theory," *Journal of the American Institute of Planners*, Vol. 44, No. 4 (October 1978), p. 391.

7. Ibid.

8. Ibid.

9. Ibid.

10. Klosterman, "Arguments," p. 152.

11. Moore, "Why Allow Planners," p. 390.

12. Elizabeth Howe, *Acting on Ethics in City Planning* (New Brunswick, N.J.: Center for Urban Policy Research, Rutgers University, 1994), p. 60.

13. Ibid., p. 62.

14. Richard Zeckhauser and Elmer Schaefer, "Public Policy and Normative Economic Theory," in *The Study of Policy Formation*, ed. Raymond A. Bauer and Kenneth J. Gergen (New York: The Free Press, 1968), p. 40.

15. William J. Baumol, *Economic Theory and Operations Analysis*, 2nd ed. (Englewood Cliffs, N.J.: Prentice-Hall 1965), p. 376.

16. Ibid., p. 378.

17. Ibid., p. 380.

18. See Kenneth J. Arrow, *Social Choice and Individual Values*, 2nd ed. (New York: John Wiley & Sons, 1963).

19. Ibid., pp. 2–3.

20. Israel Stollman, "The Values of the City Planner," in *The Practice of Local Government Planning*, ed. Frank S. So, Israel Stollman, and Frank Beal (Washington, D.C.: International City Management Association, 1979), p. 18.

21. For example, John Friedmann has equated the public interest with equity, with emphasis on equal access to resources. See "The Public Interest and Community Participation: Toward a Reconstruction of Public Philosophy," *Journal of the American Institute of Planners*, Vol. 39, No. 1 (January 1973), pp. 2–12 (including commentaries by Robert Nisbet and Herbert J. Gans).

22. Richard E. Klosterman, "A Public Interest Criterion," *Journal of the American Planning Association*, Vol. 46, No. 3 (July 1980), pp. 323–333.

23. Ibid., p. 329.

24. For an excellent discussion of this issue, see Susan S. Fainstein, "The Politics of Criteria: Planning for the Redevelopment of Times Square," in *Confronting Values in Policy Analysis: The Politics of Criteria*, ed. Frank Fischer and John Forester (Newbury Park, Calif.: Sage Publications, 1987), pp. 232–247.

25. Elizabeth Howe, "Professional Roles and the Public Interest in Planning," *Journal of Planning Literature*, Vol. 6, No. 3 (February 1992), p. 242.

26. Ibid.

27. Linda L. Davis, "Guidelines for Survival and Success," in *Planners on Planning: Leading Planners Offer Real-Life Lessons on What Works, What Doesn't, and Why*, ed. Bruce W. McClendon and Anthony James Catanese (San Francisco: Jossey-Bass Publishers, 1996), pp. 104–105.

5

The Critical Role
of Values and Ethics

VALUES

For the purposes of this discussion, values can be defined quite simply as the principles or standards that are important to us and that therefore help shape our opinions, decisions, and actions. In one sense our values are intensely personal, reflecting our belief systems (which are often—but not always—embodied in religious or philosophical stances). Values also shape our attitudes toward the people, organizations, and institutions with which we interact; our political orientations, for example, are expressions of our value systems. Indeed, values have significant effects on many aspects of our lives, including the performance of our professional roles.

It was generally assumed, during the profession's early years, that planners should be value neutral. This assumption has yielded, however, to the realities of contemporary practice. Most planners recognize that values underlie virtually everything they do under the aegis of planning. Few select a career in urban planning based on expectations of fame, a high salary, or a soft workload; more often, the decision reflects a desire to play a part in "improving our communities" or "making the world a better place for future generations." On the job, virtually every decision a planner makes must take into account the values involved in the situation—his or her own, as well as those of numerous others.

Planners spend a great deal of time analyzing things; shouldn't this part of their role, at least, be free of the influence of values?

Easier said than done. The very selection of a topic to be analyzed often reflects values, as does the selection of a methodology. Shall we rely more heavily, in making our recommendations regarding a particular neighborhood improvement, on a careful cost-benefit analysis of the major options, or on a canvass of residents' views? If the latter, shall we rely on neighborhood meetings, undertake surveys, conduct focus groups, or employ some other method? All these choices involve values. Moreover, the value biases that the planner brings to the analysis—based on social class, education, political philosophy, and other personal characteristics—will likely play a role, no matter how hard he or she tries to keep them in check. The "facts" generated by research are often subject to diverse interpretations. Indeed, the line between value and fact is frequently rather thin where planning issues are concerned.

Are there universal planning values to which all planners can subscribe, and that can therefore guide them in their work? Israel Stollman suggested such a list in 1979; it included health, conservation of resources, efficiency, beauty, equity, pluralism, individuality, democratic participation, democratic responsibility, and rational management.[1] The list is a good one, but hardly free of problems (as Stollman himself noted). These values are held differentially— that is, in different combinations and with differing interpretations and levels of priority—by different individuals and groups; in practice, such values often end up in conflict with one another. As noted earlier, values are intensely personal, so whose—in a given situation—should prevail? The planner's? Those of elected officials? Those of the planner's client? And if the client, who *is* the client?

By way of illustrating the difficulties inherent in attempting to develop a list of universal planning values, one of my favorite teaching exercises is to ask my students to identify buildings in the local community that they consider beautiful. A lively argument generally ensues, since one person's architectural masterpiece is another's eyesore. Similar arguments can be instigated around the concepts of efficiency (at what point do admirably detail-oriented bureaucrats become "bean counters"?), equity (are we talking about equality of opportunity or of results?), and virtually every other item on Stollman's list.

In a more recent (1993) article, John Friedmann listed his own professional values, which he described as being "grounded in a humanist vision":

In the late twentieth century, the following values seem to compel serious consideration: the ideals of inclusive democracy; giving voice to the disempowered; integrating disempowered groups into the mainstream of economic and social life while preserving cultural diversity; privileging qualitative over quantitative growth, including the notion of sustainability; gender equality; and respect for the natural world.[2]

This too is a good list, reflecting fewer obvious internal conflicts and manifesting greater harmony with postmodern planning sensibilities. But this list would hardly enjoy the full and enthusiastic endorsement of all those in the planner's work orbit, nor would consensus exist—even among planners—on procedures for acting on these values. Friedmann's intention, of course, was clear; he was stating his own values and urging others to consider them as well, but he was not so foolhardy as to endow them with official status for the profession.

Making a list of one's professional values is not a bad thing to do; indeed, I would encourage every planner to do so. Each such list, however, will be a reflection of the professional values of its author rather than a recitation of acquired professional doctrine; hence few such lists will look exactly alike.

Lists aside, are there any fundamental values that can be said to form the normative foundation of public planning? Back in the days when planning was generally viewed as an exercise in rational decision-making (before, say, the 1970s), theorists were inclined to see planning as a manifestation of utilitarianism, a body of theory originally developed by Jeremy Bentham, an eighteenth-century English philosopher. As described by Thomas Harper and Stanley Stein, utilitarian theory judges the best course of action to be "one that maximizes the sum total of whatever is intrinsically good— usually happiness or well-being."[3] The utilitarian view would suggest, then, that the planner's role is to produce the greatest good for the greatest number—a notion that is easily equated with the concept of the public interest and is readily served by cost-benefit analysis and other techniques aimed at maximizing positive outcomes.[4] An example of utilitarian theory in practice, offered by Harper and Stein, is "the justification of a new rapid transit line as having benefits (which go to many more people—that is, the commuters) exceeding costs (such as the harm to nearby and displaced residents, who are relatively few in number)."[5]

Today utilitarianism has, for the most part, been rejected by planning theorists. Its fatal flaw, as a fundamental value for public planning, is that it focuses on maximizing the sum total of a particular good at the societal (or community) level but pays no attention to individual shares of that good; in other words, it ignores the manner in which the benefits produced by planning are to be distributed—and in fact provides a basis for using the public interest as an excuse for actions that may do great harm to some individuals.[6]

Harper and Stein have suggested an alternative value system, described by them as classical liberalism but more commonly referred to today as libertarianism. Its basic focus is on "the free, equal, and autonomous individual person as the basic unit of society."[7] Specific principles include individual liberty, tolerance for differing conceptions of the good life, impartial application of the law, and restriction of the "coercive powers" of government, which should instead focus primarily on the protection of liberty.[8] Clearly, public planning would be a comparatively modest enterprise under a libertarian value system.

At the other extreme, stressing pluralistic rather than individualistic values, is communitarianism, a philosophy recently espoused by Amitai Etzioni and others.[9] Reacting in part to the alleged "me-first" spirit of the 1980s, communitarians argue that our overemphasis on individual rights has resulted in the loss of important community rights. This balance, they say, should be restored. An example: police roadblocks to check for drugs and illegal firearms may be inconvenient to the innocent, but their benefits to the community outweigh the inconvenience.

Yet another value system, developed by John Rawls, emphasizes justice as the primary criterion to be employed in public decision-making.[10] Instead of attempting to provide the greatest good for the greatest number, Rawls would have us provide the greatest benefits to the least advantaged. Under this value system, planning would focus on fairness and equity, striving to ensure that all residents of the community have equal access to the benefits of planning. (Norman Krumholz's style of planning in Cleveland, described in Chapter 8, reflected Rawls's value system.) Still other authors have attempted to develop value systems based on specific sets of issues—for example, building on concern for the environment to create an environmental ethic upon which a broad range of decisions might be based,[11] or building on the roles and life experiences of women in a capitalist society.[12]

Values are staples of planning theory, of course, and most of the work being done by contemporary planning theorists is intensely value based. Those committed, for example, to a "progressive" political ideology—and a significant number of theorists over the past quarter-century have been so committed—have not been shy in urging readers to adopt their perspectives.[13] As Nigel Taylor notes, a key value-based issue for planning theorists has been whether planners should

> engage in practices which involve working pragmatically with the market and compromising certain planning ideals to achieve at least something on the ground. One's view about this depends on one's political ethics and ideology. For those ideologically committed to Marxism, working "with" capitalist developers is exactly what planners should not do. For according to Marxist ideology, the aim is to replace capitalism, not perpetuate it by striking deals which further the interests of capitalist developers. Political liberals take a more positive view of the market system, and therefore also of a style of planning which works with the market.[14]

Do any of the value systems cited thus far provide a universally agreed upon foundation for the practice of planning? The answer is clearly no. Different planners subscribe to different sets of values, and what is important to one may be of no concern whatsoever to another. Moreover, our values are subject to change over time, reflecting—among other causes—changes in our life circumstances. For that matter, value systems are themselves highly fluid; this year's philosophical fad may not be in vogue next year. (Stollman's list of values, published in 1979, seems somewhat dated today; Friedmann's 1993 list is more au courant—but will it still be so by, say, 2015?)

I have argued that values are critically important to the practice of planning; indeed, values permeate every professional issue that the planner is apt to confront. The fact that an issue is being investigated systematically, with sophisticated methods of data collection and analysis, does not free it from this generalization. As Taylor notes, "the idea that something like cost-benefit analysis...can provide an uncontroversially right 'answer' is seriously misleading, for the problem of deciding which alternative is *preferable* remains. This problem is not 'solved' by means of a statistical calculation, for the act of choosing the preferable option still remains a matter of *value*."[15]

I have also concluded, however, that despite the socialization that occurs during the course of a planner's professional education and practice, there are no universal value systems to which all planners subscribe. Each of us might wish that his or her own values were dominant in the planning profession; indeed, countless books and articles have been published in efforts to persuade others that a particular set of values is the "right" one for planners. It is certainly reasonable to assume that values reflecting a concern for the well-being of the community, or for some segment thereof, are much more relevant to planning than are values related to one's personal well-being. In the final analysis, however, we planners acknowledge no central authority regarding the values we should hold; our values remain our own, and a measure of diversity continues to prevail in this regard. So where does this leave us?

Values themselves are inherently passive—abstract principles or standards that become concrete only when applied. Thinking about the application of values leads, in turn, to a consideration of planning ethics, which I view as the action component of planning values.

ETHICS

In the early 1980s, while serving as dean of the design school at a large midwestern university, I made a fund-raising trip to several cities in the Southwest. In each city I met with groups of alumni, brought them up to date on events and changes at the school, and encouraged them to support the school financially. Particularly fruitful, in this regard, was a luncheon meeting with an alumnus who had recently experienced considerable financial success. The former planning director for his city, he had correctly anticipated the coming boom in downtown real estate values and had resigned his public position to form a development partnership with several private sector colleagues. Much land was acquired at the most propitious time, and much money had been made. At the end of our meeting he told me, somewhat apologetically, that his other charitable commitments required him to restrict his gift to only $50,000 for now—but that he would try to do better in later years. Since most of the donations received on the trip had been of the $50 and $100 variety, I was understandably ecstatic, and returned to the school feeling that the trip had been a major success.

Shortly after this particular pledge became public, however, a delegation of students visited my office to request that I refuse the $50,000 donation. The students' position was that since the individual in question had made his money on the basis of information he had acquired during his service as the city's planning director—which, in their view, was ethically questionable—then it would be unethical to accept the money.

I promised to consider their position, and did so. (I will not embarrass myself by specifying the length of time during which I considered it.) Ultimately, I informed the students that I had decided to retain the gift for the school. Clearly, the alumnus had vacated his public position before making the investments that proved so profitable, and he had waited an appropriate period of time before interacting with his former department. Had he attempted to profit from his inside knowledge while on the public payroll, he most certainly would have been engaging in behavior that was unethical—and illegal as well. But this had not been the case, and I concluded that no ethical principles had been violated in this situation.

I describe this case simply to introduce the concept of an ethical dilemma. All of us face such dilemmas constantly, in both our private and our professional capacities. We know that we are facing an ethical dilemma when we ask ourselves, "What is the right thing to do here?" Ethical dilemmas typically force us to reflect upon our values and how they should be applied to the situation at hand.

In planning, I find it useful to distinguish between "micro" and "macro" ethical issues; the former pertain to individual professional behavior, while the latter involve the collective behavior of the profession as a whole.

National planning organizations have generally served as the definers and enforcers of ethical practice; today this function is the responsibility of the American Institute of Certified Planners (AICP), whose code of ethics will be discussed later in this chapter. Historically, the formal enactment of this role has focused primarily on micro ethical issues. In the 1960s and 1970s, when the American Institute of Planners (a forerunner of the AICP) concerned itself with enforcing ethical standards, the situations in question were likely to involve conflict of interest, or the unethical use of inside information, or even the violation of the principle that planning consultants who are bidding on contracts should never bad-mouth their competitors.

Today, more attention is being paid—at least in the planning literature—to macro ethical issues. Public planning entails decisions regarding the nature, distribution, and timing of a variety of potential benefits; needless to say, these decisions are quivering masses of ethical dilemmas. It is not surprising, then, that ethical complaints are voiced from time to time regarding planning departments that seem to be doing the bidding of corrupt political administrations, or seem too cozy with developers, or overlook the negative impacts of specific projects on low-income neighborhoods, or remain silent in the face of discriminatory or exclusionary policies, or appear too willing to alter their research findings and projections to comply with the biases of elected officials. The issues underlying these sorts of charges are never simple, of course; strong political forces may be at work, involving numerous players, and the stakes are typically high. Nevertheless, such charges pose genuine ethical problems for the planning profession, and we do not always cover ourselves with honor on such matters.

Other observers have charged that too many planners are living out stable and secure careers as bureaucrats, rather than serving as advocates for equity, social justice, environmental quality, and other important principles. Peter Marcuse, for example, has asserted that planning ethics as currently practiced are "system-maintaining" rather than "system-challenging." He believes that planners' professional ethics tend to reinforce established power relationships, and that we have shied away from perspectives that might yield entirely different sets of ethics.[16]

A widely discussed concept in the realm of popular philosophy in decades past was that of situational ethics. This concept is based on the proposition that few ethical principles are applicable to all situations, and that the context of an action helps to shape its ethical content. Thus what is unethical in one situation may be quite ethical in another. (Lying to an accident victim who is clearly dying, killing an armed intruder who is threatening one's family—these and similar situations are typically offered as examples.)

I suggest that planners, too, often encounter decisions involving situational ethics. Years ago, the planning director of a well-to-do Philadelphia suburb was ordered to draft a revised zoning ordinance for his county, the intention being to increase significantly the lot-size requirements for new development. The objective was clearly exclusionary. Rather than comply with this order, he resigned his position. His principled stand received much applause in planning circles, and he was soon in a position to choose from several attractive job offers. It is important to note, however, that this event occurred at a time when federal funds for planning were abundant. *Jobs in Planning,* distributed monthly at that time by the American Society of Planning Officials, was a thick "dreambook," regularly listing hundreds of available positions throughout the nation. Today's situation, of course, is quite different; staffs tend to be smaller, openings are not as abundant, and the job market as a whole is less fluid than it was in the 1970s. As a result, planners have less mobility—and more anxiety about hanging on to the positions that they have. This circumstance inevitably renders planners more cautious about making waves. I might consider resigning as a matter of principle over a particular issue—but can I be certain that I will immediately be picked up elsewhere, and by a community in which I would want to live? Can my family afford to go a few months with little or no income? Such questions do give one pause, and greater caution may result. I raise this point not to apologize for ethical lapses in planning behavior but simply to suggest that the ethical climate is indeed influenced by situational factors—and that one of these factors is the current vitality of the job market. Tight job markets undoubtedly pose special challenges to the realm of planning ethics.

A Typology of Ethical Dilemmas in Planning Practice

Much has been written about the ethical dilemmas planners face in the course of their professional practice.[17] Most of these dilemmas, I believe, involve one or more of the following five kinds of issues:

(1) *Loyalty to one's employer versus loyalty to a broader principle or group.* The planning director who resigned his job rather than produce the exclusionary zoning revisions requested by his superiors resolved his dilemma in favor of his principles. I suspect, however, that virtually every reader of this book can think of examples to the contrary—that is, situations in which planners sacrificed their principles in order to do the bidding of their superiors (whether the planning director, city manager, or elected officials). Indeed, many readers will have personal experience of this sort; sometimes there appears to be no other option, consistent with retaining one's job. Because acting contrary to their values on a

regular basis can be devastating to their personal and professional self-respect, however, many planners have defined a "resigning point," an ethical limit beyond which they are unwilling to go. This can be, in fact, a significant element in one's professional value system.

(2) The control and release of information. When, if ever, is it ethically permissible to leak confidential information? A planner might feel no temptation whatsoever to leak information—about, say, a planned entertainment complex—to developers who could benefit financially from that information, but would a planner be equally reluctant to share information with an environmental advocacy group that wishes to prevent the potentially damaging complex from being built? An African American planner learns of impending plans to clear part of a predominantly black neighborhood to allow for the expansion of a local university; is that planner justified in blowing the whistle so that the neighborhood can begin to organize in opposition to the plan? Clearly, the "loyalty to employer" principle would preclude leaking information in either case, but temptations nevertheless occur—temptations that originate with the planner's commitment to other values and principles.

(3) The accuracy and integrity of information. Martin Wachs has written about the difficulties planners encounter when they are asked to fudge or cook the numbers, in studies they have conducted, in order to place the city (and its officials) in a more favorable light.[18] His examples include publicizing the positive reactions to a proposed development while keeping the negative reactions under wraps; reworking the assumptions in quantitative models to produce the results that superiors or clients desire; and making overly optimistic projections of population or economic development.[19] Equally troubling are situations in which findings from a study in one locality are applied to another, or where clearly out-of-date data are presented as an accurate description of current circumstances (do 1990 census data accurately portray a city's housing problems in 1999?).[20]

A sizable body of planning theory focuses on the accuracy and integrity of planning communications; this literature will be examined in Chapter 9. For now it suffices to note that planners have significant ethical responsibilities regarding the accuracy and integrity of the information that they generate, analyze, and communicate to others.

(4) Conflict between what one deems right and what will sell. Planners often analyze alternatives (potential actions, developments, locations, magnitudes, timing, and so on) only to learn that those they deem best are not those that receive public or political support. Sometimes, in fact, the most popular "solutions" to a problem are those that the planner knows will render the situation worse.

A major industry wants to locate on a waterfront site in your county; you know that the site is entirely wrong, that environmental problems are sure to arise, that the subsidies promised the firm are out of line with reasonable expectations for increases in tax revenues, and that most of the jobs created by the development will go to outsiders. Your efforts to convince others on these points fall on deaf ears; local elected officials want to land this firm at virtually any cost. What do you do? Should your report to the planning board communicate what you really think, or is it safer to tell the board members what you know they want to hear? Again, one must consult one's values and ethics.

(5) Shortcuts. The results of a study done on the run—using shaky data because they were all one could find, ignoring particular sources or methods because they would have consumed more time or funds than one wanted to spend, drawing conclusions that are not really supported by the data at hand—may vary radically from those yielded by a more competent study. Shortchanging the citizen participation process—treating it as a troublesome requirement that must be carried out rather than as an opportunity to strengthen the legitimacy of a particular decision—can backfire in a number of unpleasant ways. Any situation in which a planner is tempted to take shortcuts—that is, to give something less than his or her best—is one that raises ethical issues.

The accompanying sidebar is an exercise that I have used in the classroom on several occasions. It stacks the deck, to be sure, but it does illustrate several of the types of ethical dilemmas I have described. The reader may find it useful to reflect on this case and determine how she or he would respond to the questions asked at the end.

The AICP Code of Ethics and Professional Conduct

As noted earlier, national organizations often assume responsibility for the development and enforcement of standards of professional ethics. For planners, this role is played by the AICP, whose Code of

An Ethical Dilemma

You are the planning director for Pleasantville, Virginia, a city of 70,000. You report directly to the city manager, who considers economic development to be her highest priority. She has succeeded in convincing a New England chemical firm to relocate its manufacturing facility to your community, and the firm has identified a riverside site (currently zoned for low-density residential use) as its only acceptable location. "If we can't have that site, we'll go to a community that places a higher value on economic progress," the firm's president has threatened. (Ironically, you yourself live in Happiness Estates, a neighborhood that begins only three blocks from the site.)

On the one hand, it is estimated that the facility will create two hundred new jobs for the community, and this employment increase is universally applauded. On the other hand, the firm's poor environmental record is a source of serious concern to you, especially since the river that flows through your community passes through several other populated areas on its way to the Chesapeake Bay. Given the obvious economic benefits of the firm's relocation, however, few city leaders seem concerned about the possibility of environmental problems.

When you express your concerns to the city manager, she responds angrily. "Bringing in this firm serves the public interest in our community," she asserts, "and I want you to do everything in your power—rezoning, tax incentives, any other legal means—to ensure that the deal goes through. Make it happen."

Meanwhile, the Happiness Estates Neighborhood Association, representing the area in which you live, has announced an evening meeting for the purpose of developing a strategy for opposing the proposed site. Most people in the neighborhood welcome the jobs that the firm would create, but they don't want the plant located so close to their own homes; their greatest concern is that the proximity of the chemical plant will damage property values. The president of the neighborhood association has invited you to attend the meeting as a "resource person," and has asked you to bring along any information you might have regarding the firm, its environmental track record in other locations, the details of what it wants to do on the riverside site, and the potential risks that it presents to the neighborhood.

What are the major issues that you must consider in deciding how to respond to this invitation—that is, in deciding whether or not to attend the meeting? What decisions would you make on these issues, and why?

Ethics and Professional Conduct was first adopted in 1978 and was last amended in 1991. The intent of the code is to provide planners with an ethical compass to guide them through the difficulties they may encounter in the course of their practice. It performs this task well in some regards—and not so well in others.

In my view, there are two problems. The first, and most serious, is the code's reliance on a concept that—as we have seen—has little concrete utility in practice. "A planner's primary obligation," says the code, "is to serve the public interest. While the definition of the public interest is formulated through continuous debate, a planner owes allegiance to a conscientiously attained concept of the public interest."[21] As Taylor has noted, there is a tendency to speak of the public as though it were "an undifferentiated group. This is, of course, far from the truth; the public of any modern society is composed of all sorts of different groups, with differing and some- times incompatible interests."[22] Which of these publics, then, is the planner to serve? To assert, moreover, that "the definition of the public interest is formulated through continuous debate" raises an interesting philosophical conundrum: if that debate is expected to reach an end state—yielding a truly workable definition—shouldn't we wait until we have it before attempting to operate under its terms? If, on the other hand, the debate is expected to remain forever "continuous," how can the planner be expected to serve such a fluid and undefined principle? The statement that "the planner owes allegiance to a conscientiously attained concept of the public interest" implies that the definition will vary from individual to individual (which is, of course, an accurate observation); but how will the AICP know, in any particular case, whether the public interest has indeed been served? In short, this aspect of the code is both internally contradictory and unenforceable.

In fairness, it must be noted that the statement about the public interest is followed by a list of seven "special obligations" of planners, dealing with attention to long-range consequences, the interrelatedness of decisions, the provision of clear and accurate information, opportunities for meaningful citizen participation, the expansion of choice and opportunity for all persons (with emphasis on the "responsibility to plan for the needs of disadvantaged groups and persons"), the integrity of the natural environment, and excellence in environmental design and conservation. Each of these items does suggest a useful ethic for planners, albeit at a highly general level. These special obligations stand on their own, however; they do not collectively add up to the public interest, nor do they need to be subsumed under a definition of the public interest in order to be meaningful.

The second major item in the code states that the planner "owes diligent, creative, independent and competent performance of work in pursuit of the client's or employer's interest. Such performance should be consistent with the planner's faithful service to the public interest." Here we encounter an internal contradiction. What if the client's and the employer's interests are in conflict (which is, I suspect, often the case)? To be sure, the code says "client's *or* employer's" rather than *and,* so perhaps it is acceptable to make a choice. Does this mean, however, that it is quite all right to violate the interests of a client as long as the employer's interests are being served? I doubt that was the intent. The "faithful service to the public interest" clause also presents difficulties. If we don't know what the public interest is, how can we serve it faithfully? If my personal conception of the public interest happens to conflict with that held by my client, my employer, or both, am I justified in ignoring their interests?

Once again, the major principle is followed by a list of ethical do's and don'ts, most of which (except for those that continue to ignore the possibility of client-employer conflict) are situation-specific and thus potentially useful. The other two major headings, the first of which deals with the planner's responsibility to the profession and to colleagues, the second with the importance of "high standards of professional integrity, proficiency and knowledge," both supported with useful lists of specifics, are essentially unarguable as well.[23]

In the final analysis, the code is a mixed bag. On the one hand, it does provide several useful definitions of ethical versus unethical conduct under specific circumstances. On the other hand, it leaves some of the profession's major conceptual difficulties unresolved— and may, in fact, confuse the issue by introducing the internal contradictions noted earlier. It is unfortunate, moreover, that the code relies so heavily on the concept of the public interest, for which it is unable—not surprisingly—to provide a workable definition.

CONCLUSIONS

Our lives as planners might well be less stressful if we possessed a set of rules of ethical conduct telling us how to behave in every situation; this would relieve us of the need to ponder our ethical dilemmas and to make difficult choices. No such set of rules exists, however. The AICP code offers some useful directions on specific points but does not provide an overall system of planning ethics that is well defined and internally consistent, and therefore applicable across a broad range of situations. No other individual or organization, moreover, possesses the requisite authority for articulating such a system, so planners have nowhere else to turn for this purpose.

Does this leave the planning profession in an ethically untenable position? I don't think so. I question, in fact, whether we would be well served by a uniform, overarching statement of professional values and ethics, one with which all planners would be compelled to comply in order to continue practicing. As Arthur Bassin has observed, planners are as free as others "to choose their own politics and personal commitments and to act upon these in a manner befitting responsible citizens of a democracy."[24] We have no party line—a situation that I do not consider unfortunate.

What the absence of such an overarching statement means, however, is that the most important processes involving values and ethics are ultimately internal to each individual planner. As professionals, then, each of us should be engaged in a never-ending quest for ethical behavior based on the values of greatest importance to us. Noting the unlikelihood that we could ever succeed in formulating a "single, general ethical theory of planning practice," Richard Bolan has nevertheless stressed the sense of morality that must underlie planning practice.

> As moralist, the practitioner is continually pushed to make ethical judgments and decisions in a social field that is characterized by a thicket of conflicting claims and pulls, some clearly apparent while others are ambiguous, covert, hidden or unspoken. The practitioner's role of moralist, then, is actually the more prominent in terms of professional creativity and imagination as distinct from the scientific, "puzzle-solving" role. The true task of the professional is not to display cleverness and intellectual dexterity but, rather, to create a new sense of value. Thus, the true challenge for every practitioner is to become a creative moralist.[25]

Neither I, nor any of the others who write about planning, nor your employer or elected officials, nor the AICP, nor any other person or institution of significance in your life can provide you with a definitive and universal set of ethics that will cover all situations. Self-awareness, introspection, sensitivity to the value nuances of practice—these are major virtues that every planner should possess. Each planner should be sensitive to the ethical dimensions of his or her work, and should be able to recognize an ethical dilemma when it appears. Above all, each planner should formulate an individual and highly personal conception of what constitutes ethical professional behavior, based on his or her own value system. With such a conception, planning is a distinguished and noble profession; without it, planning is simply...a job. Indeed, the bedrock of public planning is made up of the values and ethics of those who practice it. The profession's foundation is only as solid as the body of values on which it is based.

NOTES

1. Israel Stollman, "The Values of the City Planner," in *The Practice of Local Government Planning*, ed. Frank S. So, Israel Stollman, and Frank Beal (Washington, D.C.: International City Management Association, 1979), pp. 8–14.

2. John Friedmann, "Toward a Non-Euclidian Mode of Planning," *Journal of the American Planning Association*, Vol. 59, No. 4 (Autumn 1993), p. 483.

3. Thomas L. Harper and Stanley M. Stein, "A Classical Liberal (Libertarian) Approach to Planning Theory," in *Planning Ethics: A Reader in Planning Theory, Practice, and Education*, ed. Sue Hendler (New Brunswick, N.J.: Center for Urban Policy Research, Rutgers University, 1995), p. 14. Also see Nigel Taylor, *Urban Planning Theory Since 1945* (London: Sage Publications, 1998), pp. 79–80; Elizabeth Howe, "Normative Ethics in Planning," *Journal of Planning Literature*, Vol. 5, No. 2 (November 1990), p. 127; and Hilda Blanco, *How to Think about Social Problems: American Pragmatism and the Idea of Planning* (Westport, Conn.: Greenwood Press, 1994), pp. 141–142.

4. Taylor, *Urban Planning Theory*, p. 80.

5. Harper and Stein, "Classical Liberal Aproach," p. 15.

6. Ibid.

7. Ibid., p. 12.

8. Ibid.

9. See Amitai Etzioni, *The Spirit of Community: Rights, Responsibilities, and the Communitarian Agenda* (New York: Crown Publishers, 1993); and Hilda Blanco, "Community and the Four Jewels of Planning," in Hendler, *Planning Ethics*, pp. 66–82.

10. See John Rawls, *A Theory of Justice* (Cambridge, Mass.: Harvard University Press, 1971). For a commendably accessible discussion of Rawls's impact on planning thought, see Shean McConnell, "Rawlsian Planning Theory," in Hendler, *Planning Ethics*, pp. 30–48.

11. See, for example, Harvey M. Jacobs, "Contemporary Environmental Philosophy and Its Challenge to Planning Theory," in Hendler, *Planning Ethics*, pp. 154–173.

12. See, for example, Leonie Sandercock and Ann Forsyth, "A Gender Agenda: New Directions for Planning Theory," *Journal of the American Planning Association*, Vol. 58, No. 1 (Winter 1992), pp. 49–59; and Sue Hendler, "Feminist Planning Ethics," *Journal of Planning Literature*, Vol. 9, No. 2 (November 1994), pp. 115–127.

13. See, for example, Robert Beauregard, "Bringing the City Back In," *Journal of the American Planning Association*, Vol. 56, No. 2 (Spring 1990), pp. 210–215.

14. Taylor, *Urban Planning Theory*, p. 128.

15. Ibid., p. 79.

16. Peter Marcuse, "Professional Ethics and Beyond: Values in Planning," in *Ethics in Planning*, ed. Martin Wachs (New Brunswick, N.J.: Center for Urban Policy Research, Rutgers University, 1985), pp. 3–24.

17. For broad and insightful treatments of this topic, see Wachs, *Ethics in Planning*, and Elizabeth Howe, *Acting on Ethics in City Planning* (New Brunswick, N.J.: Center for Urban Policy Research, Rutgers University, 1994). Howe and Jerome Kaufman have authored, both singly and together, a number of articles reporting on their research on the ethics of planning practitioners and students. Also valuable is the work of Carol D. Barrett, who has developed a number of ethical scenarios that illustrate the types of dilemmas being described here; see, for example, "Planners in Conflict," *Journal of the American Planning Association*, Vol. 55, No. 4 (Autumn 1989), pp. 474–476.

18. Martin Wachs, "When Planners Lie with Numbers," *Journal of the American Planning Association*, Vol. 55, No. 4 (Autumn 1989), pp. 476–479.

19. Ibid., p. 477.

20. Ibid.

21. The code appears in a number of publications. A recent one—and the one I am employing here—is *Planners' Casebook* 30/31, Spring/Summer 1999. Given this diversity of sources, I will dispense with page numbers in this discussion.

22. Taylor, *Urban Planning Theory*, p. 50.

23. A somewhat more general critique of the code was published in 1988 (and thus before the last set of amendments) by William H. Lucy, who felt that it oversimplified a number of difficult issues confronted by planners. See "APA's Ethical Principles Include Simplistic Planning Theories," *Journal of the American Planning Association*, Vol. 54, No. 2 (Spring 1988), pp. 147–149.

24. Arthur Bassin, "Does Capitalist Planning Need Some Glasnost?" *Journal of the American Planning Association*, Vol. 56, No. 2 (Spring 1990), p. 217.

25. Richard S. Bolan, "The Structure of Ethical Choice in Planning Practice," in Wachs, *Ethics in Planning*, p. 87.

Alternative Paradigms
for Public Planning

INTRODUCTION

How should public planning be carried out? In Chapter 2, reference was made to the functional normative theories of planning and to theories *for* planning (as opposed to theories *about* or *of* planning). The next four chapters will focus on theories of this type, and will do so by examining the major paradigms that have been proposed for use by planners.

Such an examination requires a categorizing system, and I will employ here a scheme that I have been using for a number of years with good results. The paradigms will be distinguished from one another along two dimensions: the *locus* of planning that is assumed in the paradigm, and the *mode* of planning that is prescribed. With respect to locus, strategies that assume planning to be a centralized process will be distinguished from those that see it as essentially decentralized—more of a bottom-up process. With respect to mode, strategies that prescribe some form of rational behavior will be distinguished from those that view rationality as impossible or impractical and therefore prescribe various forms of non-rational behavior. As shown in the accompanying figure, these two dimensions yield four general types of planning strategies.

Each of the strategies will be described and evaluated in terms of its feasibility and potential usefulness in the highly political world of planning practice. The central questions are: Does the strategy work? And if so, under what circumstances?

LOCUS OF PLANNING

		Centralized	Decentralized
MODE OF PLANNING	**Rational**	The planner as applied scientist: Comprehensive rationality	The planner as political activist: Advocacy
	Nonrational	The planner confronts politics: Incrementalism	The planner as communicator: Communicative action

A typology of planning strategies.

6

Centralized Rationality: The Planner as Applied Scientist

THE NATURE OF RATIONALITY

If, as noted earlier, planning theorists have indeed thoroughly discredited the notion of planning as an exercise in rationality, why spend time on that notion here? The answer rests in the fact that, the theorists' views notwithstanding, the rational model is still widely invoked in the world of planning practice. Ask a professional planner to describe how he or she carries out the planning process, and the odds are good that you will hear some version of the rational model. Ironically, planning schools often display a split personality on this matter—trashing rationality in the planning theory class, while continuing to teach it in all its glory in the methods and studio classes. Much like the creatures in horror movies, rationality is dead—but keeps showing up in public places. Despite its purported flaws, rationality is still the dominant paradigm in planning practice, and therefore continues to deserve careful scrutiny.

The origin of the idea that rationality is the essence of planning has been attributed to a number of sources. One of the most important, certainly, was the University of Chicago's graduate program in city planning, which enjoyed a brief but productive life shortly after World War II. That program, the first to emphasize the social science aspects of planning, was staffed by several people who had participated in the exciting national planning efforts of the Roosevelt administration in the 1930s; as those teachers and their students dispersed to other graduate schools of planning throughout the nation, the gospel of rationality was spread.[1]

The Chicago scholars relied heavily on the "rational man" of classical economic theory, who always behaves in such a manner as to maximize his utility or satisfaction. This group's focus on rationality was essentially an effort to apply the tenets of the scientific method to the urban community. These scholars were, above all, applied social scientists, and rationality was the major instrument they intended to employ in the creation of a more orderly, attractive, and just urban America.

Rationality is, of course, an ambiguous term, used in a variety of ways, and it is therefore necessary to clarify how the word will be used here. To begin with, a distinction is generally made between two types of rationality: *pure* (or objective) and *pragmatic* (subjective, qualified, bounded). Pure rationality is the mode of reasoning that would be employed if we had perfect knowledge of all the factors in a given situation. For the planner, given a set of objectives to be attained, pure rationality would imply the ability to conceive of all potential courses of action that might be followed in pursuit of those objectives; it would also imply the ability to predict with certainty all the consequences of each potential course of action. Rationality of this sort is, of course, an impossibility; pure rationality is an ideal, an abstraction that constitutes the logical end point on a conceptual continuum but has no counterpart in the real world.

Pragmatic rationality, on the other hand, is simply the form of reasoning that we employ in that real world as we apply foresight and intelligence in our attempts to solve our problems or shape our future. As Niraj Verma has pointed out, it is the "opposite of intuition," and is "associated with scientific method, structured decision making, and the use of methods and analytic techniques such as mathematical modeling and hypothesis testing."[2] Rationality of this sort is bounded by constraints of many kinds; we accept these, however, as inevitable features of the human condition. Throughout history men and women have labored mightily to expand the scope of the knowable and manageable. But however far the constraints may be pushed and stretched, in the last analysis they are still there. Pragmatic rationality, then, does not require that we have perfect knowledge, but only that we make good use of the knowledge available to us. For the planner, who is no more capable of pure rationality than is anyone else, a pragmatically rational decision is thus simply one in which alternatives and consequences are considered as fully as he or she is able to consider them, given the time and other resources readily available.[3]

The process of planning in a pragmatically rational manner has been described in a number of ways, and with a highly variable number of prescribed steps. One of the most detailed and enduring descriptions appeared in the appendix of a book written in 1955 by Martin Meyerson and Edward C. Banfield, but countless other formulations have been offered since that time.[4] Rather than attempt to review that literature, I will simply note that most of these formulations present one or another variation on the following theme.

(1) Goals. What do we want to accomplish?

(2) Alternatives. What courses of action are potentially available for accomplishing our goals?

(3) Consequences. What consequences, both positive and negative, might be expected to result from the major alternatives under consideration?

(4) Choice. In light of the above steps—and given the values that are most important to us—which alternative should we pursue?

(5) Implementation. Having settled on a course of action, how shall we carry it out?

(6) Evaluation. To what extent is our chosen course of action achieving the goals at which it is aimed?

Having conceded that we must settle for the pragmatic form of rationality does not, of course, resolve the problems that inevitably accompany attempts at rational decision-making. Are we certain that our goals are appropriate, unambiguous, and endorsed by all major stakeholders? Since it is likely that far more alternative courses of action are potentially available than we can possibly conjure up, how do we know which ones to select for further consideration? Similarly, since the consequences of any major action are virtually limitless, rippling outward as when a stone is thrown into water, how do we decide which possible consequences to subject to analysis, and what do we do about those often important consequences that simply cannot be foreseen? In planning, Ernest

Alexander has argued, rationality "implies that a plan, a policy, or a strategy for action is based on valid assumptions, and includes all relevant information relating to the facts, theories, and concepts on which it is based."[5] But what basis do we have (other than the word of the analyst) for determining that the assumptions are indeed valid, and that no relevant information has been ignored?

By itself, the concept of pragmatic rationality is, unfortunately, devoid of behavior rules; it tells us to make the best of the situation at hand but does not tell us how to evaluate that situation, what constitutes "best" for what kinds of situations, or how to behave if the boundaries and constraints of the situation are less than clear. (How often is a planner told that he or she has exactly ten days and $20,000 to generate six distinct alternatives?) I suggest that pragmatic rationality is potentially useful only when it is rendered operational—that is, when it is embodied in a planning model or strategy that comes equipped with a set of instructions. Many such models have been developed, all of them intended to reduce the degree of uncertainty that is inherent in efforts to apply pragmatic rationality to planning problems. Some of these models will be examined briefly later in this chapter.

First, however, let us examine some of the arguments of those who have questioned the very feasibility of rational planning because of basic human intellectual and psychological limitations. In their classic 1953 work, Robert Dahl and Charles Lindblom observed that the "number of alternatives man would need to consider in order to act rationally is very often far beyond his limited mental capacity."[6] This constraint led Herbert Simon to articulate what he termed the "principle of bounded rationality": "*The capacity of the human mind for formulating and solving complex problems is very small compared with the size of the problems whose solution is required for objectively rational behavior in the real world—or even for a reasonable approximation to such objective rationality.*"[7]

It would be foolish to deny that our problems are sometimes larger than we can fully grasp; we have already referred to this phenomenon in noting the "wicked" nature of contemporary urban problems. But it gets worse. Our psychological impediments—our hang-ups—create a second set of constraints. Here the issue is not the bounded nature of our rationality but the irrational impulses that can undermine it. Dahl and Lindblom paraphrased the Freudian perspective on "man" as follows (note that the passage was written before the emergence of gender consciousness in scholarly writing—though the result is a depiction with which many women might be inclined to agree):

> He is autistic; he distorts reality to suit inner needs and then makes his distorted picture of reality the premise of his actions. He is compulsive. He projects his own motives and reality views on others; represses powerful and urgent wants deep into the unconscious for fear of penalties from conscience or the responses of others, only to have his repressed wants unrecognizably displaced on other goals; acquires and displays exaggerated fears; colors the world with emotional tones of forgotten childhood; expresses hatreds and resentments coming from long-buried events; rationalizes all his actions; and throws a veil of hypocrisy and dishonesty not only over his outer behavior in order to deceive others but even over his innermost wishes in order to deceive himself.[8]

And we want this guy planning our city?

Most of us would prefer to consider this a description not of a normal person but of one who is highly neurotic. Alternatively, we might take comfort in the fact that this portrayal is somewhat outmoded in the light of more recent theories of human behavior. But who can deny that each of us does indeed view reality through our own unique lens? Who can claim never to have exhibited any of the traits just described?

While the problem is undoubtedly overstated in the quotation, there is little doubt that we do possess psychological traits that tend to work against our capacity for rationality. Consider, for example, the goals we hope to accomplish through rational action. Kenneth Arrow, among others, has noted that the individual's utility function (that is, one's rank ordering of goals) is highly variable, changing virtually from day to day.[9] Nor, for that matter, is it even possible for an individual to attain a consistent utility function: "in truth the individual is a congress of selves, each pursuing values to which the other selves may be indifferent or hostile—if, indeed, they are even aware of the pursuit."[10]

Despite these constraints, most of us do succeed in mustering sufficient rationality to function on a day-to-day basis—and often rather well at that. The purpose of these comments, then, has been simply—as Dahl and Lindblom put it—to "stand as a warning not to romanticize our capacity for rational social action."[11]

It might be argued that one of our chief strategies for overcoming our individual constraints is to join with others in organizations and institutions—which, on the face of it, would seem to have many advantages over the individual with respect to the potential for rationality. Because institutions serve as the repositories of knowledge inherited from their past members, their collective available knowledge is apt to be far greater than that of any individual member. Institutions are more likely than individuals to have systematic procedures for gathering information of relevance to their functions. They also tend to keep in check their members' more blatant psychological aberrations; irrational impulses are likely to be muted in the face of organizational norms for appropriate behavior.

I suspect that these advantages are real, but they do not necessarily overcome the difficulties with rationality that were mentioned earlier. If individuals must come to terms with their internally inconsistent utility functions, moreover, how much more difficult is it for institutions to reconcile the often divergent values of their members when large-scale public policy issues are at stake?

Banfield listed six "compelling reasons which militate against planning and rationality on the part of all organizations."[12] Briefly summarized, they are that (1) the future is too uncertain, and reliable predictions can rarely be made for more than five years ahead; (2) even if a course of action can be decided upon well in advance, it is often unwise to do so since this invites organized opposition; (3) there is little use in considering fundamentally different alternatives in most organizations because conditions usually preclude them from doing anything very different from what they are doing at present; (4) organizations are preoccupied with present rather than future effects, and are no more likely to postpone gratification than are individuals; (5) the goal of organizational maintenance—of "keeping the organization going for the sake of keeping it going"—is usually paramount; and (6) planning requires money and the time of chief executives, both of which are often considered to be more appropriately deployed elsewhere (in the resolution of current crises, for example). Banfield undoubtedly overstates some of these reasons in his effort to show that organizations neither behave rationally nor plan; for most of them we would have little difficulty coming up with examples that both illustrate and contradict his claims.

To be sure, both individuals and organizations possess a number of characteristics that constrain their ability to operate in a highly rational manner. However, these characteristics are not by themselves sufficient to discredit rationality. Numerous means have been suggested to circumvent those limitations, one of which is the creation of strategies or models that make "realistic" use of rationality.

RATIONALITY-BASED PLANNING STRATEGIES

As noted earlier, rationality alone—whether of the pure or pragmatic variety—is of little help in the planning process. Rationality becomes potentially useful only when it is embodied or packaged in operational models or strategies, complete with instruction kits. Many such models have blazed across the planning sky, only to vanish when "newer, better" approaches are introduced. In his book on strategic planning, John Bryson apologetically notes that leaders and managers "are likely to groan at the prospect of having yet another new management technique foisted upon them. They have seen cost-benefit analysis, planning-programming-budgeting systems, zero-base budgeting, management by objectives, Total Quality Management, reinvention, reengineering, and a host of other techniques trumpeted by a cadre of authors and management consultants."[13] To this list might be added statistical decision-making, game theory, operations research, and systems analysis, among others. In varying degrees, each of these techniques has attempted to harness the notion of rationality for application to real-world problem solving; each has had its day in the sun, only to be brushed aside by the next highly touted strategy.

Perhaps the purest expression of the rationality idea in planning was that manifested in the development, in the 1950s and 1960s, of large-scale computer-based models of land use and transportation. The Chicago Area Transportation Study and the Penn-Jersey Study were the most prominent examples; in each case, large sums of money were expended to develop computerized mathematical models that could predict the impact of alternative developments or of changes in a metropolitan area's land use and transportation systems.[14] The proponents of the models hoped that they would "revolutionize the practice of urban policy making" by providing the data needed to "forecast and control the future of cities."[15] It didn't work out that way, of course; Michael Wegener notes that

nowhere in the world have such models "become a routine ingre-
dient of metropolitan plan-making."[16] In his view, the modeling
approach faded because of its close association with the broader
notion of rational planning; as our confidence in rationality faded,
so did the models.

It is likely, too, that the modelers were not keenly attuned to the
political dimensions of their work. An article by Alan Black
provides an informative description of the seven-year Chicago Area
Transportation Study, offering it as an example of effective rational
planning; after all, it "followed the rational model closely,
completed the planning process, and published a plan."[17] Black
characterizes rational planning as a ten-step process, and notes that
nine of the ten steps were successfully carried out by the study's
team. The only exception: implementation. Black acknowledges
that the staff had little interest in this; they were highly skilled tech-
nicians, and not oriented to the hurly-burly of citizen participation,
public hearings, and coalition building. It is hardly surprising, then,
that little or no implementation occurred. Even Black, who participated in the study and was justifiably laudatory regarding its
technical sophistication, concluded that it is "easier to carry out the
rational planning process if the planning agency is autonomous and
free from political interference. But if planners want to affect
decisions, they may have to get involved in politics and sacrifice
rationality to some degree."[18]

Despite their association with the much-maligned rational paradigm, large-scale models continue to be developed. Writing in 1994,
Wegener noted the existence of "a small but tightly knit network of
urban modelers dispersed across four continents."[19] He identified
and described twenty modeling processes (seven in the United
States, thirteen elsewhere) varying widely in their comprehensiveness and level of sophistication. He acknowledged, however, that
these models tended to deal with a rather narrow spectrum of the
problems confronting metropolitan areas, and he advocated the
development of models that would be "more sensitive to issues of
equity and of environmental sustainability."[20]

Although Wegener and other authors have documented the fact
that highly sophisticated urban models are still being developed,
these models continue to function primarily as the objects of
research activity. While they certainly have value in that regard, it is
nevertheless clear that they have made few inroads into the

processes whereby urban policy decisions are made. Like the proponents of other rationality-based strategies, the modelers might hope that the quality, elegance, and technical competence of their models would somehow carry the day—but alas, decisions within the political system continue to be responsive to other, more traditional variables.

THE LATEST CONTENDER: STRATEGIC PLANNING

This examination of rationality-based planning models should not conclude without consideration of the one that is currently most prevalent—namely, strategic planning. I suspect that the popularity of strategic planning derives, at least in part, from its roots in the private sector; any plan labeled "strategic" seems to possess an aura of respectability not necessarily enjoyed by plans with other designations. After all, every corporation worth its salt has a strategic plan in place, and what is good for our corporations must be good for government as well—right?

Despite this popularity, there is little consensus on what it means to plan strategically; strategic planning has been described in a variety of ways, with each author or short-course instructor presenting his or her own preferred version.[21] At the risk of over-generalizing, however, I suggest that policy- or decision-making processes carried out under the rubric of strategic planning often contain at least the following elements:

(1) A mission statement. What is the organization's basic purpose, and who are its major stakeholders (those whose interests are affected in some manner by the organization's activities)?

(2) A "SWOT" analysis. This focuses on (a) the organization's internal strengths and weaknesses (the "SW" part)—what is the organization doing well, what not so well; and (b) the organization's external opportunities and threats (the "OT" part)—what is happening in the political, economic, social, and other environments that should be taken into account as the organization charts its future? (The resulting analysis is often referred to as an environmental scan.)

(3) An analysis of specific issues that the organization needs to address. These will vary from case to case.

(4) The development of a detailed and compelling vision for the

organization's future.

(5) The development of a set of action strategies for achieving that vision.

How do these elements relate to the six steps of the rational planning process cited earlier? That list began with a determination of goals as the first step, and I view the first four strategic planning elements I have listed here simply as a refinement on the goal-formulation process. An organization will presumably develop more useful goals (a better-informed vision) if it has a clear sense of mission, has performed a competent SWOT analysis, and has carefully examined all the current issues that are central to its future. The vision statement, then, *is* the goal statement, describing in detail what the organization hopes to achieve or create in the future. Strategies, of course, are the implementation component—the means of getting there.

While strategic plans can be developed for any time frame, the approach tends to be applied most frequently to relatively short-term planning processes—those intended to guide actions over a three- to five-year period, say, rather than the ten- to twenty-year horizons often associated with comprehensive plans. Advocates of strategic planning tend to believe that their approach is more politically sensitive than are other models. Whether this is true depends, however, on how the political process is handled in those other models; strategic planning has no monopoly on political savvy, nor does it come equipped with a guarantee of successful outcomes.

Strategic planning is, in the final analysis, simply one more entry in the long line of rationality-based strategies that have been packaged for use by planners. With its built-in emphasis on political sensitivity (the political process is, in fact, one of the strategy's objects for rational analysis), it represents a considerable improvement over strategies that seem to suggest that a plan's inherent wisdom and sophistication are sufficient to carry the day politically. Strategic planning has indeed proved more durable than most rationality-based strategies. Bryson may be right in attributing this to its emphasis on politics,[22] though I suggest that its widespread use in the private sector has played an important role as well. But strategic planning still assumes that a central planner (or planning organization) manages a process in which a variety of phenomena are analyzed, with that analysis being used to formulate a set of strategies—in other words, a plan—for achieving desired outcomes. The concept of rationality may indeed be broadened here—to include, for example, analyses of political pressures and the preferences of various stakeholder groups—but strategic planning never completely departs from the centralized, rational camp. Accordingly, it cannot escape the fundamental problems that have bedeviled other styles of planning based on assumptions of rational behavior.

CURRENT STATUS OF THE RATIONALITY CONCEPT

Nigel Taylor suggests that the notion of planning as a rational process, coupled with the view of cities as systems that are amenable to scientifically engineered improvement, represented the "high water-mark of modernist optimism in the post-war era."[23] Clearly the emergence of a postmodern world view has shattered that optimism, and few authors today feel compelled to devote more than a paragraph or two to their rejection of rational planning. This book is an obvious exception, for reasons stated at the beginning of this chapter.

Perhaps the most compelling anti-rationality argument in recent years has been that advanced by Bent Flyvbjerg, in his fascinating case study of central city planning in Aalborg, Denmark. Flyvbjerg argues that power defines what constitutes knowledge and rationality; indeed, power ultimately defines "what counts as reality." Thus, rationality is embedded in power relationships—and is, in fact, one of the tools used by those in power to get what they want.[24] What emerges from his study "is a picture of technical expertise used as rationalization of policy, of rationality as the legitimation of power."[25] To the extent that Aalborg's planners attempted to rely on rational analysis and plan-making for their central city plan, Flyvbjerg charges, they played into the hands of those who possessed genuine power (identified, in this instance, as the Chamber of Industry and Commerce, which—contrary to the planners— wanted no restrictions on the movement of automobiles in the city's downtown) and who were therefore able to define what was ultimately perceived to be rational.

Flyvbjerg sees Aalborg's public planning failures as providing evidence of the "fundamental weakness of modernity."[26] His proposed solutions are not particularly satisfying; he concludes that we need to better understand the nature of power (a step to which his book makes a significant contribution), reject the notion of a rationality-based democracy as the major vehicle for solving our problems, and join with like-minded allies to work toward what is right.[27] In fairness, it must be noted that Flyvbjerg's primary intent was to describe and analyze a particular case, not to provide solutions to the problems he unearthed. Indeed, he is generally perceived to be one of the "dark side" planning theorists described in Chapter 2—a group more given to critical analysis than to proposals for amelioration.

While he has enriched the conceptual basis for the case against rationality, Flyvbjerg's bottom line is the same as that of numerous other authors—namely, that rational planning reflects a world view that is not in tune with the dynamics of contemporary society (and was perhaps *never* very effective). So: what happens when one of a profession's most fundamental assumptions turns out to be mired in quicksand?

In a 1984 article, Alexander identified several responses to what he termed "paradigm breakdown"—in this case, the discrediting of rationality. Some theorists, he observed, simply continued to write as though there were no problems with the concept; others acknowledged its limitations but made adjustments that, in their minds, "solved" these limitations; others abandoned rationality and attempted to replace it with ideological positions; and still others went in search of new paradigms that might fill the gap.[28]

More interesting than the responses of planning theorists, however, are those of practitioners. As noted at the beginning of this chapter, they are still inclined, when asked, to describe their plan-making and problem-solving activities in ways that sound suspiciously akin to the rational model. Why is this the case?

Several possible explanations have been offered. Howell Baum suggests that planners cling to rationality for psychological reasons; it provides a measure of insulation from "risky reality."[29] Thus if "community groups are hostile, if bosses put agency politics above rigorous analysis, if coworkers duplicitously do not share information, taking the rational view that planning is simply abstract analysis eliminates these concerns and the feelings they evoke."[30] Hey, I'm just a technician here; if things don't work out, it's because of politics—and that's none of my concern.

In addressing the same question—the persistence of allegiance to rationality in planning practice—Linda Dalton has suggested several alternative explanations, including that (1) planning has been institutionally identified with rationality so deeply, and for so long, as to render the relationship extremely difficult to terminate; (2) planning educators may reject rationality intellectually, but they continue to model it in their teaching and research—a point not lost on their students; and (3) rationality provides a "secure base for a profession that is potentially in trouble."[31] Implied in this last point is the notion that planners may find it politically useful, in some circumstances, to be perceived as dispassionate, analytical, value-neutral, rational actors rather than as skilled participants in the political process. All these forces are undoubtedly at work; all have contributed to the durability of a concept that was long ago declared dead by the profession's community of theorists.

Should we conclude, then, that the purported demise of rationality is a figment of out-of-touch planning theorists' imaginations, and that in reality it remains a useful paradigm for the practice of planning? Absolutely not. My fundamental problem with rationality is not that it is a modernist strategy in a postmodern world, as numerous theorists have alleged (although I would not quarrel with this contention). Rather, my concern is that reliance on rational models is dysfunctional because *decisions relevant to public planning are not generally made on the basis of rational planning processes.*[32] Indeed, the kinds of problems with which planners are typically involved, as well as the environments in which these problems are generally addressed, militate strongly against the use of rationality-based strategies.

Most public planning issues—and certainly all of them that we would consider major—generate outcomes that affect individuals and groups differentially. Some people win, some lose, and some win or lose more or less than others. Even in cases where a significant number of people are not directly affected by a particular outcome, many members of the community will have strong opinions about the rightness or wrongness of what is happening.

Virtually any major issue, then, has a number of stakeholders and is likely to feature a large measure of interest group involvement. This in turn guarantees that political processes will be paramount in shaping the outcomes. Sometimes these political processes include a subsidiary role for rational analysis and planning (though Flyvbjerg would suggest that when this occurs, planning and analysis may well have been co-opted by those in power); often, however, the political process ignores planning altogether. There is, in fact, a strong unwillingness on the part of many interest groups to concede to public agencies and officials the legitimacy and authority needed to make the decisions that most affect their well-being; this in turn leads to pressures for the decentralization of decision-making on key public policy issues.

These characteristics of the public planning arena undermine the usefulness of strategies and models based on rationality. Rationality-based planning works best when value conflicts have been resolved in advance, when the goal is one of optimization (that is, everybody gains) rather than redistribution, when political processes do not intervene in any major way, when decision-making authority is clear and fully legitimated by all in the community, and when decision-making is centralized in a single unit rather than diffused among many. In short, rationality-based planning works best with "tame" problems rather than with wicked ones—and public planners do not often find themselves tackling tame problems.

Reliance on rationality may, in fact, be highly damaging to the planning process because it contributes so readily to self-delusion. If we follow the tenets of rational planning, one might ask, aren't we simply doing what planning is all about—regardless of whether anything comes of our analyses and plans? An exercise I often give my students posits the existence of two firms, A and B. Firm A makes all the right planning moves—defining its mission, studying its competition, carefully analyzing the market for current and potential products, and formulating goals and strategies for its short-term future. Firm B, on the other hand, is run by a happy-go-lucky CEO who makes all decisions for the firm by flipping a coin. Let's say, for the sake of argument, that Firm A, despite its good planning behavior, goes down the tubes, while Firm B prospers and becomes an industry leader. The question is, which firm was the more rational?

My students almost always answer correctly—namely, that Firm A was the more rational because it behaved in a rational manner, while Firm B was not rational at all. This exercise illustrates the fact that "rational planning" means "planning conducted in a rational manner"; the focus is on the process, not on the results. Successful outcomes are not necessary for rational planning; it is enough that we planned rationally. But is this truly satisfactory? I don't think so. Public planning is about improving the quality of life in our communities, and we should not take comfort in methods that may soothe our psyches but have little real-world impact.

To summarize, there is a tension in our nation (and I suspect in most nations) between rational planning and the political system. Because they fail to deal with that tension, most rationality-based planning strategies will ultimately prove disappointing to the planner. What we need, then, are models or strategies that do a better job of taking the political process into account. Let us continue our search.

NOTES

1. Herbert J. Gans, *People and Plans: Essays on Urban Problems and Solutions* (New York: Basic Books, 1968), pp. 71–73.

2. Niraj Verma, "Pragmatic Rationality and Planning Theory," *Journal of Planning Education and Research*, Vol. 16, No. 1 (Fall 1996), p. 5.

3. For a related discussion, see Edward C. Banfield, "Ends and Means in Planning," *International Social Science Journal*, Vol. 11 (1959), p. 362.

4. Martin Meyerson and Edward G. Banfield, *Politics, Planning and the Public Interest* (Glencoe, Ill.: The Free Press, 1955).

5. Ernest R. Alexander, *Approaches to Planning: Introducing Current Planning Theories, Concepts, and Issues*, 2nd ed. (Philadelphia: Gordon and Breach, 1992), p. 40.

6. Robert A. Dahl and Charles E. Lindblom, *Politics, Economics, and Welfare: Planning and Politico-Economic Systems Resolved into Basic Social Processes* (New York: Harper & Row, 1953), p. 60.

7. Herbert A. Simon, *Models of Man* (New York: John Wiley & Sons, 1957), p. 198. Emphasis in the original.

8. Dahl and Lindblom, *Politics, Economics, and Welfare*, p. 60.

9. Kenneth J. Arrow, "Mathematical Models in the Social Sciences," in *The Policy Sciences*, ed. Daniel Lerner and Harold D. Lasswell (Stanford: Stanford University Press, 1951), p. 136.

10. Abraham Kaplan, "Some Limitations on Rationality," in *Nomos VII: Rational Decision*, ed. Carl J. Friedrich (New York: Atherton Press, 1964), p. 58.

11. Dahl and Lindblom, *Politics, Economics, and Welfare*, p. 60.

12. Banfield, "Ends and Means," pp. 365–367.

13. John M. Bryson, *Strategic Planning for Public and Nonprofit Organizations: A Guide to Strengthening and Sustaining Organizational Achievement*, rev. ed. (San Francisco: Jossey-Bass Publishers, 1995), p. 10.

14. For a useful overview of the modeling movement, see Michael Batty, "A Chronicle of Scientific Planning: The Anglo-American Modeling Experience," *Journal of the American Planning Association*, Vol. 60, No. 1 (Winter 1994), pp. 17–29.

15. Michael Wegener, "Operational Urban Models: State of the Art," *Journal of the American Planning Association*, Vol. 60, No. 1 (Winter 1994), p. 17.

16. Ibid.

17. Alan Black, "The Chicago Area Transportation Study: A Case Study of Rational Planning," *Journal of Planning Education and Research*, Vol. 10, No. 1 (Fall 1990), p. 27.

18. Ibid., p. 36.

19. Wegener, "Urban Models," p. 18.

20. Ibid., p. 26.

21. For works emphasizing the use of strategic planning by local government, see Bryson, *Strategic Planning*; John M. Bryson and William D. Roering, "Applying Private-Sector Strategic Planning in the Public Sector," *Journal of the American Planning Association*, Vol. 53, No. 1 (Winter 1987), pp. 9–22; and Jerome L. Kaufman and Harvey M. Jacobs,

"A Public Planning Perspective on Strategic Planning," *Journal of the American Planning Association*, Vol. 53, No. 1 (Winter 1987), pp. 23–33.

22. Bryson, *Strategic Planning*, p. 10.

23. Nigel Taylor, *Urban Planning Theory Since 1945* (London: Sage Publications, 1998), p. 60.

24. Bent Flyvbjerg, *Rationality and Power: Democracy in Practice* (Chicago: University of Chicago Press, 1998), p. 27.

25. Ibid., p. 26.

26. Ibid., p. 234.

27. Ibid., pp. 234–236.

28. Ernest R. Alexander, "After Rationality, What? A Review of Responses to Paradigm Breakdown," *Journal of the American Planning Association*, Vol. 50, No. 1 (Winter 1984), pp. 62–69.

29. Howell S. Baum, "Why the Rational Paradigm Persists: Tales from the Field," *Journal of Planning Education and Research*, Vol. 15, No. 2 (Winter 1996), p. 133.

30. Ibid.

31. Linda C. Dalton, "Why the Rational Paradigm Persists: The Resistance of Professional Education and Practice to Alternative Forms of Planning," *Journal of Planning Education and Research*, Vol. 5, No. 3 (Spring 1986), pp. 147–153.

32. Howell Baum makes the same point in "Why the Paradigm Persists," p. 127.

7

Centralized Non-Rationality: The Planner Confronts Politics

The planning strategies reviewed in this chapter were developed in response to the perceived shortcomings of rationality-based models. They acknowledge the impossibility of pure rationality in planning and decision-making, and use that fact as the point of departure for the development of models that take explicit account of our nonrational characteristics. The major similarity between the rationality-based models and those discussed in this chapter is their emphasis on planning as a centralized function—that is, a task performed by professionals working for (or advising) a central planning or policy-making agency. Beyond that, however, the differences are substantial. The models in this chapter are intended primarily to provide decision-makers with behavior rules that are realistic, in the sense that they take into account both the constraints on rationality and the nature of large-scale bureaucracies.

SIMON SAYS "SATISFICE"

I have already mentioned Herbert Simon's "principle of bounded rationality," which notes the relatively limited capacity of the human mind in comparison with the size of the problems we attempt to resolve. The result of this limitation, wrote Simon, is that we often *satisfice*—that is, settle for a course of action that is merely "good enough" for the purposes at hand.[1] One who satisfices, Simon added, "has no need of estimates of joint probability distributions, or of complete and consistent preference orderings of all possible alternatives of action."[2]

Simon's principal target was the "economic man" of classical economics, a person with no counterpart in the real world. Simon wanted to replace him with the more realistic "administrative man." Economic men maximize; administrative men *"satisfice because they have not the wits to maximize."*[3] Economic man strives to deal with the real world in its full complexity; administrative man perceives a highly simplified model of the real world, omitting consideration of all but its most relevant and crucial aspects.[4] Thus, for example, he never attempts to consider all the alternatives open to him but only those that seem most plausible.[5] Having constructed a simplified model of the real situation, Simon wrote, administrative man does behave rationally with respect to that model—which, however, is "not even approximately optimal with respect to the real world."[6]

Administrative man satisfices with regard to ends as well as means. If a goal proves too ambitious, he simply lowers it; if progress toward the goal exceeds expectations, he can then raise it again. In business, for example, rather than search for the course of action that will maximize profit, the satisficer begins with an idea of the profit that the business should generate, then simply adopts the first course of action that will satisfy that profit requirement. If no such course of action is readily discovered, the profit requirement will probably be revised downward, to be raised again later if circumstances permit. In short, the search is for a course of action that is good enough rather than for one that is best.

While this point has been debated, it appears to me that Simon was more interested in describing how people actually make decisions than in prescribing how those decisions should be made; in other words, his theory was more positive than normative. Indeed, the satisficing idea would have serious shortcomings if its intentions were prescriptive. It fails, for example, to specify criteria for determining when we have an alternative that is "good enough." Do we take the first acceptable alternative that comes along, even if it means lowering our goals? Do we postpone lowering the goals until we have devoted X dollars, or Y days, to analysis? Clearly, the definition of a satisfactory solution will vary with the situation, and will depend on a number of factors—such as values, costs, and time—unique to each. It is one thing to observe, however correctly, that people tend to satisfice; it is quite another to tell them how to do it.

To be sure, all planners—along with, I suspect, everyone else—sometimes engage in decision-making behavior that might reasonably be described as satisficing. There is something about such behavior, however, that is antithetical to the planner's role. Public planning often requires outcomes that are more than merely "good enough." Indeed, planning based on satisficing would appear to be the exact opposite of the visionary spirit being advocated in this book (see Chapter 13). Yes, much planning reflects satisficing—but planning at its best transcends this approach.

INCREMENTALISM

Charles Lindblom's first major reference to incrementalism appeared in 1953 in a book that he coauthored with Robert A. Dahl.[7] By 1959 Lindblom had become sufficiently impressed with the explanatory powers of the concept of incrementalism to publish an article about it entitled, descriptively enough, "The Science of 'Muddling Through.'"[8] By this time he had decided that in addition to describing how people make their plans and decisions, incrementalism was in fact a very good way to do so; hence he offered it as both a positive and a normative theory. In that article he referred to his strategy as "the method of successive limited comparisons," which he contrasted favorably with the traditional "rational-comprehensive method."

In 1963 the strategy—now called "disjointed incrementalism"—was developed more fully in a book coauthored with David Braybrooke, a philosopher; this book provides a thorough exposition of the strategy for those interested in its theoretical rationale, minute details, and empirical illustrations.[9] Finally, in 1965 Lindblom published another book dealing largely with other issues but containing a concise and highly useful description—in a single, fifteen-page chapter—of the strategy's central features.[10] (I have long considered this a better description of the concept than the more frequently cited "Muddling Through" article.)

Like Simon, Lindblom was concerned about the divergence between the methods that planners and decision-makers claimed to use (that is, those based on rationality) and those that they actually used. Thus he devoted considerable attention to a systematic demolition of the "synoptic model," which is roughly akin to what I have been calling "pure rationality." In its place he proposed an approach that he believed to be more realistic. As Nigel Taylor observes, Lindblom "suggested that, in most situations, planning has to be piecemeal, incremental, opportunistic, and pragmatic, and that planners who did not or could not operate in these ways were generally ineffective. In short, Lindblom presented a model of the 'real world' planning as necessarily 'disjointed' and 'incremental,' not 'rational' and 'comprehensive.'"[11]

Lindblom listed several "adaptations" or "tactics" that decision-makers use in order to cope with the realities of the policy-making environment. Briefly summarized, they are as follows:

(1) Decision-makers compare and evaluate increments only.[12] No attempt is made to analyze alternatives in great depth; on the contrary, they are considered only at the margins, where they differ from one another or from what is being done at present. This approach is, moreover, highly practical, since most political systems cannot tolerate more than incremental changes from the existing situation.

(2) Decision-makers consider only a restricted number of policy alternatives.[13] They ignore those that entail more than incremental change or that lie outside the "familiar path of policy making."[14]

(3) Decision-makers consider only a restricted number of important consequences for any given policy alternative. They ignore, for a number of practical reasons, many other important consequences.[15]

(4) Decision-makers engage in "reconstructive analysis."[16] That is, ends are adjusted to means as well as vice versa; the problem is continuously redefined. In this way potentially impossible problems are rendered manageable.

(5) Decision-makers carry out their analyses and evaluations serially.[17] That is, they approach a problem through a series of attacks rather than a one-shot effort. Values or consequences omitted in one attack can thus be added later if their importance becomes apparent.

(6) Decision-makers have a remedial orientation.[18] Most planning, in other words, is geared to solving existing problems rather than to achieving desired future states. Certain general ideals (such as justice or economic growth) may be kept in mind, but in practice

their importance will be minor compared to that of the problems that the decision-maker is endeavoring to solve.

Lindblom himself summarizes the process as follows:

> The decision-maker makes an incremental move in the desired direction and does not take upon himself the difficulties of finding a solution. He disregards many other possible moves because they are too costly (in time, energy, or money) to examine; and, for the move he makes, he does not trouble to find out (again, because it is too costly to do so) what all its consequences are. He assumes that to the extent that his move was a failure or was marked by unanticipated adverse consequences, someone's (perhaps even his) next move will attend to the resulting problem.[19]

The last sentence reflects one of the strategy's most interesting characteristics—namely, the idea that one's decisions need not always be right. Given the serial nature of public policy decision-making, if a particular decision turns sour, it can always be fixed in the next iteration. To his credit, Lindblom noted that a "great deal of damage" could occasionally occur before corrective steps are taken; this is unavoidable, however, since the only alternative is the unworkable rational approach. A major feature of the strategy, in fact, is that it is often better to let adverse consequences develop and deal with them as separate problems than to attempt to anticipate all such consequences in advance.[20]

CURRENT STATUS OF INCREMENTALISM

Much about the concept of incrementalism is intuitively appealing to practicing planners. It does seem to describe a great deal of the planning that goes on at the local level—and it provides a welcome rationalization for the fact that so much of that planning is being done in a way that can hardly be considered rational. While Lindblom was a public administrator rather than a planner, he made a significant contribution to planning thought by pointing out that rationality need not be the only conceptual basis for the planning process—that in fact it is possible to develop alternative strategies that pay greater attention to the political realities of planning practice. Given the overwhelming dominance of the rational paradigm in the 1950s and 1960s, it would be difficult to overestimate the importance of Lindblom's work in loosening that paradigm's stranglehold on the profession.

It should come as no surprise, however, that incrementalism has also been widely criticized. Among the most significant arguments are the following:

• Lindblom may have been correct in his description of the way in which many public planning decisions are made, but he offered little empirical evidence to support his assertions. The illustrative cases that he presented did indeed support his theory—but they were selected to do so, after all, and hardly reflected a representative sampling of planning situations. Each of us, certainly, can think of real-world policy or planning decisions that have not conformed to his description—that is, were not incremental. Rapid developments in health, electronic communications, recreation, and other fields come immediately to mind; the world is undoubtedly changing at a faster pace than was the case in the 1960s.

• A closely related problem is simply that there are many circumstances in which we would not want to settle for an incremental approach. It can hardly apply, for example, to situations where there is substantial public dissatisfaction with current policies; when new problems emerge (or old situations are redefined as problems), thus necessitating new approaches; when new organizations or programs are created to tackle previously unrecognized problems; when new methodologies or action policies become available because of technological or other breakthroughs; when elected officials are given mandates for major reform; or when disasters or crises render new approaches both feasible and essential. In short, incrementalism ignores the very processes of innovation through which societies often change and grow. Such situations may occur relatively infrequently, compared with more routine decision-making situations, but they are of fundamental importance—and incrementalism ignores them.

• Some analysts have claimed that incrementalism is politically conservative (a weakness or strength depending, of course, on one's political orientation) because it pays great respect to past traditions and institutions, viewing them as givens and thus leaving them essentially unchallenged. It is therefore a rather unattractive strategy for those interested in fundamental change or reform.

• It has also been suggested that incrementalism favors the powerful members of a society at the expense of those who are underrepresented and politically weak because decision-makers, in their quest for moves that are practical and feasible, will accommodate their decisions to those who are most capable of blocking implementation—namely, those with power.[21]

• On the other hand, incrementalism contains its own political risks because it tends to offer small solutions for large problems (opening fire hydrants to deal with neighborhood unrest; appointing commissions to study problems that merit immediate action; combating drugs by "just saying no"; dealing with the nation's urban school crisis by having cities endorse a list of goals, as in the first President Bush's America 2000 project; and so on).

• Some critics have also suggested that incrementalism discourages activities that, while closely associated with rationality, are nonetheless important to any community's planning process. Incrementalism is rather cavalier, for example, in its treatment of goals and in its attitude toward analysis; neither is seen to have much practical value.[22]

• While intended to be more prescriptive than Simon's satisficing concept, incrementalism is similarly devoid of behavior rules. How small is incremental? How many alternatives make up the restricted number that are to be considered, and by what criteria should they be identified? How do we determine which important consequences to consider and which to ignore? Indeed, as Yehezkel Dror has noted, "the very concept of 'incremental' change is vague, because the same change may be both 'incremental' and 'radical' in different systems and at different times."[23]

• Finally, the strategy is thoroughly inefficient when it comes to correcting a course of action that proves to be inappropriate. Incrementalism posits no formal evaluation mechanisms; it assumes that if actions go sour, others will point this out to decision-makers, who will then make the necessary adjustments. This is, of course, a wildly rash assumption. Most readers of this book would have little difficulty generating a list of governmental programs that have been continued long beyond their useful life—and even long after beginning to have adverse effects—simply because no one noticed or had sufficient clout to change the situation. (William H. Whyte offered a good example in his case study of incentive zoning in New York City; initiated in 1961, the program operated for nearly twenty years before planners began to realize that its impact was precisely the opposite of that which had been intended.)[24] To rely on a process of "partisan adjustment" (Lindblom's term), of reaction to the corrective observations of the decision-makers' colleagues and professional rivals, is to rely on a process that has proven remarkably inept in dealing with the major problems confronting America's cities.

Incrementalism may indeed describe the way in which certain decisions (typically those that are relatively routine) are made, but it hardly presents a model to be emulated. The strategy applies to a relatively narrow range of planning situations, excluding those that might lead to large-scale change; it is deferential toward the existing social order, paying great respect to current power configurations; and it is inefficient in its approach to corrective action. One could argue, in fact, that incrementalism is not a planning strategy at all, but is more appropriately viewed as the antithesis of planning—that is, as the way in which decisions get made when, for one reason or another, planning is not possible.

Recognizing some of these drawbacks, Amitai Etzioni proposed a "mixed scanning" strategy, intended as a compromise between the rational and incremental approaches—supposedly containing the virtues of both and the defects of neither.[25] A key element in the mixed scanning strategy is its distinction between "contextuating" decisions and "bit" decisions. The former are the more fundamental policy-shaping decisions, tend to be made by those higher in an organization's hierarchy, and are more apt to be based on a careful analysis of the options. Bit decisions, on the other hand, focus more on implementation than on policy-making, tend to be made at lower levels, and are thus more apt to reflect the characteristics of incrementalism as described by Lindblom. In discussing the interplay between these two levels of decision-making, Etzioni accurately noted that policy occasionally results from an agglomeration of bit decisions—in other words, by default—rather than from top-down decision-making. To its credit, his model also provided a "set of instructions for the unimaginative decision-maker," including strategies for assessing alternatives repeatedly until only one is left.

Mixed scanning is indeed an improvement on incrementalism; by distinguishing between contextuating policy decisions and bit implementation decisions, it acknowledges the rather obvious fact that some decisions are not incremental—and thus it applies, at least theoretically, to a broader range of decision situations. Like the rational model and incrementalism, however, mixed scanning assumes a centralized decision-making process. It leaves unresolved the identity of those who will participate in that process or the possibility of conflict among the values held by those participants (the strategy seems to assume a benevolent decision-maker with all the right values; but which values are indeed the right ones, and who is empowered to make this decision?). The centralized, top-down character of incrementalism and mixed scanning ultimately undermines their potential utility, just as it undermined that of the rationality-based models.[26]

Public planning occurs in an environment characterized by conflicting ideologies and values, vigorous competition for scarce resources, and vast differentials in power. These aspects of the environment are expressed through the political system, of which the planning process is inescapably a part. As interest groups vie with one another in the political system, therefore, they tend to view planning as simply another tool to be used in pursuit of their ends.

We planners, then, find ourselves squeezed on both sides. On the one hand, we lack a workable and widely acceptable definition of the public interest—which, if available, would at least let us enter the political fray with a keen sense of moral compass. On the other hand, interest groups press their claims upon us in such a way that even if we had all the intellectual and conceptual tools needed to "plan rationally in pursuit of the public interest," we would still be politically constrained from doing so.

This is but another way of describing the tension between planning and politics to which I referred in the previous chapter. If we did possess a model or strategy that would enable us to make decisions in accordance with a highly developed sense of the public interest (however defined), we would need sufficient centrality of position, legitimate authority, and freedom from political interference to carry out that strategy. These are, however, concessions that a capitalist democracy is unwilling to make to us.

Incrementalism and mixed scanning acknowledge the impact of political power on the planning process—but they cave in too easily, failing to search for ways in which the dynamics of the political system might be harnessed to good purpose. We can do better. A good starting point is an examination of models that view planning as a decentralized process. That is the task of the next two chapters.

NOTES

1. Herbert A. Simon, *Models of Man* (New York: John Wiley & Sons, 1957), p. 205.

2. Ibid.

3. Herbert A. Simon, *Administrative Behavior*, 2nd ed. (New York: The Macmillan Company, 1957), p. xxiv. Emphasis in the original.

4. Ibid., p. xxvi.

5. Ibid., p. 99.

6. Simon, *Models of Man*, p. 199.

7. Robert A. Dahl and Charles E. Lindblom, *Politics, Economics, and Welfare: Planning and Politico-Economic Systems Resolved into Basic Social Processes* (New York: Harper & Row, 1953), pp. 64–88.

8. Charles E. Lindblom, "The Science of 'Muddling Through,'" *Public Administration Review*, Vol. 19 (Spring 1959), pp. 79–88.

9. David Braybrooke and Charles E. Lindblom, *A Strategy of Decision: Policy Evaluation As a Social Process* (New York: The Free Press, 1963). Also useful in this regard is Michael T. Hayes, *Incrementalism and Public Policy* (New York: Longman, 1992).

10. Charles E. Lindblom, *The Intelligence of Democracy: Decision Making through Mutual Adjustment* (New York: The Free Press, 1965).

11. Nigel Taylor, *Urban Planning Theory Since 1945* (London: Sage Publications, 1998), p. 72.

12. Lindblom, *Intelligence of Democracy*, pp. 144–145.

13. Ibid., p. 145.

14. Ibid.

15. Ibid., pp. 145–146.

16. Ibid., pp. 146–147.

17. Ibid., p. 147.

18. Ibid., pp. 147–148.

19. Ibid., p. 148.

20. Ibid., pp. 148–151.

21. Amitai Etzioni, *The Active Society: A Theory of Societal and Political Processes* (New York: The Free Press, 1968), pp. 272–273.

22. For counterarguments to these and other critiques of incrementalism, see Andrew Weiss and Edward Woodhouse, "Reframing Incrementalism: A Constructive Response to the Critics," *Policy Sciences*, Vol. 25, No. 3 (August 1992), pp. 255–273.

23. Yehezkel Dror, *Public Policymaking Reexamined* (San Francisco: Chandler Publishing Company, 1968), p. 146.

24. William H. Whyte, *City: Rediscovering the Center* (New York: Doubleday, 1988), pp. 229–255.

25. See Amitai Etzioni, "Mixed Scanning: A 'Third' Approach to Decision-Making," *Public Administration Review*, Vol. 27 (December 1967), pp. 385–392; and Etzioni, *Active Society*, pp. 282–305.

26. An anonymous reviewer of a draft of this book took issue with this claim, arguing that both incrementalism and mixed scanning are "mainly decentralized, hence bottom up, sideways, and top down." I disagree. Both Lindblom and Etzioni were clear in their intentions; they were proposing strategies intended to improve the role performance of policy makers.

8

Decentralized Rationality: The Planner as Political Activist

ADVOCACY PLANNING

The authors whose strategies will be considered in this and the following chapter place a high value on democratic process. This is not to say that the rationalists and the incrementalists are not similarly inclined. In their preoccupation with the intellectual task confronting the central decision-maker, however, they reflect an implicit assumption that the important decisions will indeed be made (or recommended) by duly authorized planners, administrators, bureaucrats, and elected officials, either directly or in an advisory capacity.

The strategies examined under the "decentralized" heading, on the other hand, generally assume that major decisions should be in the hands of the citizenry itself. The role of the professional planner, then, is to facilitate decision-making by the citizenry. As with the centralized strategies, I have divided the decentralized models into those that assume rational planning behavior and those that do not. The former category offers only one strategy to consider: advocacy planning.

The central themes of advocacy planning are widely known—namely, that many groups are not adequately represented in standard or customary planning practices; that to correct this situation, various interest groups should be able to put forward their own plans for public consideration; and that professional planning assistance should be made available to such interest groups to assist them in that process.

Advocacy planning emerged as a major movement in the urban planning profession during the 1960s and 1970s, a time of considerable turbulence in American society.[1] Large-scale migration processes, accompanied by widespread racial discrimination and residential segregation, had concentrated hundreds of thousands of low-income and minority citizens in central city neighborhoods, where social problems abounded. The failures of the federal urban renewal program (generally perceived to have done more harm than good), incidents of property-destroying neighborhood violence in several major cities, growing concerns over an unpopular war in Vietnam—these and other elements combined to destabilize the society and to create a sense of crisis in the American spirit. Those readers old enough to have lived through that time will remember it as a period of considerable turmoil. Clearly, the old ways of doing things were simply not working; new approaches were called for—in planning as much as in most other major social institutions and processes.

Many of us have had professional heroes during our careers, and one name has always headed my own list: Paul Davidoff, who introduced the concept of advocacy to the planning profession. As Barry Checkoway has noted, Davidoff

> was an unyielding force for justice and equity in planning. He viewed planning as a process to address a wide range of societal problems; to improve conditions for all people while emphasizing resources and opportunities for those lacking in both; and to expand representation and participation of traditionally excluded groups in the decisions that affect their lives. He challenged planners to promote participatory democracy and positive social change; to overcome poverty and racism as factors in society; and to reduce disparities between rich and poor, White and Black, men and women.[2]

Davidoff was a lawyer-turned-planner whose career featured a blend of university teaching and direct social action. He was one of the few planners ever to run for the U. S. Congress—an aspiration not supported, as it turned out, by the vast majority of voters in Westchester County. By the time of his premature death in 1984, Davidoff had fundamentally and permanently altered the ideology of the planning profession.

While hints are detectable in some of his earlier writings, the major statement of the concept of advocacy planning appeared in a 1965 article in the *Journal of the American Institute of Planners*—an article that has probably been read and cited by more planning students than any other single work.[3] In that article, Davidoff took strong exception to the supposed value neutrality of the urban planner; any decision to act, he said, must be based on someone's conception of desired objectives. Having decided what objectives to pursue, the planner should not only make explicit the values underlying his or her prescription for a course of action but should also *affirm* them—in other words, become an advocate for what is deemed proper.[4] The planner should be able to engage in the political process as an advocate "of the interests both of government and of such other groups, organizations, or individuals who are concerned with proposing policies for the future development of the community."[5] Thus the advocacy planner bypasses the lack of a universally agreed upon public interest by concentrating on the values of a subunit of the larger community (thereby pitching a tent squarely in John Rawls's camp rather than in that of the utilitarians).

For Davidoff, public planning decisions are the end product of competition in the political arena. Hence:

> The recommendation that city planners represent and plead the plans of many interest groups is founded upon the need to establish an effective urban democracy, one in which citizens may be able to play an active role in the process of deciding public policy. Appropriate policy in a democracy is determined through a process of political debate. *The right course of action is always a matter of choice, never of fact.*[6]

The major innovation needed, in Davidoff's view, was a process whereby "plural plans" would be prepared, rather than continuing to rely upon a "unitary plan" developed by a single agency. This was quite a revolutionary idea for a body of planners who, at the time, tended to see the development of a community's master plan as the ultimate expression of their professional expertise.

The advocacy planner would be responsible to a particular interest group in the community and would attempt to express that group's values and objectives in the plans that he or she produced. If these values and objectives were unclear, the planner should assist the group in clarifying them. The planner could certainly have his or her own ideas, of course, and might attempt to educate or persuade clients regarding the wisdom of certain policies or actions; in the last analysis, however, the client group's preferences must prevail. The planner might also "become engaged in expanding the size and scope" of the client organization—words suggesting participation in community organization and development activities.[7] Overall, however, the planner's primary role would be "to carry out the planning process for the organization and to argue persuasively in favor of its planning proposals."[8] Clearly, then, Davidoff's advocacy planning consisted of two major elements: technical assistance and representation.

In theory, at least, all major groups in the community should generate plans reflecting their interests. Davidoff wanted to see plans emerging from political parties; from protest organizations; and from special interest groups such as "chambers of commerce, real estate boards, labor organizations, pro– and anti–civil rights groups, and anti-poverty councils."[9] In practice, however, most proponents of advocacy planning viewed it primarily as a vehicle for providing assistance to low-income and minority groups, these being the groups that Davidoff and other observers believed had been neglected—and even harmed—by past planning processes.

Not surprisingly, a sizable literature emerged in response to Davidoff's arguments, and many fine points were debated at conferences and in journals. For example, must the advocacy planner be employed directly by the client groups whose interests he or she is furthering? Marshall Kaplan, at that time a consultant whose firm frequently undertook advocacy-related projects, distinguished between "inside advocates," those employed by City Hall and linked to a *constituency* rather than to a *client*, and "outside advocates," those employed by the client group itself. While noting that the inside advocate has a particularly difficult task, he concluded that both have useful roles to play.[10]

Why have I categorized advocacy planning as a *rational* form of decentralized planning? At least so far as Davidoff's formulation is concerned, such a label is entirely appropriate. For he was suggesting a change not in what the planner *does,* but only *for whom he or she does it.* Davidoff's own conception of the planning process was spelled out in a 1962 article coauthored with Thomas A. Reiner.[11] The "choice theory" presented in that article is clearly one more version of the rational planning model, and it positions Davidoff squarely in the mainstream of the rational planning tradition. His argument was not that we should abandon rational planning, but that we should make its benefits available to those who have previously been excluded from the rational planning process.

Nor did Davidoff suggest that planners should necessarily take on new substantive concerns. A specialization in social planning enjoyed brief popularity in the profession in the 1960s and early 1970s, instigated by the social problems of the era and fueled by the flow of federal funds for community action programs (focused on poverty) and the Model Cities programs (which attempted to better integrate social and physical planning for the amelioration of inner-city problems).[12] It is often assumed, because of his concern for social equity, that Davidoff played a key role in the social planning movement. This was not the case, however; he was, and remained, primarily a physical planner. Davidoff's advocacy planner would still prepare land use and site plans, zoning ordinances, and schedules for improvements in municipal facilities; he or she would do so, however, in a way that reflected the needs and priorities of a specific subgroup of the community.

In theory, then, the advocacy planner continued to plan in a pragmatically rational manner, but defined the client in far narrower terms than had the more traditional community-wide comprehensive planner. In so doing, by the way, the advocacy planner improved the likelihood that the client group's values—at least those relevant to the problem at hand—would be somewhat homogeneous, and thus more susceptible to rational treatment.

I must concede, however, that my categorization of advocacy as a form of rational planning breaks down when advocacy is examined as practiced rather than as presented in theory. Davidoff himself may have been loyal to the concept of rationality, but most of those who actually functioned as advocates were more likely to view a plan simply as one of many tools available to the advocate in the pursuit of what is right. The advocacy planning initiatives of the 1960s and 1970s were often transformed into social protests, community organizing efforts, and other forms of political activism, with relatively little emphasis on the development of plans *per se.*

Because, I suspect, of the extent to which it reflected the political concerns felt by many young men and women in the 1960s, advocacy planning was tremendously popular in graduate schools of planning at that time. Well into the 1970s, when I would ask a class of students how many of them wanted to become advocacy planners, virtually every hand would be raised. Ironically, however, the extent of advocacy planning practice was never consistent with the concept's impact on planning thought. In several cities that housed major schools of planning and architecture, groups of graduate students, faculty members, and recent graduates banded together to offer their services to low-income neighborhoods, often under the auspices of "community design centers" (the Architects' Renewal Committee, in Harlem; Boston's Urban Planning Aid; and San Francisco's Community Design Center were the best-known examples).[13] A few concerned professionals of more advanced years and experience contributed *pro bono* services to such groups. A handful of consulting firms declared themselves to be interested primarily in advocacy planning projects (at least as long as federal funds were available for such projects); an occasional planner, acting alone, gave up an agency job to work for low-income groups for little or no pay; and a fairly sizable number of planners working for city planning agencies, Model Cities programs, and community action programs came to satisfy themselves—if not those they served—that they were in fact advocacy planners working inside the system.

Overall, however, only a small number of planners—that is, people who continued to identify with the planning profession—played advocacy roles of the sort called for by Davidoff in his 1965 article. When the national mood shifted in the 1980s and federal funds for social programs dried up, advocacy planning lost what little financial support it had enjoyed in the previous two decades. Nor did the idea of plural plans ever take hold in American cities; political decisions continued to be made without them.

In 1971, the American Institute of Planners created the Advocate Planners' National Advisory Committee, which was charged with recommending steps that the AIP should take to further the practice of advocacy planning, and I was asked to chair the group. Three years later (and they were turbulent years indeed, with many viewpoints vying for preeminence), we issued our report, which called for (1) the creation of a national clearinghouse for information about advocacy planning projects, intended to enable those running such projects to benefit from each others' experiences; (2) technical assistance to local groups attempting to organize for and carry out advocacy projects; (3) several forms of assistance to planners who had lost their jobs because of advocacy activities; and (4) the appointment, by the AIP, of a director of advocacy planning to over-see all these activities. A director was indeed hired but the position was short-lived, and little came of the other recommendations; by that time—the mid-1970s—the idea of advocacy planning was receding in popularity.

Advocacy too, it seems, had developed feet of clay. Several practical reservations had been expressed along the way. For example, Roger Starr, a prominent housing official, argued that advocacy fosters conflict, whereas planners would do better to focus on building consensus;[14] and Richard Bolan warned that multiple plans could result in decision-making gridlock.[15] More important in bringing about the decline of advocacy planning, however, were two fundamental issues.

The first surfaced at a unique and memorable event—the First (and, as it turned out, the last) Annual Advocacy Planning Conference, held in New York City in 1970 under the sponsorship of Hunter College, where Paul Davidoff was a member of the planning faculty. Billed as an opportunity to share experiences in order to advance the practice of advocacy planning, the conference was attended by several hundred faculty members and students from throughout the nation—and by a number of grass-roots leaders of New York City neighborhood organizations. It quickly became apparent that the latter group was not happy with the concept of advocacy planning as Davidoff had conceived it.

The gathering was raucous and unruly from beginning to end. In the spirit of the times, few speakers—including Davidoff—were able to complete their talks without being hooted down; platforms were stormed, microphones were wrested from the hands of speakers, and their messages were decried as "colonialist bullshit." All in all, it was heady and exciting stuff (and, if I remember correctly, more than a little daunting) for the many young advocacy enthusiasts in attendance.

The message communicated by the stage-stormers, most of them affiliated with New York neighborhood groups, was approximately this: "Advocacy has become the plaything of white middle-class professionals who receive sizable salaries for their efforts. We don't need their help, and we resent their patronizing behavior. The money spent on advocacy would serve our needs much more directly if it were simply given to us; we are capable of developing our own plans and strategies, and we can certainly speak for ourselves. If you planners are really serious about doing something for the poor and minorities, go root out racism where it operates most virulently—in the affluent, segregated suburbs."

All those who attended the conference went home with a new perspective on advocacy planning; what had previously seemed principled and noble had instead been described as colonialist, elitist, self-serving, top-down, and repressive. Clearly some of the luster had been lost from the advocacy ideal. Indeed, it was not long after this conference that Davidoff resigned his teaching post at Hunter and created the Suburban Action Institute, for the purpose of combating housing discrimination in Westchester County.

The second issue was a growing concern that the advocacy concept might be politically naive—that in fact it seemed to offer little hope of affecting the ways in which political decisions are actually made. Assuming that a number of plans are produced to compete with one another in the political arena, but assuming also that the distribution of power in the community remains unchanged, why should decisions on planning issues differ from those made in the past? What new tribunal can be called upon to render verdicts more pleasing to the advocacy planners' clients? According to this view, interest groups will be better represented only when the balance of power shifts in their favor. (But if such shifts occurred, would the interest groups need a planner to represent them?) The principal point was simply that the services of an advocacy planner did not automatically endow a group with additional power, and that advocacy planning without an increase in power was probably a fruitless undertaking. (Offered as evidence of this point was the frequency with which advocacy projects began as technical assistance in research and planning, only to shift eventually to community organizing and social protest.) This was the view of advocacy planning that was reflected by most of the progressive theorists discussed in Chapter 3, who tended to see advocacy as typical of the naive thinking of liberal reformers and rejected the notion that advocacy planners could have any significant impact on the power relationships inherent in the capitalist state. Advocacy planners were certainly well-intentioned, said the progressives, but they simply didn't understand how capitalist society operates.

CURRENT STATUS OF ADVOCACY PLANNING

Has advocacy planning, then, been discredited and largely disappeared? On the contrary, it remains a strong element in the language and culture of the planning profession, even if it appears in forms that depart rather sharply from those originally conceived by Davidoff.

In a small number of instances, the spirit of advocacy has come to permeate the day-to-day operations of local public planning programs. The critical requirement is a political administration sufficiently progressive to allow that spirit to flourish. The leading example in this regard was the city of Cleveland from 1969 to 1979, when Norman Krumholz served as an advocacy-oriented planning director. During his term, the needs of low-income communities were given highest priority, and equality of access to the city's facilities and resources was a basic criterion for the recommendations made by Krumholz and his staff.[16] Equity planners (his preferred term) were, for Krumholz, those who deliberately sought, in their work, "to redistribute power, resources, or participation away from local elites and toward poor and working-class city residents."[17] Not surprisingly, this ride ended abruptly when a more traditional, business-oriented administration came into power. (Indeed, personal correspondence from a Cleveland planner in the post-Krumholz years refers to a "scorched-earth policy" toward any remaining traces of the 1969–1979 planning program.)

A useful overview of equity planning programs in American cities was published by John T. Metzger in 1996. He defined equity planning as advocacy planning carried out inside government, and cited Berkeley, Boston, Burlington (Vermont), Chicago, Cleveland, Hartford, San Francisco, and Santa Monica as cities that have, at one time or another, provided conditions hospitable to equity planning.[18] Equity planning, according to Metzger, "is a framework in which advocacy planners in government use their research, analytical, and organizing skills to influence opinion, mobilize underrepresented constituencies, and advance and perhaps implement policies and programs that redistribute public and private resources to the poor and working class in cities."[19] The plans and policies that result from such efforts, he noted, "diverged from the downtown-oriented land-use planning tradition of most U.S. cities."[20]

Despite the equity planners' accomplishments, however, Metzger's review concludes with some doubts about the future of equity planning. Most of the equity planners working in the "progressive cities" of the 1980s had left their positions by 1996, as less supportive administrations had taken office. At present, Metzger notes, equity planners "are more likely to work as administrators of housing, community development, and economic development programs or as city managers than in traditional planning agencies, which continue to resist the concept in many places."[21]

The reality, of course, is that the prospects for equity planning— like those of all other modes of planning—are highly dependent on the political environment in which it is practiced. Obviously, equity planning is more apt to flourish under progressive political leadership than under more conservative administrations. Equity planning nevertheless remains a strong element in the profession's ethos, ready to emerge wherever and whenever conditions permit.

The spirit of advocacy lives on in other ways as well. Most often it continues to take the form of *people* advocacy, focusing on specific groups. Peter Marris asserts that today "there are far more planners trying to help poor communities than there were in 1965. These planners have fewer illusions about the ability of planning to redistribute resources, but they are also less anxious about justifying their professional status."[22] A sizable literature has developed on feminist advocacy, dealing with the experiences and specific needs of women in the planning process.[23] Many planners would argue, moreover, that they are advocates for future generations.

Issue advocacy has become a central feature of our society, with special interest groups laboring diligently to advance their goals or values. Many of these are directly relevant to planning, and thus inevitably engage the attention and involvement of planners; organizations dealing with the environment, economic development, affordable housing, regionalism, recreation, tourism, health, education, and historic preservation offer good examples. Indeed, one could argue that the spirit of advocacy lives on most directly in the efforts of the growing number of planners who choose to work for private nonprofit organizations that deal with such issues. Here, I have been told, they are free to advocate for their values without fear of retribution from overly cautious bosses or elected officials. It is a mistake to think that such employment offers freedom from all political pressures, however, and the planner who takes the private nonprofit route to escape from politics is in for a keen disappointment. Political relationships must still be maintained with clients, governmental bodies from whom various approvals are needed, funding sources, governing boards, and a host of other entities. On the other hand, private nonprofit employment may well be a more supportive environment for advocacy than can be found elsewhere, at least under current political conditions.

Advocacy planning has also left its mark, however, on the more conventional modes of planning practice. Many large-city planning departments devote some portion of their staff and other resources to neighborhood-level planning, giving planners the opportunity to develop advocacy-style relationships with grass-roots organizations. The ultimate loyalties and reporting responsibilities of such planners may remain at issue, but progress has definitely been made in this regard—progress that owes a large debt to Paul Davidoff and his advocacy colleagues of the 1960s and 1970s.

I conclude this review with two observations. First, I suggest that the most important and lasting contribution of the advocacy movement was its success in pulling planners away from the idea that planning's primary purpose was to serve a unitary public interest. Advocacy made it legitimate for planners to focus their efforts on the needs of particular subgroups—the poor and powerless, certainly, but many others as well.

Second, advocacy is largely about values. It entails a conscious decision to act in accordance with a particular set of values. And since virtually all planners have values that are important to them in their professional practice, it follows that virtually all planners are advocates as well. This underscores, once more, the importance of being introspective about what we are doing, and for whom we are doing it.

The spirit of advocacy is exactly that: a spirit. As such, however, it does not provide us with a planning strategy, complete with a set of instructions. For that we must continue our search.

NOTES

1. Barry Checkoway, "Paul Davidoff and Advocacy Planning in Retrospect," *Journal of the American Planning Association*, Vol. 60, No. 2 (Spring 1994), p. 140.

2. Ibid., p. 139.

3. Paul Davidoff, "Advocacy and Pluralism in Planning," *Journal of the American Institute of Planners*, Vol. 31, No. 4 (November 1965), pp. 331–338.

4. Ibid., pp. 331–332.

5. Ibid., p. 332.

6. Ibid. Emphasis added.

7. Ibid., p. 333.

8. Ibid.

9. Ibid., p. 334.

10. Marshall Kaplan, "Advocacy and the Urban Poor," *Journal of the American Institute of Planners*, Vol. 35, No. 1 (March 1969), pp. 96–101.

11. Paul Davidoff and Thomas A. Reiner, "A Choice Theory of Planning," *Journal of the American Institute of Planners*, Vol. 28 (May 1962), pp. 103–115.

12. For an overview of that specialization, see Michael P. Brooks, *Social Planning and City Planning*, Planning Advisory Service Report No. 261 (Chicago: American Society of Planning Officials, September 1970).

13. For a description of these programs, see C. Richard Hatch, "Some Thoughts on Advocacy Planning," *The*

Architectural Forum, Vol. 128 (June 1968), pp. 72–73, 103, 109.

14. Roger Starr, "Advocators or Planners?" *ASPO Newsletter*, Vol. 33 (December 1967), p. 137.

15. Richard S. Bolan, "Emerging Views of Planning," *Journal of the American Institute of Planners*, Vol. 33 (July 1967), p. 239.

16. For a description of this program, see Norman Krumholz and John Forester, *Making Equity Work: Leadership in the Public Sector* (Philadelphia: Temple University Press, 1990). Also useful is Krumholz, "A Retrospective View of Equity Planning: Cleveland 1969–1979," *Journal of the American Planning Association*, Vol. 48, No. 2 (Spring 1982), pp. 163–174.

17. Norman Krumholz, "Advocacy Planning: Can It Move the Center?" *Journal of the American Planning Association*, Vol. 60, No. 2 (Spring 1994), p. 150.

18. John T. Metzger, "The Theory and Practice of Equity Planning: An Annotated Bibliography," *Journal of Planning Literature*, Vol. 11, No. 1 (August 1996), p. 113.

19. Ibid.

20. Ibid.

21. Ibid., p. 115.

22. Peter Marris, "Advocacy Planning As a Bridge between the Professional and the Political," *Journal of the American Planning Association*, Vol. 60, No. 2 (Spring 1994), p. 145.

23. See, for example, Leonie Sandercock and Ann Forsyth, "A Gender Agenda: New Directions for Planning Theory," *Journal of the American Planning Association*, Vol. 58, No. 1 (Winter 1992), pp. 49–59; and Jacqueline Leavitt, "Feminist Advocacy Planning in the 1980s," in *Strategic Perspectives on Planning Practice*, ed. Barry Checkoway (Lexington, Mass.: Lexington Books, 1986), pp. 181–194.

9

Decentralized Non-Rationality: The Planner as Communicator

POSTMODERNISM

In Chapter 2 I noted that much of the current planning theory literature is grounded in an explicitly postmodern view of the world. While this term has an unfortunate tendency to mean different things to different authors (to say nothing of different professional groups), it certainly implies movement away from the sense of order, comprehensibility, predictability, and rationality that prevailed in the modernist era.[1] The postmodernist view recognizes the complexity of our problems, the elusiveness of solutions to those problems, and the often chaotic nature of the social, economic, and political environments in which those problems occur. Most important for planners, the postmodernist view rejects the notion that the major problems of our communities can be resolved through the diligent exercise of rationality-based planning.

Modernist planning, writes George Hemmens, sought "to organize the parts of the urban environment into a coherent whole,"[2] emphasizing the relationships among the various elements—land use and transportation, for example. Postmodernism, on the other hand, entails a recognition that there are "multiple, irreconcilable stories in every social phenomenon," which leads to the conclusion that "there cannot be one best choice for action."[3] The postmodernist, concludes Hemmens,

> argues that all of the supposed virtues of modernism are faults. They can be summed up as one great fault: Modernist thinking creates a "totalizing discourse" that oppresses all those in the multicultural, multiracial, and gender-, time-, and space-specific communities whose reality is not reflected in the modernist plan.... And what does a postmodern planner believe in? First, that it's up to us as a profession to promote radically democratic urban forms, institutions, and development practices. Second, that we should be far more assertive in expressing the local and particular interests of our constituents.[4]

These views are echoed in much of Judith Innes's recent writing; she argues, in fact, that we planners must "systematically reinvent our field for the post-modern era."[5] Innes provides an excellent summary of the postmodern world view and its potential implications for the planning profession as follows:

> The world of the late 20th century is characterized by fragmented power; distrust of government and experts; multiple, seemingly incommensurable discourses; and a new tribalism, where groups celebrate their differences. All over the world, new processes and new institutions are being invented to deal more effectively with the future. Technological change and globalization of economies require professionals who can both see the big picture and creatively respond to a rapidly changing context. Under these conditions collaborative, communicative planning is proliferating in its applications. This "post-modern" planning involves making connections among ideas and among people; setting in motion joint learning; coordinating among interests and players; building social, intellectual and political capital; and finding new ways to work on the most challenging tasks. This kind of planning, when it is done well, builds its own support and changes the world. Post-modern planning confronts the challenge of continuous change, not by creating blueprints or rigid regulatory regimes, but by trying to influence its direction and preparing to meet uncertainty.[6]

This is, to be sure, a most ambitious set of marching orders for planners, and does call for a profession that is radically different— in its knowledge, skills, and modes of action—from that which has existed to this point. To date, however, there is little evidence to suggest that the profession as a whole has been lining up to march in the direction Innes proposes. (The neotraditional communities designed by Andres Duany and his colleagues have been held up as examples of postmodern planning.[7] It is difficult, however, to see Innes's characterization of postmodernism reflected in Seaside, Florida.) Is it possible that the postmodern theorists are incorrect in their reading of contemporary planning processes? Alternatively, have they simply identified changes that they believe should occur in planning, based on their particular value systems, but that have not materialized (at least thus far) to any great extent? Are they perhaps describing processes that are indeed being carried out by other actors in the public arena but have not yet become key aspects of urban planning practice? *Should* the planning profession be moving more vigorously to reinvent itself in the manner Innes prescribes?

The search for answers to these questions requires a closer examination of the ideas and prescriptions of some of the most prominent postmodern theorists. Their strategies are clearly decentralized, in that the planner is viewed not as a top-down plan-maker but as a facilitator of community-based decision processes. The strategies are also non-rational, in the sense that they rely very little on rational analysis and planning.[8]

PLANNING AS COMMUNICATIVE ACTION

Postmodern planning theory places particular emphasis on the communicative aspects of planning practice. Clearly, planners communicate information and ideas to the many people and organizations with whom they interact, and receive information and ideas in return. This communication occurs not only through formal plans and reports but in a variety of other ways as well—through phone calls and e-mail messages, at meetings, over the front counter, in casual conversation, and so on. Communication also takes place in nonverbal ways, ranging from facial expressions and gestures to the messages that are transmitted through one's actions.

The communicative action theorists place great emphasis on the fact that planning communications are not just exchanges of words but reflect a variety of institutional, political, and power relationships.[9] During the course of these exchanges, a collective sense of meaning is gradually created among the participants, and subsequent actions will be heavily influenced—for good or ill—by these shared understandings.[10] Communication in planning can be done well or badly, of course; it can be true or false, valid or invalid, manipulative or empowering. But one way or another, it does have effects—that is, things happen as a result of it.

As Nigel Taylor notes, the idea is not simply that communication is an important aspect of the planning process, but rather that it is the very *essence* of that process. For communicative action theorists, planning "can best be viewed as a process of practical deliberation involving dialogue, debate, and negotiation among planners, politicians, developers, and the public."[11] The planner who follows this approach, Connie Ozawa and Ethan Seltzer write, "is not an analyst working behind closed doors to eventually produce the most rational recommendation but an active and intentional participant in a process of public discourse and social change."[12]

The seminal writings in communicative action theory are those of John Forester, who has long argued that we need to view what planners do as "attention-shaping, communicative action rather than as instrumental action, as means to particular ends."[13] Planners' actions, he says, "shape others' expectations, beliefs, hopes, and understandings, even though planners do not strictly control any of these outcomes."[14] Forester wants planners to better understand the extent to which their "ordinary actions" produce these communicative effects, and he argues that planners can use this understanding to avoid potential problems and improve the quality of their practice.

Building upon the work of the critical theorist Jurgen Habermas, Forester suggests four characteristics of good communication in planning. It should be (1) *comprehensible* (a point to bear in mind when one is tempted to dazzle the audience with the latest planning jargon); (2) *sincere*, in order to establish a relationship of mutual trust; (3) *legitimate*—that is, appropriate to the situation at hand, and justifiable in view of the nature of that situation; and (4) *true*, to the best of the planner's knowledge and ability.[15] Communication that falls short of these principles is *distorted*, which fuels distrust.

Much of Forester's work has dealt, in fact, with the unfortunate potential for the dissemination of distorted information by planners. Planners can serve to increase the amount and quality of useful information available to the members of a community—or, alternatively, they can abet (knowingly or unknowingly) the processes whereby powerful interest groups manipulate channels of communication in pursuit of their own ends.[16] We have a responsibility, he writes, "to prevent and correct false promises; to correct misleading expectations; to eliminate clients' unnecessary dependency; to create and nurture hope; to spread policy and design questions to those affected; to nurture dialogue about options and about the 'values' and 'interests' by which those options for policy and design may be evaluated; and, thus, to communicate genuine social and political possibilities."[17]

It is impossible to adequately characterize, in only a few paragraphs, the richness of the communicative action approach to planning. It has generated a sizable literature, and numerous aspects and issues have not been mentioned here. I hope this will suffice, however, to give the reader a general sense of its major themes. What, then, are the major implications of communicative action theory for planning practice?

IMPLICATIONS FOR PRACTICE

Clearly, the planner who wants to practice in a manner consistent with the communicative action approach will pay careful attention to the messages conveyed in his or her professional communications, scrutinizing them in terms of Forester's criteria and being sensitive to their potential effects. Beyond this, however, communicative action theorists emphasize the importance of "cultivating community networks of liaisons and contacts; supplying technical and political information to citizens; educating citizens and community organizations about the planning process; listening to the concerns and the interests of all participants; ensuring access to planning information for community and neighborhood organizations...."[18] One author has concluded that communicative action is best understood, in fact, as another version of the advocacy planning of the 1960s and 1970s, and there are indeed many similarities in the underlying values and concerns of the two approaches.[19] Other elements of communicative action, however, clearly differentiate it from advocacy.

One of these is the notion of mediated negotiation, wherein the planner attempts to forge a working agreement among two or more groups that approach an issue with differing viewpoints or goals.[20] Conflicts between developers and environmental groups, between adjacent neighborhoods, between citizens' groups with conflicting agendas, between regulators and the regulated—these and numerous other situations present ample opportunity for the intervention of skilled mediators. Often the planner turns out to be one of the parties in the conflict, of course, and negotiating skills are useful on those occasions as well.

Forester is particularly interested in the potential role of mediated negotiation in achieving the sorts of equity-oriented results that he and other communicative action theorists consider most important. Planners, he writes,

> can use a range of mediated negotiation strategies practically to address power imbalances of access, information, class, and expertise which perpetually threaten the quality of local planning outcomes.

> Mediated negotiations in local land-use processes are no panacea for the structural problems of our society. But when local conflicts involve many issues, when differences in interests can be exploited by trading to achieve joint gains, and when diverse interests rather than fundamental rights are at stake, then mediated negotiation strategies for planners make good sense, politically and practically.[21]

The ability to serve as an effective negotiator does not emerge full-blown from reading a few articles on the subject, of course; mediated negotiation is a reasonably specialized undertaking, and thus requires training and practice. I suspect that only a small percentage of planning practitioners have acquired such training, whether through university courses, sessions at national planning conferences, or attendance at proprietary short courses and training programs. To expect all planners to be competent negotiators is surely unrealistic; if mediated negotiation came to be considered the essence of planning practice, the profession would need to become radically different from what it is today (that is, it would indeed need to "reinvent itself"). It is nevertheless clear, however, that mediated negotiation is a highly useful item in the planner's tool kit, and it would certainly be advisable for large planning departments to include at least one staff member who possesses this skill.

Somewhat broader in scope is a second role associated with communicative action theory: the planner as consensus builder. Innes, at present the principal exponent of this approach, describes consensus building as

> a method of group deliberation that brings together for face-to-face discussion a significant range of individuals chosen because they represent those with differing stakes in a problem. Facilitators, training for participants, and carefully designed procedures are intended to ensure

that the mode of discourse is one where all are heard and all concerns are taken seriously. Little is taken as given in the wide-ranging discussion. The process requires that participants have common information and that all become informed about each other's interests. When the group has explored interests and agreed on facts, they create options, develop criteria for choice, and make the decisions on which they can all agree. Citizens, public agencies, or even legislatures create consensus-building groups to supplement traditional procedures for policy development and plan preparation. Such groups have built consensus for planning and policy tasks on geographic scales ranging from the neighborhood to the nation.[22]

The role of facilitator has been around for a long time; what is new here is Innes's emphasis on facilitation as a major technique for planners, and her linkage of this role to some of the historically elusive concepts of planning practice. Skillfully facilitated decisions can be "communicatively rational," Innes suggests, as long as they "come about because there are good reasons for them rather than because of the political or economic power of particular stakeholders."[23] But can we always distinguish the good reasons from those based on political or economic interests? In the spirit of Flyvbjerg's analysis, is it possible that the possession of power also entails the privilege of defining what constitutes a good reason? Even more ambitiously, Innes argues that a properly designed consensus-building process "can produce decisions that approximate the public interest."[24] In the eyes of that particular set of participants, perhaps, but in absolute terms?

Again, it is clear that facilitation skills—along with other group dynamics techniques, the ability to run an effective meeting, and so on—are highly valuable for any planner whose role regularly includes work with citizens' groups.[25] Some planning situations will lend themselves to consensus-building processes, while others will not—and the astute planner will be able to tell the difference.[26] To suggest that consensus building is emerging as a major paradigm of the planning process, however, probably overestimates its centrality to planning practice.

CURRENT STATUS
OF THE COMMUNICATIVE ACTION CONCEPT

Writing in 1995, Innes asserted that communicative action theory was "beginning to dominate the field."[27] It is certainly true that a number of the planning profession's most prolific authors have been attracted to this body of theory, and its impact on planning thought at the outset of the twenty-first century is incontestable. On the other hand, given that rationality was the last paradigm to enjoy genuine dominance in the profession and that planning theorists have long been searching for a new body of theory to take its place, it is no small matter to claim such dominance for communicative action theory. How well does this claim hold up, both in the realm of theory and in its implications for practice?

In April 1998, a major international conference on planning theory was held in Oxford, England. Reporting on the conference, Oren Yiftachel notes that a number of those in attendance challenged the purported dominance of communicative action theory.[28] According to Yiftachel, the papers presented were quite diverse in content, and the issues they addressed ranged from "rationality (yes, still alive) to communication, consensus, participation, postmodernity, environmental sustainability, values, control, oppression, and more."[29] Another participant in the conference, James Throgmorton, writes that a clear majority of the conferees rejected the claim of dominance for communicative action theory. Most of the participants, he says, wanted to replace it

> with their own preferred theoretical approaches. Some argued, for example, that planning should be based on the principles of ecological sustainability. Others argued that it should be based on spatial processes and the regulation of space. Still others promoted a return to Rationality. And so on.[30]

Yiftachel does note that communicative action was one of the two approaches afforded the greatest attention at the conference, the other being what he calls the "critical approach" (which he equates with analysis of the "dark side" of planning, featuring "a range of perspectives that critically examine the role of planning in creating, maintaining, or reproducing social control, oppression, inequalities and injustices").[31] Overall, however, it is clear—based not only on that conference (a number of planning theorists, after all, were not in attendance), but on an ongoing perusal of the planning literature as well—that a number of planning theorists have abstained from accepting communicative action as the discipline's dominant paradigm. It is worth noting, of course, that the members of the planning theory community—as is the case, I suspect, with theorists in most other professions—tend to be a rather disputatious lot, enjoying nothing more than a good argument over concepts and values. If that community achieved complete consensus around a single theory, what else would there be to write about, or to debate at conferences? It is difficult to conceive of a paradigm that could be so compelling as to enjoy genuine dominance in the field— especially now, in the postmodern era.

But enough about the status of communicative action in the world of theory. More important, in keeping with the overall purpose of this book, how useful is the communicative action approach for practicing planners? Not surprisingly, the answer is mixed. On the negative side, several potential issues have been raised.

First, only some of a planner's activities are indeed communicative.[32] Others are more mundane: thinking about a particular issue or assignment, getting organized to tackle it, and trying to get a handle on it (including the collection of information about it); thinking through alternative approaches; assessing budgetary parameters; developing timetables; thinking through the legal and political aspects; deciding how to proceed (including whom to involve); managing and being managed; and so on. To be sure, communicative action theory kicks in as soon as exchanges begin to occur among the various participants in the process. But it says relatively little about the many activities that the planner carries out before (and after) getting to that point. If communication is indeed the essence of planning, then significant portions of many planners' days are excluded from relevance.

Second, it is my impression that the communicative action literature tends to romanticize the inherent nobility of citizens' values and preferences. The approach seems to assume that if we make sure (1) that all stakeholders are involved and empowered, (2) that our communications with those stakeholders are comprehensible, sincere, legitimate, and true, and (3) that the stakeholders are fully informed of the possibilities open to them, then better decisions will result—that is, decisions that approximate a consensus and come closer, than might otherwise have occurred, to serving the interests of all participants. On the other hand, I have already noted the extent to which communities are made up of individuals and organizations with radically divergent values, aspirations, and operating styles—which are often in conflict with one another and are often manifested in political processes that defy management by planners.

One of my students recently described a dilemma he faced during his internship with a county planning department. As part of his duties, he served as the front-desk respondent to citizens' telephone calls. His marching orders heavily emphasized customer service: giving his name and title when he answered the phone, listening courteously, communicating understanding and concern, either providing an answer or referring the caller to someone who could, and so forth. The problem, he said, was that a significant proportion of the callers were expressing narrow-minded, self-serving, even prejudiced viewpoints—opposing, for example, the establishment of residential social care facilities in their neighborhoods. He was frustrated because he could not argue with these callers; his instructions surely precluded such a response (nor would it likely have done much good in any event), and he had great difficulty expressing "understanding and concern." What was he to do about this? In short, how should planners communicate with citizens whose values and aims are deemed patently ignoble?

Might the fears and biases of these callers be resolved by bringing them to the table for some mediated negotiation or consensus building? To be sure, any reasonable idea is worth a try—but it would be terribly naive to assume that such an approach will always work (or even always be feasible; people cannot be forced to participate in such processes against their will). This discussion leads, then, to a third concern about communicative action theory—namely, that it seems to presume the existence of a more structured, polite, reasonable, manageable—even rational—set of political processes than are generally said to characterize the postmodern era. A fundamental characteristic of both mediated negotiation and consensus building is agreement at the outset, among all participants, that the process will likely lead to a decision on the issue at hand, and that the participants, by virtue of having a place at the table, should be willing to abide by that decision. This is not a characteristic, however, of the give-and-take typically observed in the broader political arena, where there are winners and losers—and where the losers, far from accepting the outcome gracefully, often look for ways to reverse it (and perhaps to get even as well). To be sure, there are undoubtedly many issues that lend themselves to ministrations of the sort recommended by communicative action theorists, and planners should be prepared to deal with them appropriately when they arise. It is also important to bear in mind, however, that many of the issues planners confront are probably not amenable to resolution by such means.

Fourth, even when an issue is deemed appropriate for mediated negotiation or consensus building, there is no guarantee that such a process will succeed. While a number of examples of successful intervention have been cited,[33] there are also times when a compromise or consensus simply cannot be reached, despite the planners' best efforts. The "goals for the region" project briefly described in Chapter 1 is a case in point; despite highly professional facilitation of a number of meetings intended to generate consensus on the region's principal goals, the process ultimately collapsed because of fundamental differences between the goals of activist, change-oriented citizens and those of elected officials more interested in preserving the status quo. Similar results have occurred in collaborative visioning or goal-setting projects in other cities.[34]

Fifth, even when a compromise or consensus can be reached, it will sometimes be accompanied by (and perhaps even result from) the continued domination or marginalization of one or another individual or group participating in the process. Much as we might wish to the contrary, power relations are not erased by legitimate communications; power continues to operate after all the communication has occurred.[35]

Sixth, Michael Neuman has criticized communicative action theory for its emphasis on process at the expense of content.[36] Specific images of the good community, as well as plans embodying those images, are largely absent from the literature of communicative action; as long as the right people are involved and the communications are of the right kind, one conception of the future city seems to be as good as another. By failing to incorporate images and plans into their theories, Neuman charges, communicative action theorists refuse "to allow planning's past to be experienced with its present. We can rest somewhat easier knowing that practice has gone ahead of theory by reincorporating the image and rediscovering the plan."[37]

Innes argues that communicative action theory has closed the gap between planning theory and planning practice:

> These theorists make the gap complaint moot because they take practice as the raw material of their inquiry. In this they differ from their predecessors, who did primarily armchair theorizing and systematic thinking

about planning. These new theorists pursue the questions and puzzles that arise in their study of practice, rather than those which emerge from thinking about how planning could or should be. These new planning scholars do grounded theorizing based on richly interpretive study of practice. Their purpose is, on the one hand, to document what planners do and, on the other, to reflect critically on that practice. They apply intellectual lenses that are new to planning to illuminate and critique what they see. They see planning as an interactive, communicative activity and depict planners as deeply embedded in the fabric of community, politics, and public decision-making.[38]

This approach, she says, does not offer "bottom-line prescriptions or simple models for how to proceed, but it has helped students and academics to see planning, and has helped planners to see themselves."[39]

As discussed in Chapter 2, I cannot agree that the gap between planning theory and planning practice has been significantly narrowed by communicative action theory. It is significant to note that most of the claims regarding the closing of that gap have come from the academic wing of the profession. I will begin taking such claims more seriously when they are routinely voiced by practitioners as well.

The mere fact that planning scholars focus their theoretical work on practice does not close the gap; indeed, if they are planning scholars, one might reasonably ask what *else* they would focus on. Communication between practitioners and theorists is a two-way street, and the traffic will be light, I suggest, as long as the role of practitioners in the planning theory enterprise continues to be primarily that of serving as objects of analysis and critique, rather than as full partners in a process aimed at maximizing the quality of the profession's performance. (High-quality performance will be defined differently by different observers, of course, depending on the values that they bring to the task.)

While communicative action theory cannot legitimately claim total dominance in the realm of contemporary planning thought, and while it has probably not succeeded in closing the theory-practice gap, it has nonetheless made several important contributions to the planning profession. First, directing a spotlight on the communicative aspects of planning has been highly useful. Planners should take very seriously the communicative effects of their work; they should ensure that their words and actions are not used in ways that perpetuate inequalities and oppressive power relations but are instead liberating and empowering; they should indeed strive diligently to communicate in ways that are comprehensible, sincere, legitimate, and true. In short, communicative action theorists have made an important contribution to the profession's value system, and all planners should be encouraged to incorporate these values into their own practice.

Second, communicative action theorists have emphasized a set of methods—mediated negotiation, consensus building, and other dispute-resolution and group decision-making techniques—that can be quite useful under certain circumstances (typically where a decision is needed, where stakeholders are well-defined and willing to participate in the process of reaching a decision, and where power relations can be kept in check at least temporarily). Thus, communicative action theory has made important contributions to the profession's body of methodology as well.

Finally, communicative action theory offers a vast array of research opportunities for the profession's academic wing. There is still a great deal to be learned about the communicative content and effects of many types of planning activity, and researchers will likely be exploring these issues for many years to come. The challenge will be to do so in a manner that engages the objects of that research—the practitioners—as full partners in the process, with benefits flowing to both groups. I am eagerly awaiting—but not holding my breath for—the first journal article written by a planning practitioner in which she or he critically analyzes the communicative effects of the work being done by planning theorists.

In short, communicative action theory is a rich source of insights, values, and methods that make significant contributions to the planning profession. It is not necessary to accord it status as an all-encompassing paradigm in order to derive these benefits, however. Planning—the process by which we attempt to shape the future—certainly involves a great deal of communicative content, but it also includes a number of elements that do not fit neatly under the communicative action umbrella.[40] This is perhaps one of the reasons, among others, that so few planning practitioners have thus far shown much interest in embracing communicative action theory as a practical guide to their daily activities.[41]

NOTES

1. For a discussion of alternative meanings of postmodernism, see Beth Moore Milroy, "Into Postmodern Weightlessness," *Journal of Planning Education and Research*, Vol. 10, No. 3 (Summer 1991), pp. 181–187.

2. George Hemmens, "The Postmodernists Are Coming, the Postmodernists Are Coming," *Planning*, Vol. 58, No. 7 (July 1992), p. 20.

3. Ibid., p. 21.

4. Ibid.

5. Judith E. Innes, "The Planners' Century," *Journal of Planning Education and Research*, Vol. 16, No. 3 (Spring 1997), p. 227.

6. Ibid.

7. See, for example, Hemmens, "Postmodernists Are Coming."

8. Howell Baum suggests that communicative theorists do indeed practice a rationality of sorts, one that "reflects the interplay and negotiation of interests, statuses, and meanings." I won't quibble with this, but it certainly necessitates a broader definition of rationality than the one I have been using. See "Practicing Planning Theory in a Political World," in *Explorations in Planning Theory*, ed. Seymour J. Mandelbaum, Luigi Mazza, and Robert W. Burchell (New Brunswick, N.J.: Center for Urban Policy Research, Rutgers University, 1996), p. 369.

9. Ibid., pp. 368–369.

10. For a discussion of the role of information in communicative planning, see Judith E. Innes, "Information in Communicative Planning," *Journal of the American Planning Association*, Vol. 64, No. 1 (Winter 1998), pp. 52–63.

11. Nigel Taylor, "Mistaken Interests and the Discourse Model of Planning," *Journal of the American Planning Association*, Vol. 64, No. 1 (Winter 1998), p. 71.

12. Connie Ozawa and Ethan Seltzer, "Taking Our Bearings: Mapping a Relationship among Planning Practice, Theory, and Education," *Journal of Planning Education and Research*, Vol. 18, No. 3 (Spring 1999), p. 259.

13. John Forester, *Planning in the Face of Power* (Berkeley: University of California Press, 1989), p. 138. Also see Forester, "Critical Theory and Planning Practice," *Journal of the American Planning Association*, Vol. 46, No. 3 (July 1980), pp. 275–286.

14. John Forester, *Critical Theory, Public Policy, and Planning Practice: Toward a Critical Pragmatism* (Albany: State University of New York Press, 1993), p. 25.

15. Forester, "Critical Theory and Planning Practice," p. 278. Also see Hilda Blanco, *How to Think about Social Problems: American Pragmatism and the Idea of Planning* (Westport, Conn.: Greenwood Press, 1994), p. 138.

16. For an interesting case study revolving around this issue, see Patsy Healey, "A Planner's Day: Knowledge and Action in Communicative Practice," *Journal of the American Planning Association*, Vol. 58, No. 1 (Winter 1992), pp. 9–20.

17. Forester, *Face of Power*, p. 21.

18. Blanco, *Social Problems*, pp. 138–139.

19. Peter Hall, "The Turbulent Eighth Decade: Challenges to American City Planning," *Journal of the American Planning Association*, Vol. 55, No. 3 (Summer 1989), p. 280.

20. See Forester, *Face of Power*, pp. 82–103; and Lawrence Susskind and Connie Ozawa, "Mediated Negotiation in the Public Sector: The Planner As Mediator," *Journal of Planning Education and Research*, Vol. 4, No. 1 (August 1984), pp. 5–15.

21. Forester, *Face of Power*, p. 103.

22. Judith E. Innes, "Planning through Consensus Building: A New View of the Comprehensive Planning Ideal," *Journal of the American Planning Association*, Vol. 62, No. 4 (Autumn 1996), p. 461. See also Judith E. Innes and David E. Booher, "Consensus Building and Complex Adaptive Systems: A Framework for Evaluating Collaborative Planning," *Journal of the American Planning Association*, Vol. 65, No. 4 (Autumn 1999), p. 412;

and Innes, "Information in Commun-icative Planning," p. 60.

23. Innes, "Planning through Consensus Building," p. 461.

24. Ibid., p. 469.

25. A useful discussion of group process techniques is found in Kem Lowry, Peter Adler, and Neal Milner, "Participating the Public: Group Process, Politics, and Planning," *Journal of Planning Education and Research*, Vol. 16, No. 3 (Spring 1997), pp. 177–187.

26. One of my faculty colleagues argues—persuasively, I must concede—that attitudes toward consensus are somewhat gender based. Women, she suggests, are more concerned with the affective elements of a planning process, while men are more oriented toward the bottom line; accordingly, women are more willing to spend the time and energy needed to secure a consensus, while men soon lose patience and want to vote. Obviously there are exceptions to these generalizations, but overall there may be some validity here—and if the reader has any doubts in this regard, I'll be happy to set up a profession-wide vote on the matter!

27. Judith E. Innes, "Planning Theory's Emerging Paradigm: Communicative Action and Interactive Practice," *Journal of Planning Education and Research*, Vol. 14, No. 3 (Spring 1995), p. 183.

28. Oren Yiftachel, "Planning Theory at a Crossroad: The Third Oxford Conference," *Journal of Planning Education and Research*, Vol. 18, No. 3 (Spring 1999), p. 267.

29. Ibid.

30. James A. Throgmorton, "Learning through Conflict at Oxford," *Journal of Planning Education and Research*, Vol. 18, No. 3 (Spring 1999), p. 269.

31. Yiftachel, "Planning Theory," p. 268.

32. I attribute this point to comments made by Ann Forsyth during a session at the 1999 annual conference of the ACSP.

33. See, for example, Lawrence E. Susskind, Sarah McKearnan, and Jennifer Thomas-Larmer, eds., *The Consensus Building Handbook: A Comprehensive Guide to Reaching Agreement* (Thousand Oaks, Calif.: Sage Publications, 1999).

34. See, for example, Amy Helling, "Collaborative Visioning: Proceed with Caution! Results from Evaluating Atlanta's Vision 2020 Project," *Journal of the American Planning Association*, Vol. 64, No. 3 (Summer 1998), pp. 335–349.

35. This point is illustrated quite effec-tively in a case study by John Foley and Mickey Lauria presented at the 1999 Annual Conference of the ACSP: "Plans, Planning, and Tragic Choices," Working Paper No. 62, College of Urban and Public Affairs, University of New Orleans, no date.

36. Michael Neuman, "Planning, Governing, and the Image of the City," *Journal of Planning Education and Research*, Vol. 18, No. 1 (Fall 1998), pp. 61–71.

37. Ibid., p. 68.

38. Innes, "Planning Theory's Emerg-ing Paradigm," p. 183.

39. Ibid.

40. Concern for the implementation and effectiveness of plans, says Emily Talen, entails a recognition that "they are more than communicative devices." See "After the Plans: Methods to Evaluate the Implementation Success of Plans," *Journal of Planning Education and Research*, Vol. 16, No. 2 (Winter 1996), p. 90.

41. Jerome Kaufman suggests that the roles posited for planners under commu-nicative action theory are difficult for most public agency planners to pursue, even when they sympathize with the underly-ing values of the approach. "The prevalent social, political, and institutional system in which U.S. planning operates poses too many obstacles for these roles to work in practice." Kaufman, "Making Planners More Effective Strategists," in *Strategic Perspectives on Planning Practice*, ed. Barry Checkoway (Lexington, Mass.: Lexington Books, 1986), p. 100.

Toward a More
Practical Strategy

INTRODUCTION

Throughout the history of the planning profession, authors have been urging planners to embrace a seemingly endless array of roles. A case has been made, at one time or another, for the planner as master designer, rational analyst, social change agent, visionary, negotiator, monitor of communication flows, storyteller, advocate, social interventionist, political strategist, specialist in comprehensiveness, customer service specialist, deal maker, designer of social institutions, group process facilitator, and others too numerous (and in some cases too humorous) to mention. Most of these roles are subsumed under, or are closely affiliated with, one of the four umbrella paradigms—rational planning, incrementalism, advocacy, and communicative action—that were reviewed in Chapters 6 through 9.

Each of these paradigms has made a significant contribution to our understanding of the planning process. Each has also provided advice to planners about how that process should be carried out— advice that, as we have seen, can be useful under some circumstances but not under others. It is quite likely, then, that we would do well to abandon our quest for a single, overarching, discipline-defining paradigm. Instead, we should celebrate the rich diversity of the strategies that are available, and focus on learning how to match particular strategies to the circumstances at hand.[1] John Forester asserts—correctly, in my view—that when different paradigms "compete and pose problems differently, that is a sign of health, not intellectual poverty. We should stop looking for a unified field theory, a single common measure of excellence,...and we should instead explore the real possibilities to improve planning practices so that they serve human need."[2] Doing so will entail the use of many planning strategies, not just one.

It is unrealistic, however, to assume that any one planner can be skilled in the application of each and every strategy that is available for use by members of the profession. Indeed, just as the planning profession has its content specialists—those who are particularly knowledgeable about land use, transportation, geographic information systems, and so on—so does it have its process specialists. Every large planning organization needs its analysts, its front-counter workers, its designers, its creative idea people, its political strategists and negotiators, its skilled communicators, its detail people, its big-picture people, and its staff possessing excellent "people skills." Smaller planning organizations are probably unable to cover all these bases, but would do well to incorporate as many of them as possible in the few positions available. Ironically, these characteristics are rarely given significant weight, at least explicitly, in the recruitment of new staff members; ultimately, however, the array and balance of such skills and orientations within an organization can have a tremendous impact on its record of accomplishment.

All of this is simply to reiterate that each of the approaches examined thus far has made significant contributions to the planning profession, but none has been so all-powerful, in its explanations of planning and in its advice to planners, as to earn for itself the mantle of "dominant planning paradigm."

The strategies discussed in Chapters 6 through 9 were presented more or less sequentially: rationality emerged as the dominant paradigm in the post–World War II years; incrementalism made its initial splash in the late 1950s and early 1960s, followed in short order by the profession's preoccupation with advocacy from the mid-1960s through the 1970s; communicative action theory, at least as it applies to planning, has been evolving since the early 1980s. Clearly, our changing conceptions of the planning process have also reflected significantly different notions about the relationship between planning and politics.

Early writers on rationality tended to portray planning as a highly efficacious undertaking that required planners to pay little heed to politics; a well-crafted and creative plan was expected to carry the day on its own merits, rendering unnecessary any interaction with the unsavory political arena. Charles Lindblom's incrementalism introduced recognition of the fact that political realities did indeed affect the planning process and should therefore be taken into account. Paul Davidoff's advocacy planning raised the political ante even further, suggesting that planners would succeed only if they joined the political fray; the content of planning was still important, but plans could also function as effective political weapons. Finally, with communicative action theory, the triumph of politics was complete. There is little emphasis on the content of plans, or on planners' images of the future city; instead, it is assumed that plans will emerge from the prevailing political economy and that the planner's most important role is to strive to create a level playing field.

Critically weakened by political naivete, rationality-based planning tended to ignore the realities of politics. My concern is that the pendulum has now swung all the way in the opposite direction. Politics is perceived as controlling everything, so there is little need for the planner to develop and articulate visions of a better community; ultimately, all that matters is whether all stakeholders have had an opportunity for meaningful participation in the planning process. Gone, then, is any conception of the planner as a skilled and creative formulator of alternative futures; in short, the planner no longer *plans*, but simply facilitates the planning processes of others.

I am not content with this conception of the planner's role. The next two chapters present a perspective—and ultimately a strategy—intended to strike a workable balance between planning as a political process and planning as a creative act of shaping the future. Such a strategy entails focusing sharply on the dynamics of the relationship between the planner and his or her working environment. Chapter 10 examines three such dynamics—idea generation, feedback, and goal formulation—each of which plays a major role in the strategy described in Chapter 11. I hasten to note that the strategy is not being proposed for "dominant planning paradigm" status. I hope, however, that some planners, in some circumstances, will find it helpful.

NOTES

1. I first discussed this issue in "A Plethora of Paradigms?" *Journal of the American Planning Association*, Vol. 59, No. 2 (Spring 1993), p. 143.

2. John Forester, "Bridging Interests and Community: Advocacy Planning and the Challenges of Deliberative Democracy," *Journal of the American Planning Association*, Vol. 60, No. 2 (Spring 1994), p. 157.

10

Setting the Stage: Ideas, Feedback, Goals— and Trial Balloons

---

I have suggested that the profession has a strong need for strategies that can assist planners to play roles that are both efficacious and politically realistic. The Feedback Strategy described in Chapter 11 is intended to meet that requirement[1]. Like many of its predecessors, it is an action strategy of planning, one that prescribes a set of procedures that the planner might follow in the pursuit of planned change.

The Feedback Strategy is grounded in some assumptions about the context in which planning occurs; indeed, it makes the context a *part* of the strategy. This chapter examines several aspects of that context, each of which plays a major role in the Feedback Strategy.

WHERE DO PLANNING IDEAS COME FROM?

Regardless of the approach a planner opts to follow, planning inevitably entails choosing among alternatives: deciding what to do, or recommend, or incorporate into a particular plan, or even whom to involve and how. It is reasonable, then, to ask from what sources the planner acquires those alternatives, and what impact the social and political context has on the planner's ultimate choice among them. Herbert Simon's administrative man may have satisficed—but where did the satisficing alternative itself come from? Many of the steps taken by planners may indeed be, as

Charles Lindblom suggests, only incremental departures from the current mode of operation, but the fact that they are departures at all makes it meaningful to inquire about their sources.

Lindblom said little about this question, noting only that the planner or administrator, in designing courses of action incrementally, would "outline those relatively few policy alternatives that occurred to him."[2] Nothing was said about the reasons why some alternatives occurred to the planner while others did not. Amitai Etzioni was only slightly more specific in advising the decision-maker, as the first step in the mixed scanning strategy, to "list all relevant alternatives that come to mind, that the staff raises, and that advisers advocate."[3] More recently, Patricia Bayne has suggested that planners rely primarily on two kinds of "memories" for their ideas. The "internal" memory "comprises the store of information contained within each practitioner's cognitive structures by virtue of his particular experience, education and information storage and retrieval capabilities."[4] The '"external" memory, on the other hand, consists of the journals, books, documents, and people that a planner regularly consults.[5] More specificity is needed, however, if we are to better understand the ways in which planning behavior is influenced by the context in which it occurs.

Etzioni addresses the question of sources for ideas by positing a three-filter screen through which ideas pass on their road to implementation. In Etizioni's view, each of three kinds of societal elites—intellectual, expert, and political—constitutes a "filter."

> The intellectual filter is the most open one; ideas are approved with comparative ease, especially if they are not in open conflict with a major body of known facts. Intellectual screening is more evaluative than empirical and more concerned with value-relevancy and "coverage" than with reality-testing. The expert filter is considerably less open and admits mainly ideas that withstand some kind of empirical test. The political filter is the most narrow for it allows only one or two alternatives to pass through it—those which the elite will seek to implement.[6]

Etzioni's construct is an appealing one, and I would certainly agree with his conclusion that a "society that is free to test its ideas and to try out fundamentally new ones cannot be restricted to approaching the world and itself merely through the narrow political filter of the elites in power."[7] This view can also be related to my assessment of past and present planning theories; because they emanate primarily from the field's intellectuals, planning the-ories have certainly tended to be more evaluative and value-relevant than empirical. Nevertheless, I cannot agree with Etzioni's observation that intellectuals constitute the best, or even the major, source of ideas for application by experts (into which category most practicing planners would presumably fall). One of the distinguish-ing marks of the postmodern era, I should think, is the notion that the ideas propelling our society forward are as likely to emerge from the grass roots (and, for that matter, from experts and occasionally even politicians) as they are from universities, think tanks, and laboratories. Certainly the sources of sound ideas for community improvement are far more numerous and diverse than Etzioni suggests in this formulation.

The list shown in Figure 10-1 is a typology of the sources of alter-natives that are most relevant to the planner.[8] It is difficult, of course, to assess the relative importance of these sources, which undoubtedly differ from situation to situation and from planner to planner. Were we able to count the frequency with which each of these sources is tapped, however, my guess is that we would find influence-wielders to be the most common sources of alternatives—followed, in declining significance, by reference groups, the legal framework, one's self—and, finally and regrettably, client groups.

Different planners will tend to derive their alternatives from dif-ferent sources, of course, and in fact a major element in planners' individual operating styles may be the relative weights that they give to such sources. The advocacy planner, for example, selectively screens out other sources in order to focus on the ideas emanating from the client group (as well as those coming from his or her own value system); the junior planner hoping to rise rapidly in the local planning hierarchy may be particularly attuned to the ideas of influ-ence-wielders and local reference groups; other planners may strive vigorously to implement the ideas they acquired in graduate school or at professional conferences; and so on. None of the sources iden-tified here can be assessed, on their face alone, as either good or bad; all are potentially productive—and all can generate atrocious ideas as well.

While planners may give more or less weight to various sources, depending on the circumstances, they often experience difficulty when they feel the need to be equally responsive to two or more sources simultaneously—for example, neighborhood leaders and the city's business leaders. (This is an ongoing dilemma for the "inside advocates" mentioned in Chapter 8.) The plight of the planner who attempts to follow the dictates of professional standards or federal guidelines in the face of intense local sentiments to the contrary is equally familiar. Difficult choices must often be made under such circumstances.

Other factors undoubtedly influence the planner's reliance on different sources over time—for example, a change in the planner's position in a bureaucratic hierarchy; changes in personal or family

---

1. **Internal**
    - Reason, knowledge
    - Ideology, values
    - Intuition

2. **Reference groups**
    - Local (for example, colleagues within the same organization, other public officials, friends and social contacts)
    - Professional (for example, graduate schools and professional societies whose members have been socialized to conform to a set of professional standards, ethics, and modes of behavior)

3. **Influence-wielders**
    - Superiors (in the planner's bureaucratic hierarchy)
    - Elected officials
    - Social and economic power figures
    - Providers of resources (for example, local, state, and federal governments, as well as foundations)
    - Special interest groups (which vary widely in their lobbying expertise and in their ability to wield other forms of political clout)
    - The media

4. **The legal framework (which may mandate the consideration or adoption of specific alternatives)**

5. **Client groups**

Figure 10-1. A typology of the sources of alternatives typically used by planners.

circumstances, social status, or psychological state; changes in the kinds of decisions the planner is asked to make; or the emergence of new reference groups.

One point deserving special emphasis is that the planner's own inner resources—his or her knowledge, experience, and so forth—make up only one of the several sources from which alternatives are drawn, and perhaps not the most important one at that. Recognition of this fact is an important antidote to the potential pitfalls of professional arrogance, and is a reality worthy of consideration in the development of viable planning strategies.

Reliance on particular sources for ideas or alternatives may have implications beyond those mentioned thus far. First, with respect to internal resources, a variety of factors—favorable and unfavorable past experiences, the desire for job security and advancement, and so on—will often combine to impel the planner toward relatively "safe" proposals. Nor are local government agencies and departments often the source of ideas for radical change. While exceptions do surface now and then, the same must be said of elected officials. Edward Banfield observed several decades ago that for big-city mayors, the generation of support and the avoidance of conflict are key objectives; thus they are apt to be less concerned with the content of a given proposal than with the identity and political power of its proponents.[9] (One would be hard-pressed to argue that Banfield's comments have no validity today.) Chief executives, he wrote, "are slow to take up an issue presented to them by the 'civic leaders.' They know from experience that what one organization wants is almost certain to be opposed by others."[10] When the mayor finally imposes a settlement, "it deals only with those aspects of the issue which cannot be put off; it does not go beyond the particular, concrete problem at hand in order to settle general principles or larger issues; and it is based, not on the merits of the issue, but on the principle that everyone should get something and no one should be hurt very much. The political head is satisfied to patch matters up for the time being."[11]

The point here is simply that many of the more important sources from which the planner derives alternatives—his or her own intuition, local reference groups, supervisors, elected officials, and so on—are often characterized by a cautious and conservative spirit, favoring changes that are small and gradual (that is, incremental) over those that are large and rapid. On the other hand, sources more likely to generate alternatives calling for large-scale change include the planner's own ideology and values, supra-community reference groups (for example, national organizations promoting reform), supra-community providers of resources (foundations and, on occasion, the federal government), and client groups. While it is often tempting to feel that the forces of incrementalism in our society tend to overwhelm those fostering large-scale change, it is important to bear in mind that there *are* sources for alternatives of the latter type as well.

Thus far I have discussed some of the major sources of the alternatives considered by planners, and have noted that external forces often influence both the planner's selection of alternatives to consider and the nature of the alternatives themselves. Many of these same dynamics come into play when the planner attempts to select a single alternative to be implemented—and in both cases, the mechanism at work can best be described as *feedback*.

THE CRITICAL ROLE OF FEEDBACK

Just as the social and political context affects a planner's choice of alternatives to consider, so does it affect his or her choice among those alternatives. People in the planner's work environment—superiors and colleagues, clients, power figures, and so on—are often aware of at least some of the alternatives under consideration, and will "feed back" a variety of responses and pressures that inevitably help to shape the planner's decision. Some of this feedback will be positive, advocating the selection of a given alternative, and perhaps offering intangible rewards (quick approval, praise, improved relationships, and so on); other feedback will be negative, threatening sanctions (dismissal, the withdrawal of support, the loss of friends or status, decreased or terminated funding, civil unrest) if a particular alternative is selected. Such feedback need not occur in every decision-making instance in order to be effective; anticipated approval or penalties can be as powerful as those that are actually experienced.

It is important to recognize that feedback also occurs, frequently and with great intensity, during the time between the selection of an alternative and its implementation. Such feedback often comes from the same sources as did the alternatives themselves (politicians, other bureaucrats, clients, and so on). Once the planner has openly recommended a given course of action and received feedback from interested and affected parties (or stakeholders), it is often necessary to undergo several rounds of negotiation—featuring bargaining, compromises, trade-offs—with one or more such parties before a course of action can be undertaken. That action may well be different, moreover, from the one on which the planner had earlier decided.[12] Once implementation is under way, the flow of feedback continues, and adjustments in the course of action may continue as well. (This stage of the planning process can be particularly troublesome; the strategy proposed in the next chapter attempts to deal more systematically with post-implementation feedback.)

The point here is that the entire planning process—from the emergence of a problem to be tackled to the implementation of a course of action for dealing with it—is strongly affected by a number of forces external to the planner. These forces are communicated to the planner most concretely, I suggest, in the form of feedback to actions proposed or taken. The planner learns from this feedback, gaining insight into the preferences, values, and goals of the individuals and groups with whom he or she is interacting.[13]

Feedback can be transmitted in a number of ways. Some is instigated by the planner, whether through surveys, focus groups, attendance at neighborhood meetings or public hearings, work with citizen committees, or other techniques. Other feedback originates externally to the planner: newspaper and television stories, letters to the editor, telephone calls and e-mail messages from public officials or affected citizens, requested meetings, and countless other sources. Either way, feedback cannot be ignored; the planner must decide how to deal with it.

FORMULATING WORKABLE GOALS:
EASIER SAID THAN DONE

Planning practice has long been characterized by a citizen participation conundrum. On the one hand, most planners are deeply and fully committed to the idea of citizen participation. On the other hand, this commitment operates in a postmodern milieu characterized by problems of vast, and seemingly unfathomable, complexity. We encourage people to take the lead in solving their own problems, then, at precisely the time when those problems seem most intractable—and thus seem most likely to require the efforts of highly skilled experts if solutions are to be found. Not surprisingly, this conundrum leads to a measure of cynicism on the part of planners about citizen participation; they practice it because it is compatible with their value systems, but they rarely expect it to work any special magic in the search for solutions to major community problems.

Virtually every major federal program since the 1960s has included a requirement for citizen participation as a condition for receiving funds, and the notion of citizen involvement is firmly embedded in all planning activity. Discuss it publicly, and practicing planners salute it. Discuss it privately, however, and many of them will talk about the ways in which it complicates their lives. (Citizens: can't plan with 'em, can't plan without 'em.) As anyone who has attended many public meetings or hearings knows, public involvement tends to be expressed negatively, as opposition to something, far more often than positively. The most prominent grass-roots action stories of the past quarter-century have tended to focus on how citizens managed to block a proposed highway, a university's expansion, an unwanted housing development, a theme park, or some other major project. On the other hand, planners have no sure-fire strategies for pulling people away from the TV or the Internet to come to an evening meeting for a rather abstract discussion of what they want their community to be like in the future.

Planners know that the more opinions and preferences that must be taken into account in a particular decision-making process, the more difficult it is to arrive at a consensus, and the greater the risk that the outcome will reflect the lowest common denominator (that is, nobody is left unhappy—but nothing of any significance has taken place).

We know that the preferences expressed in citizen participation processes vary with the type of participation strategy employed; for example, research by Carl Patton showed that the predominant sentiments expressed at public meetings often differed dramatically from those obtained through surveys of the relevant population.[14] We also know that the citizen participation arena is hardly a level playing field, despite our desire that it be so; people differ widely in their resources, patience, interest in (and time to devote to) public issues, level of education, ability to conceptualize and articulate, skill in group dynamics, and number of friends in high places. Nor do those who participate most vigorously necessarily represent the broader community viewpoint—or even, on some occasions, positions that can be considered admirable. ("Grass-roots activism" recently squelched the extension of mass transit into a suburban county in my metropolitan area; racial and class prejudices and fears were clearly the primary motivations. Grass-roots sentiments can be, on occasion, every bit as ignoble as those of economic elites.) How do planners deal with all of this? In general, we simply muddle through, continuing to voice our support for citizen participation while struggling with it in practice—and harboring private doubts about its efficacy.

I suggest, however, that the planner's relationship to citizen participation could be improved significantly by a more realistic division of labor between citizens and planners. I further suggest that a reasonable, and potentially fruitful, division is one in which citizens are responsible for goal formulation, while the planner's primary task is the design of courses of action intended to achieve those goals.

Concern with goals is a central feature of the planning process. As Robert Young observed many years ago, planning "differs from engineering, designing, or just plain problem-solving in that for these activities the goals or objectives are given; in planning, the determination of the goals assumes equal importance with the design that is meant to achieve them."[15] I am suggesting that this act—the determination of goals—is one of the most important vehicles for effective citizen participation in the planning process.

Elected officials, and many public agency officials as well, tend not to be overly concerned with goals. Young wrote that most public policy goals are "the desire components of 'problems' which the policy-making officials are unable to avoid because of the impetus of public opinion and pressure."[16] Most goals, in other words, are posited grudgingly; it seems to be a rule of political life that, all other things being equal, the fewer goals one articulates, the safer one is from public attack. A case in point would be a president or governor who promises "no new taxes" but later feels compelled by events to support a tax increase—and thereafter pays the political price.

This situation does not suffice for the planner, whose professional *raison d'être* is the creation of a better future state of affairs than would have occurred in the absence of planning, and who looks rather silly pursuing that better state of affairs unless he or she has some idea of what it might be.[17] In other words, planners need goals. Unfortunately, however, we often face situations in which "there are no commonly accepted goals or for which the existing goals are inadequate, irrational, ambiguous, or conflicting."[18]

How does the planner deal with such situations? Stated more generally, from what sources does the planner obtain workable goals? To some extent this question could be answered by referring to the typology of sources listed in Figure 10-1; many of the sources listed undoubtedly generate goals as well. Figure 10-2 offers another way of addressing this question, however, arraying potential sources of goals along a continuum ranging from reliance on the planner's own goals (the "worst" way) to the acquisition of goals directly from the public (the "best" way). The remainder of this section considers each of these potential sources.

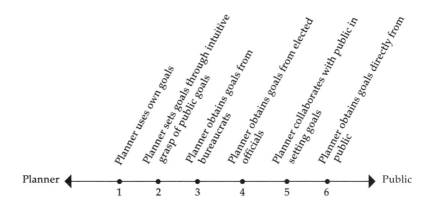

Figure 10-2: A continuum of goal sources for planners.

(1) The planner uses his or her own goals. Some of the master designers of the profession's distant past might have relied heavily on their own goals, but virtually no one today would suggest this as an appropriate, or even ethically valid, source of goals; it simply isn't what the profession is all about. (Which is not to say, of course, that it never happens…)

(2) The planner sets goals through an intuitive grasp of public goals. This, I would suggest, was at one time a common procedure in planning practice. It was assumed that while goals should indeed come

from the community, the planner was uniquely qualified, through training and experience, to sense the wants and desires of that community; it was the planner, more than any other public servant, who had his or her finger on the public pulse.[19] Today, however, this approach enjoys as little credibility as the first; there is nothing to suggest that planners are uniquely endowed with the extraordinary powers of intuition that would be necessary to justify this approach, and political support for it is nonexistent.

(3) The planner obtains goals from bureaucrats. This approach might characterize the work of an engineer, an architect, or even a planning consultant who assumes that the political and value-related aspects of a situation are, quite simply, someone else's problem. The planner is simply a technical advisor, to whom goals are of little concern; someone else is dealing with them and has managed, in some fashion, to articulate the goals that are to guide the planner's work. This approach will almost never work for an in-house planner, however, since he or she is unlikely to encounter a bureaucrat who has been authorized to determine the community's goals!

(4) The planner obtains goals from elected officials. The argument for this approach is that the people elected to office somehow embody the public (or at least the majority) will; people's voting patterns reflect their goals, and the officeholder who suggests goals that are inconsistent with public values will soon be voted out of office. Hence the planner is justified in turning to elected officials for an appropriate set of goals.

Countless political analysts have described, however, the extent to which irrationalities in voting behavior render the political arena a less than perfect reflection of public preferences. Earlier, I mentioned the natural reluctance of elected officials to propose concrete goals, since to do so is to invite opposition, and perhaps to foreclose future desired policy changes as well. Politicians want flexibility, and therefore prefer to avoid the commitments that goals entail. If an elected official *must* issue a goal statement, there is a preference for goals that are as abstract and vague as possible (from the politician's perspective, the best goals are those that allow people of opposing views to feel that their positions are being supported). Elected officials are no more able than anyone else, moreover, to be equally responsive to the needs of all citizens; some individuals and groups will feel underserved, but they too should have access to the community's planning processes. For these and many other reasons, then, elected officials constitute a questionable source of goals for the planner, who needs goals stated as concretely and operationally as possible.

(5) *The planner collaborates with the public in setting goals.* This procedure is certainly a substantial improvement over the previous four. An excellent example of this approach is the "collaborative planning" proposed by David Godschalk and William Mills in the 1960s—an approach that merited considerably more attention, in my view, than it received.[20] Collaborative planning, according to Godschalk and Mills, is "similar to the collaborative marketing approach which assumes that the consumer is not sure of his exact desires but would be interested in defining them with the help of a skilled counselor who knows the range of possible alternatives."[21] A key feature of this approach is its emphasis on a dialogue between planner and citizens; the planner strives to educate citizens' groups regarding the possibilities inherent in the situation, then attempts to gain a clear picture of what these groups want. Discussion groups (today we would call them focus groups) and creative use of the mass media play important roles in this process.

Attractive though it may be, this approach also has some drawbacks in practice. First, few large jurisdictions have planning staffs that are large enough to reach, educate, and listen to all stakeholders (both groups and individuals) over an extended period. There is a natural tendency, then, to focus on those who are the most articulate, responsive, insistent, or powerful. Second, important public policy decisions must often be made relatively quickly, which militates against extensive citizen education on, and discussion of, the issues at hand. Third, unless the issue is a hot one, generating widespread public concern, it may be difficult to enlist a significant number of discussants at all. Fourth, collaborative planning does not come equipped with instructions for dealing with the diversity of values and goals that tends to characterize any major community issue; instead, it seems to assume that there is a latent consensus out there somewhere, if only the planner can tease it out.

Collaborative planning may well be useful for dealing with the internal problems of individual organizations—and hence, by extension, it might work in a small town, where participation by most of the important groups is a realistic possibility. Indeed, this approach bears a close resemblance to contemporary strategies that cast the planner in the role of group facilitator; one can view it, in fact, as an early manifestation of communicative action theory. As a device for formulating the goals of large jurisdictions, however, collaborative planning probably doesn't hold much promise.

(6) The planner obtains goals directly from the public. The value systems of most planners would suggest that virtue resides at this end of the continuum. The problem is, how do we do it? There are a number of possibilities, including the following.

(a) Attitude and opinion surveys. The major advantages of attitude and opinion surveys are the directness of the approach (how better to ascertain people's goals than to ask them?) and the potential, through sampling if necessary, for comprehensive coverage. But there are disadvantages too. Competent surveys are expensive. Surveys often ask people to make choices without full knowledge of current conditions or of the entire range of possible alternatives (a respondent can hardly express a preference for options of which he or she is unaware). Surveys often force choices among alternative answers, none of which may accurately reflect the respondent's true position. Surveys rarely measure the intensity of opinion, the trade-offs respondents would be willing to make among various positive preferences, or the preferences that respondents are likely to have at some future time. Politicians and other civic leaders often express skepticism about survey results, especially if those results are not to their liking; this sentiment is frequently reflected in a charge that "the sample was biased." Worse yet, the very concept of sampling seems to be poorly understood by a significant number of citizens (after all, "nobody came to my door!").

Good survey design requires appropriate training and expertise; many planners have struggled with attempts to extract meaningful information from poorly designed or badly administered surveys. In short, surveys can be highly useful tools under some circumstances, but they also have their shortcomings—and these shortcomings may be particularly pronounced in surveys that ask people about their goals for the future.

(b) Focus groups. Focus groups can be useful in formulating goals for small groups or organizations. Ed Zotti has reported, for example, on a project that used focus groups to determine what people do or do not like about downtown Chicago.[22] He noted that focus groups were less expensive than surveys, generated excellent discussions, and featured a measure of spontaneity less likely to be

achieved with other techniques. On the downside, however, were concerns that the results of focus groups were not quantifiable and were easily skewed by particularly vocal or aggressive participants. Zotti concluded that their primary value was in pointing toward further research.[23]

The applicability of focus groups to an entire community is somewhat limited, moreover, for the reasons discussed in connection with the collaborative planning approach. No planning organization has the time or resources that would be required to involve all of a jurisdiction's citizens in a series of focus groups. By way of example, the "goals for the region" project described briefly in Chapter 1 was considered a major success because approximately 600 people showed up, on a given day, to discuss the region's future. This constituted, however, less than one-tenth of one percent of the region's approximately 750,000 residents. Do we really want to base goals for an entire region on the preferences of those 600? (An added complication, of course, was the many differences of opinion among the 600, and between change-oriented citizens and the elected officials who sponsored the event. There was no need, as it turned out, to lose sleep over the potential goal-formulating power of the 600 in attendance.) In short, focus groups provide excellent vehicles for exploring ideas and opinions that might later be followed up with other methods, but they do not offer a workable means of ascertaining a community's goals.

(c) Analysis of market behavior. Might the analysis of market behavior be a good way to "read" the goals of citizens? This approach would entail, for example, monitoring consumer purchases, business investments, patterns of movement, and the use of public and private facilities. One can argue that what people do in real life is a better indicator of their goals than what they say they would do, or what they do in simulated situations. Computer advances, moreover, have greatly enhanced the technology needed to do this sort of monitoring.

On the other hand, a number of factors combine to render market behavior a less than ideal reflection of citizens' goals, including imperfect knowledge on the part of consumers, the relative ease with which market behavior can be manipulated (fads and the billions of dollars spent on television advertising serve as examples), and barriers to full participation in the market (race, class, and income can all function in this manner). Good data about market behavior is useful for many purposes—especially to those offering products or services—but it has a number of shortcomings as a device for ascertaining a community's goals.

(d) Political processes. Finally, various political processes have been suggested for the formulation of goals. Some of the short-comings of deriving goals from *elections* have already been discussed; additional problems include the frequency with which political promises are broken, the intentional vagueness of party platforms, the frequent lack of major differences between parties and candidates, the strong role played by the media and special interest groups in elections, the impact of personality politics, and the low turnouts that characterize far too many local elections.

Referenda provide citizens with an opportunity to express their sentiments on a limited range of expenditure and policy decisions, but are hardly effective instruments for formulating basic goals. Referenda work best on simple yes or no decisions—and, as planners in America's West and Southwest often relate, can be vehicles for egregious political mischief. The activities of *pressure groups* are pervasive in our political system, and might be "read" as expressions of public goals; certainly they can play a major role in formulating the implicit goals that guide public policy and programs. They too have their shortcomings for our purposes, however; they typically feature a short-run perspective, tend to be biased in the direction of money and power, and, of course, focus on special interests at the expense of broader concerns.

There is, however, a political process that offers great potential, in my opinion, for assisting planners in determining a community's goals. I refer to the creative use of *trial balloons.*

THE BENEFITS OF CREATIVE TRIAL BALLOONING

For purposes of this discussion, I define the trial balloon as an idea presented, or an action undertaken, for the express purpose of generating feedback. This feedback, I suggest, can then be used to "read" the goals of those who are affected by the idea or action.

My argument is as follows. As noted throughout this book, public goals are diverse and often in conflict. It is impossible, there-fore, to produce a single, rank-ordered set of goals that reflects the collective preferences of an entire community. This being the case, the planner must ultimately identify, in any given planning activity,

that subgroup whose needs he or she is most interested in addressing. This group is the planner's primary client group for that
particular activity. So far, this sounds like advocacy planning. I suggest, however, that most planners do this regularly in any event;
that is, they do have particular clients in mind as they set about
formulating plans. These clients might indeed be residents of
low-income neighborhoods; they might just as easily, however, be
suburb-to-city commuters, the owners of new businesses, the home-
owners in a new suburban development, the users of a particular
park, or the potential users of a new community center. The point is
simply that, if forced to do so, planners can usually identify the
specific groups—the clients—whom they hope to benefit through a
particular planning activity. Sometimes, of course, there will be two
or more client groups, rather than just one.

What if, as often happens, the goals of the planner's client group
conflict with those of other groups in the community? In this case
the planner has three options. First, opt out of the situation, on the
grounds that it is too politically controversial. Second, attempt to
mediate an acceptable outcome. Third, become an advocate. Most
planners, I suspect, eventually get around to the third option. (Even
the second, mediation, is frequently conducted from an underlying
advocacy position.)

Here we are, then, involved in a planning activity, and with one
or more client groups whose needs we are particularly interested in
addressing. But how do we go about developing a set of goals for
that client group? For reasons already discussed, it is often futile to
assume that we can obtain a complete picture of a group's goals
merely by canvassing its members—whether through surveys,
focus groups, or other techniques. On the contrary, I suggest that
*most people are able to express their goals most effectively when these goals
are embodied—whether positively or negatively—in something real or
concrete to which they can react:* a program that claims to serve them,
a policy that affects their lives, land use configurations that structure their mobility or use of space, and so on.[24]

This point is consistent with Terry Moore's observation that, in
practice, goals tend to have little impact on public policy. "Decision
makers and their constituents," he writes, "reserve their judgments
and most of their participation until after the preliminary steps,
waiting to see specific policies and assess the effects of those
policies on their interests."[25]

For example, planners whose specialty is land use know that most citizens reserve comment about a comprehensive plan until they see planning and zoning maps—until they see what happens to the property where they live or that they own. The maps expose what the goals could not. Similarly, while no one may object to municipal goals to preserve environmental quality and provide public services efficiently, many will object to a specific plan to assess them for a new sewer line. Most citizens lack interest until they see specifically how a plan will affect them.[26]

It follows, then, that the trial balloon should be an effective device for deducing the goals of a given client group. If a program, policy, or action is consistent with the goals of the client group, its members will tend to support it—or, at worst, benignly ignore it. If it conflicts with their goals, however, they will generally find ways to oppose it.[27] A key feature of the trial balloon concept—and of the Feedback Strategy described in the next chapter—is that it calls for the planning process to be conducted in a manner that maximizes the flow of feedback from the client group (and, for that matter, from other stakeholders as well). Under this approach, planning must not only be designed to solicit and receive feedback, but must be prepared to take that feedback into account in successive steps in the process.[28] It is worth noting, of course, that the generation of feedback has become much easier—and the potential volume of such feedback considerably greater—as a result of developments in electronic communications and the emergence of the information superhighway.[29]

The trial balloon, I suggest, is a useful tool for the planner who wants his or her work to be both efficacious and politically feasible. Those who plan in this manner have a strong and creative role—namely, the design of courses of action that are consistent with the goals of their client groups. This role includes, moreover, full scope for the application of a wide range of methodologies and skills—but subject at all times to the test of compatibility with the client group's goals. Let us turn, then, to the strategy itself.

NOTES

1. A briefer version of the material in Chapters 10 and 11 was presented in Michael Brooks, "Planning and Political Power: Toward a Strategy for Coping," in *Explorations in Planning Theory*, ed. Seymour J. Mandelbaum, Luigi Mazza, and Robert W. Burchell (New Brunswick, N.J.: Center for Urban Policy Research, Rutgers University, 1996), pp. 116–133. In that article I called my model the "political feedback strategy," but have dropped the modifier because of the skittish reactions I often receive to the word *political*.

2. Charles E. Lindblom, "The Science of 'Muddling Through,'" *Public Administration Review* 19 (Spring 1959), p. 79.

3. Amitai Etzioni, *The Active Society: A Theory of Societal and Political Processes* (New York: The Free Press, 1968), p. 286.

4. Patricia Bayne, "Generating Alternatives: A Neglected Dimension in Planning Theory," *Town Planning Review,* Vol. 66, No. 3 (July 1995), p. 310.

5. Ibid., p. 311.

6. Etzioni, *Active Society*, p. 187.

7. Ibid., p. 189.

8. Note that I have not included cultural or societal norms and mores as primary sources of alternatives. These are important, to be sure, but at a much more general level; they provide a framework within which the sources I have mentioned operate, setting parameters on both the content of the pressures exerted and the nature of the planner's response to those pressures.

9. Edward C. Banfield, *Political Influence* (New York: The Free Press of Glencoe, 1961), pp. 250–253.

10. Ibid., p. 270.

11. Ibid., p. 272.

12. In the early 1990s I was in charge of preparing a strategic plan for my university, working with a small staff and with a twenty-three-member Commission on the Future of the University. After months of analysis of all the university's academic programs, we released a preliminary list of those programs that would be enhanced—and of those to be "diminished." Feedback was swift and impassioned. Countless negotiations ensued, and the list of winners and losers in the final report, approved several months later, differed significantly from the preliminary one.

13. Attention to feedback is also a key element in the social learning central to John Friedmann's "transactive planning," an approach that focuses on "linking expert with experiential knowledge in a process of mutual learning." See "Toward a Non-Euclidian Mode of Planning," *Journal of the American Planning Association,* Vol. 59, No. 4 (Autumn 1993), p. 484.

14. Carl V. Patton, "Citizen Input and Professional Responsibility," *Journal of Planning Education and Research,* Vol. 3, No. 1 (Summer 1983), pp. 46–50.

15. Robert C. Young, "Goals and Goal-Setting," *Journal of the American Institute of Planners,* Vol. 32 (March 1966), p. 77.

16. Ibid., p. 76.

17. "Ultimately," writes Jill Grant, "planning provides the means to an end. If we have no shared vision of a desirable end state, then how can we expect planning to show us how to get there?" Grant, *The Drama of Democracy: Contention and Dispute in Community Planning* (Toronto: University of Toronto Press, 1994), p. 219.

18. Ibid.

19. This role for the planner was advocated by Roger Starr in "Pomeroy Memorial Lecture: The People Are Not the City," *Planning 1966: Selected Papers from the ASPO National Planning Conference* (Chicago: American Society of Planning Officials, 1966), pp. 133, 136. For a description of this approach in operation, see Alan A. Altshuler, *The City Planning Process: A Political Analysis* (Ithaca, N.Y.: Cornell University Press, 1965), pp. 97, 142.

20. David R. Godschalk and William E. Mills, "A Collaborative Approach to Planning through Urban Activities," *Journal of the American Institute of Planners,* Vol. 32 (March 1966), pp. 86–95.

21. Ibid., p. 86.

22. Ed Zotti, "New Angles on Citizen Participation," *Planning,* Vol. 57, No. 1 (January 1991), pp. 19–21.

23. Ibid.

24. Giovanni Ferraro makes a similar point with regard to values, arguing that "planners cannot presuppose the existence of knowable collective values as independent points of reference for the plan. Values cannot be taken as a starting condition and a source of information for the planning process. To the contrary, values often appear to be a product of the planning process itself and cannot offer any preliminary criteria for drafting guidelines or a rational definition or evaluation of the plan's choices." See "Planning As Creative Interpretation," in Mandelbaum, Mazza, and Burchell, *Explorations in Planning Theory,* p. 315.

25. Terry Moore, "Planning without Preliminaries," *Journal of the American Planning Association,* Vol. 54, No. 4 (Autumn 1988), p. 525.

26. Ibid., p. 527.

27. Robert Tennenbaum provides an example of "feedback by usage" in describing his work in Columbia, Maryland. Through their usage patterns, citizens supported a mixture of housing types and densities; open spaces; cul-de-sacs and village centers; and pedestrian paths. On the other hand, they didn't like teen centers (teens congregated elsewhere), the minibus system, and certain signage and safety measures. In this instance, the planners were sufficiently perceptive to act upon the received feedback. See "Hail, Columbia," *Planning,* Vol. 56, No. 5 (May 1990), pp. 16–17.

28. For a related discussion, see Melville C. Branch, *Comprehensive Planning for the 21st Century: General Theory and Principles* (Westport, Conn.: Praeger, 1998), p. 124.

29. The impact of these developments on planning is discussed by Edward J. Kaiser and David R. Godschalk in "Twentieth Century Land Use Planning: A Stalwart Family Tree," *Journal of the American Planning Association,* Vol. 61, No. 3 (Summer 1995), p. 382.

CHAPTER

11

The Feedback Strategy of Public Planning

PLANNING AS SOCIAL EXPERIMENTATION

The Feedback Strategy presented in this chapter reflects an explicitly experimental orientation to the planning process, and there are compelling reasons for planning in this manner. Rarely, if ever, do we know with certainty what the single best course of action is with regard to a particular problem, yet we often behave as though there were no doubt about the correctness of our decision. Once such a decision has been made—a particular plan has been adopted, say— policy-makers tend to consider the matter at an end, and promptly turn their attention to other problems. As noted in Chapter 7, inefficient and even harmful programs or policies can continue for years because no "social learning" has taken place.

If, on the other hand, each planning action were conceived and designed as an experiment—as a means of acquiring additional information about the effectiveness of a given course of action in achieving the goals of a client group—then our body of knowledge about problem-solving and goal-achieving strategies would expand continuously.[1] Indeed, it is not unreasonable to view planning as a process of social experimentation wherein ideas are tested—and continuously evaluated—against the possibilities and constraints of reality.[2] Such an orientation requires the courage to accept negative feedback now and then, and a willingness to change policies or programs when the accumulated evidence suggests the need to do so.

An experimental orientation requires that evaluations be carried out on a regular basis. Two kinds of evaluation are important to the planning process. *Impact* evaluation entails assessing, by means of the appropriate research methodologies, whether a course of action has been effective in solving the problems, or achieving the goals, it was intended to address. *Attitude* evaluation, on the other hand, assesses a client group's attitudes and opinions about that course of action. In planning, neither type of evaluation is complete without the other.

Planning theorists have long advocated evaluation as an important element in the planning process.[3] In practice, however, it tends to occur only rarely; pressing current problems have a way of moving the evaluation of past actions to the back burner—often with unfortunate results. William H. Whyte has offered New York City's incentive zoning program, begun in 1961, as an example. According to Whyte, the program soon began producing effects quite contrary to those intended—but in the absence of any evaluation, continued to crank out its negative effects for a number of years. "In planning in general," wrote Whyte, "there has been no systematic effort to find out what has been working and what has not been. Nor is there training for it in most schools of planning and design."[4] He found this "odd," given the frequency with which words like *evaluation, monitoring,* and *feedback* appear in the planning literature. He concluded that planners were simply too busy with other tasks to engage in these activities.[5]

If a planning director is asked to assess his or her agency's accomplishments over the past year, the answer is often expressed in terms of budgets or staffing ("We received funds for a new position," "Other departments had their budgets cut but ours was left intact"), documents produced ("We finally finished the revisions to our comprehensive plan"), or the volume of cases processed ("We handled a record number of rezoning requests last year"). I have even heard this question answered in terms of survival: "It was a pretty good year, I guess. I didn't get fired." All too rarely is the question answered in terms of the agency's impact on the quality of life in its jurisdiction. I consider this unfortunate; among other things, it deprives us of information that could be highly useful in persuading citizens and elected officials of the critical importance of a high-quality planning program.[6]

The Feedback Strategy is based on the assumption that the planning profession would benefit significantly from a greater emphasis on evaluation, focusing both on the impact of planning activity and on the attitudes of those who are involved in the process. In this sense, then, the Feedback Strategy—like most of the other strategies that have been discussed—calls for a modification of the profession's prevailing behavior patterns. I don't consider this modification—the adoption of an experimental orientation to planning, entailing greater emphasis on the evaluation of planned action—to be so drastic as to undermine the strategy's potential feasibility. Moreover, such a modification could yield substantial benefits.

THE HABITS OF EFFECTIVE PLANNERS

An important caveat must be offered at this point. As diagrammed and described in the sections that follow, the Feedback Strategy consists of six stages. These six stages are presented sequentially, implying that the first stage should be completed before the second is initiated, and so on. In reality, however, few planning situations are characterized by the degree of orderliness that would be required in order to implement the strategy in such a neatly sequential manner. In practice, then, the Feedback Strategy is more appropriately viewed as an *attitude toward the planning process* than as a set of procedures to be carried out in lockstep fashion. Critical elements of that attitude include the conceptualization of planning initiatives as trial balloons; sensitivity and responsiveness to feedback from stakeholders; creative use of that feedback in formulating subsequent steps; and the importance of evaluating the results of plans and planned actions. Planners can employ the strategy's key elements, then, without necessarily doing so in discrete and orderly steps.

Indeed, although the strategy is presented in normative terms, I suggest that it is also descriptive of the way that effective planning often occurs. Anecdotes passed along to me over the course of many years suggest that elements of the Feedback Strategy are regularly employed by planners—albeit intuitively and partially, rather than intentionally and systematically—in their approaches to planning problems.[7]

I have come, then, to view the six stages of the Feedback Strategy as reflecting "the habits of effective planners." Skillful users of the strategy's key elements are not overwhelmed by political constraints but instead use them to expand the parameters of the possible. To be sure, a careful assessment of the political constraints in a given planning situation can serve to reinforce tendencies toward caution and timidity in planners who are naturally inclined in that direction. For those who are more given to boldness and risk taking, however, assessment of feedback can provide the knowledge needed to devise strategies for circumventing those political constraints. In either event, charging ahead without such an assessment all too often results in frustration and failure. In short, I offer the Feedback Strategy as a set of guidelines to assist planners in playing roles that are both politically realistic and efficacious.

THE FEEDBACK STRATEGY

As noted in Chapter 10, the Feedback Strategy pays particular heed to the interaction between the planner and his or her social and political environment, thus incorporating the sorts of political dynamics that have been discussed throughout this book. The strategy in fact *builds in* politics as a component of the planning process, rather than viewing it as a dysfunctional external disturbance or barrier. The strategy recognizes that every stage of a planning process generates feedback from "relevant others" (such as clients, superiors, elected officials, peers, and influence-wielders), and it calls upon the planner to analyze and act upon that feedback. The strategy views planning explicitly as an exercise in trial ballooning, and includes instructions for learning from and responding to the feedback generated by the trial balloons floated by the planner. So that the trial balloons can be used most effectively, the strategy emphasizes the dissemination of information about each stage in the process to those whose responses are most significant. It also requires the planner to make some ethical choices regarding the relative weight assigned to various sources of feedback in the political environment.

The six stages of the Feedback Strategy, diagrammed in Figure 11-1, are described as follows:

Step 1: Define the Problem Operationally

A planning project or activity generally begins with the emergence or identification of a problem that appears to fall within the range of the planner's professional concern and that requires action

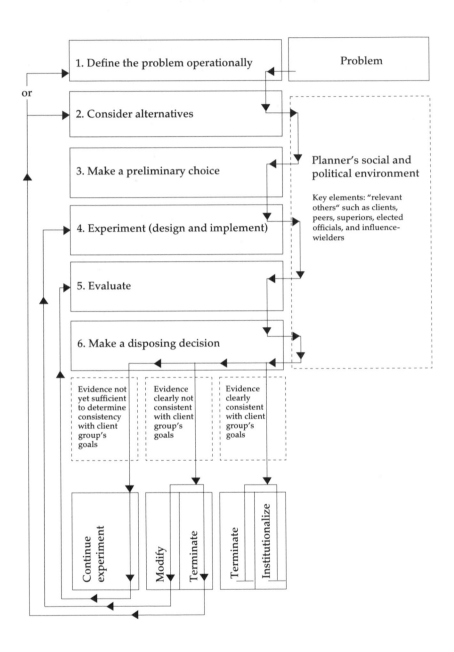

Figure 11-1: The Feedback Strategy.

of some sort. I am not troubled by the lack of well-defined boundaries around the planner's range of concern. The parameters of
planning have expanded and contracted frequently through the
years, depending on a variety of factors both internal and external
to the profession. In any event, a planner who oversteps his or her
boundaries will be alerted or challenged by feedback from the social
and political environment, and will have to decide whether to drop
the matter or to engage in a jurisdictional dispute.

The initiating problem may come from one or more of a number
of sources. Examples include the following: (1) The planner may
identify the problem on the basis of personal values, recent experiences, data, or other sources. (2) An elected official or other
influence-wielder may ask the planner to devote attention to a
particular problem. (3) A developer may present a proposal that
would not be permissible under the current zoning ordinance. (4)
Existing planning documents—such as the comprehensive plan,
zoning ordinance, or subdivision regulations—may need to be
updated or totally overhauled. (5) An interest group may place one
or more problems before the local government or the planning
body, requesting action. (6) A crisis situation—a flood, a recurrent
traffic jam, an epidemic, the closing of a major plant, civil unrest—
may require immediate attention. (7) A new grant program established by the federal government or by a foundation may bring into
the spotlight a problem that has long existed but that has received
only periodic or conventional treatment. (8) Funding may become
available for new public facilities—schools, libraries, parks, for
example—for which appropriate sites must be determined. (9)
Legislation may be enacted that creates a new planning organization or requires an existing one to deal with a previously ignored
problem. (10) Studies may generate new data showing that a long-
recognized problem—suburban sprawl, homelessness, or traffic
congestion, for example—has reached a point where "bold new
approaches" are needed. (11) A human interest story that appears in
the news media may generate a public outcry for action on a particular issue. This list could go on and on; there are few limitations on
sources where planning problems are concerned.

The effective planner will take pains to ensure that the problem
is defined operationally at the outset. That is, he or she will break
the problem into its constituent parts (if any) and identify those
aspects that are susceptible to treatment, alleviation, or resolution

through a program of action. If it is clear that the problem, or some of its component parts, cannot be addressed through the local planning process, the problem should be transferred to a more appropriate arena (for example, it may be a purely political issue that should be resolved by a political body).[8]

Having defined the problem in operational terms, the planner should communicate that definition to relevant others—interest groups, colleagues, superiors, and so on—in his or her social and political environment. It is at this point that the feedback process begins in earnest. For if the planner's own definition of the problem is inconsistent with that held by relevant others, this fact will soon be fed back, and the planner will need to decide what adjustments in the definition, if any, are to be made.

The client group—those people whose interests the planner intends to serve in a particular planning activity—should be identified at this point. In some instances this will be a simple matter, with circumstances clearly pointing to commuters, the elderly, the residents of a particular neighborhood, or working parents in need of day-care facilities. Future residents may be deemed the appropriate client group in some cases, while in others the nature of the problem—or the way it arrives on the planner's desk—may suggest the planning commission or the city council to be the principal client. More difficult, of course, are the situations involving multiple interest groups with differing, perhaps even conflicting, interests. Here the planner may select one of these groups or focus on some combination of groups among whom a measure of agreement or compromise can be anticipated.

In identifying the appropriate client group, the planner will generally rely on a mix of personal values and situational constraints. The planner may be free to choose the client group independently, or may be severely constrained by legislative mandate or power dynamics. The relevant client group will vary from activity to activity, of course, and may even change during the course of a single project.

Whether simple or complicated, however, the task of identifying the appropriate client group should indeed be carried out at the outset. Without such a determination, action tends to proceed without direction or rationale. To resort to "the public interest" at this point, thereby trying to give client status to the entire community, generally entails indulging in self-delusion. As noted previously, planning projects almost never distribute their benefits and costs to all citizens equally; some people gain while others lose (or at least gain differentially). In reality, planners inevitably benefit some groups more than they do others, though the beneficiaries of the planner's efforts will change from case to case. The point here is simply that the identification of those beneficiaries—the client group for a particular planning activity—should be a matter of conscious and thoughtful choice rather than an unplanned resultant. It is not always necessary for the planner to make a public announcement of this choice, however. At times it may be prudent, in fact, to keep one's client choice an internal matter. As has been the case throughout this book, I am concerned primarily with introspection and self-awareness on the planner's part.

Finally, I also suggest—and here I depart from the tenets of rational planning—that no effort be made at this point to formulate goals and objectives. The critical goals are those held by the client group whose interests the planner intends to serve; these will become apparent in feedback from the clients to the planner once that group confronts a specific course of action, whether conceptually (for example, in reaction to a proposal) or experientially.

This aspect of the Feedback Strategy underscores the importance of identifying the client group at this first stage, because a course of action will stand a greater chance of being consistent with the client group's goals if the planner is knowledgeable about that group and its needs, and in fact seeks the group's advice and opinions at each stage of the process. To translate a preliminary understanding of the client group's needs into a goal statement at this point, however, is premature, unnecessary, and perhaps even risky. The most important goals will be those expressed later, in the form of responses to actions that are proposed or undertaken.

It might be argued, of course, that since a goal is usually the "desire component" of a problem—that is, we set a goal because we want to change something about existing circumstances—then a problem statement implicitly assumes a goal as well. This is certainly true. The critical issue, however, is the appropriate point of departure. A goal characterizes a desired future state; the need to revise present realities so as to achieve that state may well be implied, but any resulting actions are subsidiary to the goal itself and are typically not addressed until full agreement on the goal has been achieved. A problem statement, on the other hand, simply describes an undesirable current state; provided that there is agreement that the problem is indeed a problem, the need for ameliorative action is taken for granted. Problem statements are more conducive to action than are goal statements, I suggest, because—as discussed earlier—people are far better able to express their reaction to something concrete or tangible in their present experience than to describe what they would like to experience in the future. The distinction has practical implications, then, for the nature and extent of public attention to and involvement in the planning process.

Step 2: Consider Alternatives

The effective planner will typically consider several alternative actions that might be taken to deal with the problem. This step sounds suspiciously akin to rational planning approaches, but this should not be considered a drawback; after all, when confronted with a problem we do indeed try to think of various ways to address it. (The temptation to dismiss any planning action that bears even the slightest resemblance to any element of the discredited rational model is probably dysfunctional and should be resisted.)

The process of identifying and analyzing alternatives can be aided, I suggest, by addressing two questions. First, given the virtually unlimited number of alternatives that are potential candidates for adoption, which ones should be selected for consideration? In Chapter 10 I discussed five major sources of alternatives in a planning situation: the planner himself or herself, reference groups, influence-wielders, the legal framework, and client groups. Typically, the planner will consider both those ideas that he or she thinks of and feels worthy of further analysis (whether based on values, experience, intuition, available data, or other grounds), and those ideas that are suggested—with varying degrees of intensity—by any of the four categories of external sources. As part of this step, the planner should make relevant others in the planning environment aware of the fact that alternatives are under consideration, and encourage them to offer any ideas or opinions they may have about appropriate courses of action. In other words, the planner should make certain that feedback channels are open and working.

The likelihood that the planner will seriously consider an externally generated alternative generally depends on (1) the extent to which the planner finds the idea an attractive one, and (2) the strength of the pressure that may be brought to bear on the planner to consider it. Generally, only one of these processes needs to operate in order for an externally generated idea to be given careful consideration. For example, if a particular client group suggests an alternative that strikes a responsive chord with the planner (either because of the idea's intrinsic merit or because of the planner's positive feelings about the group itself), the planner will probably consider it carefully even if the client group is a relatively powerless one. Similarly, an idea suggested by a group with a large measure of power over the planner's working conditions (say, the ability to withdraw funds or block action) will probably be considered even if the planner finds the idea unattractive.

The weights that the planner accords to various sources of alternatives will be determined largely by his or her personal values and by the degree of freedom inherent in the situation (for example, is the planner constrained by commitments to or potential sanctions by relevant others?). My own value system leads me to suggest that, all other things being equal, alternatives generated by the planner's client group, as defined for that particular planning activity, have a measure of ethical superiority over those coming from other sources, and should therefore be given high priority as candidates for further consideration. It would be naive, however, to assume that such ideas will always be more effective in dealing with the problem than are those that originate elsewhere—or to deny that the exertion of influence from other quarters will occasionally play a part in the planner's selection of alternatives for consideration.

At the end of the period of time available for the identification of alternative courses of action, the planner will typically have a list of several alternatives, each of which is viewed with favor by someone—whether the planner or relevant others—in the planning system. The planner need not be concerned with the countless other alternatives which, though theoretically possible, have not surfaced during this part of the process. It is impossible to specify the number of alternatives that the planner will have at this stage; typically, however, it will not be large.

The second question of concern at this point is: how extensively, and by what methods, should each alternative be assessed? My answer is that effective planners generally evaluate each alternative as fully—and with as sophisticated a set of methods—as the situation permits. Before proceeding to evaluate a set of alternatives, then, the planner should determine with reasonable precision just what the situation *does* permit.

In most planning situations, a number of constraints serve to limit the comparative analysis of alternatives. The most important of these are

• The resources at the planner's disposal, especially funds, staff, expertise, and equipment (such as computers and software).

• Deadlines—which, in turn, often depend on such factors as the extent to which the problem is viewed as a crisis, the anticipated life span of the planner's organization (is it temporary or ongoing?), whether the problem is one on which elected officials have promised rapid action, and the fiscal year of the funding body ("All funds not committed by June 30 will revert to the city budget").

• The political constraints on analysis, involving some combination of the number of people and organizations that have generated alternatives, the relative intensity of their feelings, and the amount of power they possess.

The planner should assess these and other constraints at the outset, deciding how much time, resources, and analytical objectivity can be applied to the evaluation of alternatives; to enter this stage of the process on an open-ended basis is to invite frustration later. In some cases there may be sufficient time, expertise, equipment, and freedom from political constraints for the development of simulation models or sophisticated cost-benefit studies; more typically, the planner will have but a few days (sometimes a few hours) to prepare a recommendation. The shorter the period of time available for the analysis of alternatives, the greater the likelihood that the process will be subjective and intuitive rather than rational and "scientific."

Step 3: Make a Preliminary Choice

The effective planner next makes a preliminary choice among the various alternative courses of action that he or she has considered. The choice is preliminary in the sense that it is not necessarily the final decision about a given course of action; that decision will be made only after appropriate evaluations have been carried out.

The most important concerns at this point are those of criteria and feedback. Several types of criteria are potentially applicable to the preliminary choice. If the planning situation is characterized by low visibility and generates little interest on the part of client groups or the public, then it may be possible to use economic efficiency criteria of the sort featured in cost-benefit analysis. As discussed earlier, however, the planner will rarely encounter this situation, especially on matters featuring high levels of visibility and significance in the community. Some alternatives may lend themselves to a much more simplistic form of economic analysis, of course; the most cursory inspection may reveal, for example, that they are too costly in relation to the anticipated benefits. Having eliminated one or more alternatives on this basis, however, the planner will generally still have to contend with several others that are deemed economically feasible, thereby reducing the utility of further economic comparisons.

Other criteria therefore come into play, the most important being (1) political feasibility and (2) the planner's perception, whether based on data or merely subjective, of the fit between a given alternative and the needs of the client group for this particular planning activity. Again, the relative importance of these two criteria will be determined by the values of the planner and by the number and intensity of external constraints.

All other things being equal, the best alternative is the one that, within the economic and political constraints of the situation, best fits the client group's needs. Ideally, "best fit" should be determined through sophisticated analysis, but the realities of the workplace often require the planner to determine best fit on the basis of inadequate data, hurried analysis, and his or her subjective conclusions. Given the critical role of feedback, however, these limitations are of little concern.

The planner will generally receive feedback both before and after the preliminary choice is made. Once an array of alternatives has been identified for consideration, the effective planner will take pains to ensure that feedback is indeed generated, in this instance by communicating the range of alternatives under consideration to all relevant groups. Typical vehicles for this purpose include written reports, Web sites, effective use of the media, and attendance at relevant meetings.

Some alternatives will quickly be labeled as politically infeasible, no matter how attractive their projected benefits in relation to costs. In such cases, the planner can attempt to play an educative or lobbying role, endeavoring to persuade relevant groups as to why they should favor one or another alternative. But planners should not expect too much to result from this role; many of the reasons for which groups will favor or oppose a given alternative will have little to do with the sorts of criteria—reflecting public rather than private benefits—typically espoused by planners.

To summarize, it may be useful to think of the preliminary choice process as the application of a set of filters. Some alternatives may be screened out by an economic filter; these are the alternatives whose costs are obviously too high, either absolutely or in relation to such benefits as they can reasonably be expected to produce. Other alternatives will be screened out by a political filter, as manifested in feedback from relevant others. Finally, with respect to the remaining alternatives, the planner can do little more than make a subjective judgment as to which will best serve the needs (or, stated alternatively, solve the problems) of the client group. This would be a hopelessly inadequate criterion for a public policy decision if, as has typically been the case in the past, the decision were considered final and definitive. As will be seen, however, the preliminary choice in the Feedback Strategy functions as a hypothesis; hence the desperate need for the choice to be the "right" one is lessened somewhat. Indeed, one of the strategy's key features is its acceptance of, and attempt to build upon, the fact that we almost never have sufficient knowledge for claiming our policy decisions to be correct in any absolute sense. Referring to the choice made in this stage as a preliminary one implies that the *final* decision is to be deferred until a later time, when more knowledge is available. The critical pieces of knowledge needed to make a valid final decision are, quite simply, how the course of action actually turns out in practice and how it is perceived by those whom it is intended to serve.

Once the planner has made a preliminary choice, feedback again comes into play—more heavily, in fact, than at any point thus far. As noted earlier, a number of bargains, compromises, and trade-offs may be required before the chosen alternative is implemented— which means, of course, that the action finally taken may differ significantly from what was initially chosen and announced by the planner.

Step 4: Design and Implement an Experiment

Having made a preliminary choice of an alternative (as modified, if necessary, in response to post-choice feedback), the effective planner will proceed to experiment with the idea—that is, to design and implement a course of action embodying that alternative. It is in this stage—program development or design—that the planner's creative capabilities are often given the widest scope. (The actual management or administration of the chosen course of action may or may not fall to the planner, depending on the nature of the organization; most often this role will be played by others, leaving the planner free to oversee the workings of the strategy's feedback mechanisms.)

Conceiving of the course of action as an experiment has several implications for its design. The hypotheses on which it is to be based—that is, what is going to be done and what is it supposed to accomplish—should be clearly stated; indicators by which these hypotheses can be tested should be identified; and a methodology for evaluation should be decided upon and built in at the outset.

Time parameters should be established; if the course of action is intended to solve a given problem in a relatively short time (say a year or two), then the final result will be the primary object of evaluation. If, on the other hand, it is likely that the problem can be alleviated only in the long run, then a series of short-run guideposts should be identified, against which progress can be assessed.

Step 5: Evaluate

Given the Feedback Strategy's experimental orientation, the evaluation of the course of action being implemented is perhaps the most critical step in the process. In brief, the strategy urges us to learn from experience. Evaluation gives both planners and relevant others information on which to base final decisions (referred to later as "disposing decisions") about a course of action.

Evaluation can take a number of forms. At one end of the scale are "scientific" evaluations, employing research methodologies developed by social scientists and conducted by those with the requisite training and skills. At the other end are the more informal, but nonetheless important, evaluations that continuously affect any planning operation—news stories, op ed pieces, and editorials in newspapers; local television specials; articles in organization newsletters; citizens' statements at public hearings; constituents' letters to elected officials; case studies written as term papers by planning students; and numerous others. Multiple evaluations of the same planning situation may yield widely divergent conclusions. Rather than being frustrated by numerous and diverse evaluations, however, the planner should remember that evaluation is important not because it produces "facts" but because it provides information that is extremely important—both analytically and politically—to all participants in the process of making informed decisions about a course of action. Evaluation results of all kinds should be broadly disseminated; they are part of the critical information needed by those who choose to participate in the decision-making process.

As noted earlier, evaluation should be focused on two primary questions. First, to what extent is the course of action successfully alleviating the problem it is designed to address? Second, what are the attitudes and opinions of relevant others toward that course of action? The former question is the "impact evaluation" component; it is here that the planner tries to learn about the problem-solving efficacy of the course of action as measured in terms of the problem-specific indicators identified at the outset. (It is important to remember, however, that two or more "scientific" evaluations of a single course of action may yield widely divergent conclusions, and that different consumers of evaluation results will often interpret the findings in different ways.) The latter question, on the other hand, is attitudinal, entailing the systematic collection of reactions—likes, dislikes, and other opinions. As the planner receives these two types of evaluation results, they should be disseminated broadly, as should any analyses that the planner carries out based on these results.

Armed with this information, relevant others in the planner's social and political environment will thus be readied for their final act of feedback—namely, their efforts to influence the planner during the final stage of the Feedback Strategy.

Step 6: Make a Disposing Decision

As in all other stages of the strategy, the planner's choice (or recommendation) of a disposing decision will reflect his or her interpretation of the information acquired from various feedback and evaluation processes. Here too, however, the planner will be subject to a number of pressures from relevant others.

It is at this point, finally, that the planner is best able to perceive the goals of the client group. If the planner has performed the evaluation task fully and competently, the client group (or its chief representatives) will have received information regarding the impact of the course of action on its problems; how various relevant groups feel about that course of action; and the nature of those issues that remain unresolved even after the evaluation has been completed. It should not be too difficult, then, to deduce the group's goals from its reaction to the course of action at this point.

It is in this sixth and final stage that feedback from the planner's client group should be accorded top priority. If the trial balloon is indeed a way of obtaining goals directly from the affected public, and if the tension between citizen participation and postmodern complexity is (as I have suggested) to be resolved somewhere in the realm of goals, then *the single legitimate criterion for making the disposing decision is the compatibility of a course of action with the goals of the client group whose well-being it is intended to address.* In short, the disposing decision should be controlled by the planner's client group. When I say, then, that the planner makes the disposing decision at this point, I mean only that he or she should determine, from the client group's feedback, what its goals are, and should act accordingly. Only in this way will the planner be serving goals obtained directly from the public, as discussed in the previous chapter.

Through the first five stages of the Feedback Strategy, I noted that the planner will receive feedback from many relevant others in his or her political and social environment. While I expressed the opinion, clearly labeled as a value position on my part, that it was ethically important for the planner to pay the greatest heed to the feedback received from his or her client group, I nevertheless noted that it may not always be possible to follow that principle; political imperatives may sometimes cause the planner to respond to pressures emanating from other sources as well. In the sixth and last stage in the process, however, I have stated unequivocally that feedback from the client group must be given first priority; in fact, the legitimacy of the entire strategy depends on doing so.

But why should the planner expect the rest of the world to stand idly by and allow the decision to be made on this basis? Obviously it won't. In the sixth stage, as at every other, political forces will be at work, and it is quite possible that the disposing decision will end up being made—contrary to the planner's recommendation—on bases other than the compatibility of a given course of action with the goals of the planner's client group. This might occur, for example, if the local legislative body decides that the vast majority of the voting public does not want to support a given program for a particular group, or if an interest group other than the planner's client succeeds in obtaining a reallocation of resources that is more favorable to its own needs, or if a local government agency has sufficient clout with elected officials to subvert the planner's recommended decision. In cases like these, the planner can attempt to alter the decision through advocacy, negotiation, and the use of other political strategies of the sort described in Chapter 12. Neither this nor any other strategy is capable, however, of forcing the political system to stop operating while the planning process runs through its six—or eight, or ten, or twelve—steps. Nor should it. By continuously interacting with the political environment in the first five steps, the planner is likely to strengthen the possibility that the sixth step—in which the goals of the client group are positively asserted—will be politically feasible as well. There are no ironclad guarantees, however.

At this point, in keeping with the goals that the client group has revealed, several disposing decisions can be made (see Figure 11-1). First, it may be that at the predetermined time when a disposing decision is to be made, there is insufficient evidence to enable the client group to determine whether the course of action is indeed consistent with its goals. This circumstance indicates the need for more information; the experiment continues, the planner returns to the fifth stage (evaluation), and a new time frame is established for a disposing decision. Second, the client group may determine that the course of action, as currently conducted, is not consistent with its goals. In this event, two options are open. If the approach appears to be on the right track but requires relatively major adjustments nonetheless, it should be modified; here the planner returns to the fourth stage (experimentation) and retools or redesigns the course of action. If, on the other hand, it is by now clear to the client group that the course of action is totally wrongheaded and inconsistent with (perhaps even harmful to) its goals, then it should be terminated; here the planner must either return to the second stage to consider a new set of alternatives or to the first stage to redefine the problem.

Third, the client group may determine that the course of action is indeed fulfilling its goals. Here again, there are two options. In some extremely rare cases, the course of action may have completely alleviated the problem, and the action can be terminated. Ideally, of course, this is the final disposition to which all public action aspires in the long run, at least theoretically—everyone has been appropriately housed, travel time has reached an irreducible minimum, sprawl has been stopped dead in its tracks, street crime has been completely eliminated, and so on. The likelihood of such "total solutions" occurring very often, however, is implicit in those examples; only on rare occasions have we been able to celebrate something like, say, the complete eradication of a major disease. Far more common, then, are situations in which the client group determines that the course of action is indeed consistent with its goals, but that the problem will likely be around for many years, if not permanently. In this case the course of action may be *institutionalized;* that is, it loses its status as an experiment and is turned over in its entirety to the realm of administration (as opposed to planning).

Needless to say, extreme caution should be exercised in reaching this decision; courses of action deemed successful in one setting— appropriately funded, implemented by well-trained and dedicated personnel, operating at the right time and in a highly supportive environment—are capable of turning sour when circumstances change. In most instances it is advisable to make the "insufficient evidence" decision and circle back for several rounds of evaluation before a course of action is finally institutionalized.

In summary, the Feedback Strategy may be outlined as follows.

Step 1. The planner begins with a problem (not a goal), which is quickly defined and operationalized to his or her own satisfaction, but subject to modification through feedback.

Step 2. The planner considers several alternatives, derived from several sources (including his or her own insights and those of relevant others), and analyzes each within a set of resource, time, and political constraints.

Step 3. The planner makes a preliminary choice of the alternative that seems best in the light of gross economic considerations, political feasibility, and fit between the alternative and the needs of the client group; considerable feedback, both before and after the selection, has a strong impact on this choice.

Step 4. The planner designs and implements the selected course of action in the form of an experiment.

Step 5. The planner evaluates the effects of the chosen course of action, devoting particular attention to (1) the extent to which the course of action alleviates the problem and (2) the attitudes of relevant others toward the course of action.

Step 6. On the basis of feedback from the client group concerning the extent to which the course of action is consistent with its goals, the planner makes a disposing decision to continue, modify, terminate, or institutionalize the course of action, circling back to earlier stages of the strategy if necessary.

As noted earlier, I am not advocating use of the Feedback Strategy in the rather lockstep manner that this summary might seem to imply. Real-world circumstances almost never permit a planning process—this one or any other—to be carried out in such an orderly fashion. Instead, the strategy's primary purpose is to suggest a set of attitudes toward the planning process—specifically, a recognition of the utility of experimentation, trial ballooning, feedback, and evaluation, as well as a commitment to serving the goals of the client group.

HOW THE FEEDBACK STRATEGY RELATES TO OTHER PARADIGMS

The Feedback Strategy draws some of its elements from each of the paradigms discussed thus far in this book. Indeed, my intention has been to build upon the best features of each of those paradigms, while avoiding their worst (typically least realistic in practice) characteristics.

Like most of the rationality-based planning models, the Feedback Strategy recommends a series of steps that seem to manifest a logical, orderly, and somewhat analytical approach to the planning process. Its emphasis on planning as social experimentation also suggests a degree of kinship with rationality-based planning. Unlike most rationality-based models, however, the strategy does not assume that the plan emanates primarily from the planner's own creative ideas or competent analysis, or that the planner's task ends with the preparation of the plan, or that the quality of the plan itself determines the likelihood of its being implemented. Instead, the Feedback Strategy acknowledges the strong role typically played by the planner's social and political environment in shaping the planner's decisions and actions—and, in fact, makes that environment an integral part of the process.

Given its emphasis on identifying and attempting to achieve the goals of a specified client group, the Feedback Strategy also manifests a strong normative base; values are central elements of the strategy, not dysfunctional intruders. The strategy does ask the planner to analyze the feedback received at each stage of the process, so it hardly abandons the need for systematic decision-making; this analysis occurs, however, within an explicitly normative context. In short, the Feedback Strategy retains some elements of rationality-based planning but includes political and normative dimensions that ultimately differentiate it from the rational paradigm.

Like incrementalism, the strategy does not assume that the first approach to a particular problem is always the correct one, and it stresses the importance of taking corrective action when an approach turns out to be the wrong one. Unlike incrementalism, however, the Feedback Strategy does not assume that corrective action will occur automatically; on the contrary, we know that this is frequently not the case. By emphasizing the importance of evaluation, the Feedback Strategy increases the likelihood that ineffective plans, policies, and programs will be corrected in a timely manner—and in a direction that is consistent with the goals of the specified client group. Armed with careful analyses of the feedback he or she has received, moreover, the planner is more likely to be able to undertake courses of action that transcend the bounds (and bonds) of incrementalism.

The Feedback Strategy is strongly influenced by the spirit of advocacy, as reflected in its emphasis on the selection of a client group for each planning activity, and on the use of that group's goals to validate or invalidate a course of action. Indeed, opportunities to advocate on behalf of a selected client group, or on behalf of a particular set of values, abound at every stage of the strategy— but with the added responsibility of analyzing the feedback that the advocacy has generated and using that analysis to formulate subsequent steps.

Finally, it is clear that the Feedback Strategy cannot work without effective communication at every stage. Planners should indeed communicate their problem definitions, the alternatives under consideration, decisions, and evaluation findings to relevant others in ways that are comprehensible, sincere, legitimate, and true; in turn, they should listen carefully and analytically to the feedback that they receive. Although these elements of the Feedback Strategy suggest at least a modicum of kinship with the communicative action approach to planning, that approach tends to emphasize specific values and methodologies that, while not incompatible with the Feedback Strategy, are not central to it.

POTENTIAL SHORTCOMINGS
OF THE FEEDBACK STRATEGY

As noted earlier, I have been teaching one or another version of the Feedback Strategy for a number of years. I always invite critiques or reservations, and those expressed most frequently have been the following. First is a concern that the strategy calls for planners to play an unaccustomed role—namely, to evaluate the plans and actions that they engender. There is irony in this critique, of course, since many of the models or strategies employed by planners in the past—especially those based on rationality—have explicitly identified evaluation as a major component. In practice, however, evaluation rarely occurs. I am indeed suggesting the need for greater emphasis on this aspect of the planning process—which implies, in turn, that more attention should be given to evaluation in planning degree programs and in continuing-education offerings. It is folly, I suggest, for a profession to develop plans for action, and then to pay no heed to the extent to which those plans did or did not accomplish their intended purposes.

A second critique has to do with the already-noted observation that evaluation does not necessarily generate objective facts about the results of a given course of action. On the contrary, evaluation reports often reflect the values and biases of their authors or sponsors, and two or more evaluations of the same action may well yield widely divergent "findings." Any major and reasonably controversial policy or program is apt, in fact, to generate an evaluation *system* consisting of (1) one or more primary evaluations, which may or may not be in agreement; (2) one or more counterevaluations generated specifically to counteract the findings of the primary evaluations; and (3) a number of opinions expressed in op ed pieces, letters to the editor, organizational publications, and other vehicles, which are interpreted by relevant others to be just as significant as the more formal ones.

Is this profusion of evaluations a problem? I don't think so. I have already suggested that evaluation results should be viewed not as "facts" or "truth" but rather as information to be shared, reviewed, interpreted, and acted upon by all those who have a stake in a particular planning case. Evaluations are fodder for the feedback process; far from telling people what they should think, they simply provide the raw material people need to formulate their own reactions to a particular idea, plan, or course of action. The planner aids this process by distributing all evaluations to relevant others and by attempting to clarify (but not resolve) the issues that they highlight.

A third and potentially more serious concern is one suggesting that the Feedback Strategy may be difficult to apply in cases where the end product of planning is a physical entity of some sort—a building, highway, reservoir, or housing subdivision, for example. According to this argument, a planner cannot make a preliminary choice to put a major highway in a particular location, experiment with it, then rip it out (a "disposing decision," to be sure) if the evaluations are negative (for example, it is used too much or too little, it stimulates unwanted sprawl, it increases the social and economic gulf between inner-city and suburban residents). This would be a highly costly and inefficient way to make governmental decisions.

True enough. I offer three responses, however. First, if the time span of the analysis is long enough, it is clear that we *do* eliminate, from time to time, physical entities that have proven to be ineffective. Pruitt-Igoe, a failed public housing project in St. Louis, is an obvious case in point; downtown expressways, pedestrian malls, and numerous other structures and facilities deemed unsuccessful have also been removed. Second, architects regularly design buildings in which interior spaces can be altered to reflect patterns of usage and preference; the same principle can be applied to other physical entities as well. Third and most important, however, is a reminder that the Feedback Strategy is more an attitude toward planning than a set of steps that must be carried out sequentially and fully. If we maintain an experimental orientation toward planning for our public facilities, we will regularly evaluate the extent to which they succeed in achieving their purposes—and we will use that information in subsequent decisions about other, similar facilities. We will learn, for example, how to replicate the best features of the freeways we have built in recent years and how to avoid the problems that were associated with them. This, in my view, is an approach fully in keeping with the spirit of the Feedback Strategy.

Finally, a shorter version of the Feedback Strategy published in 1996 engendered the following critique from Glen McDougall, who wrote that the strategy's "political neutrality (or perhaps 'defeatism' may be more appropriate), combined with an anti-theoretical stance, has defined a narrow role for the planner—confined by institutional constraints and the existing political agenda. I would argue that it is this blindness to the power of agency as much as the failures of planning theory that has dulled the creativity and effectiveness of planning and denied planners the choice to act differently."[9]

"Political neutrality?" To be sure, the Feedback Strategy is not predicated upon a specific ideology. It does assume that the planner's values are critically important at every stage of the planning process. Unlike much of the contemporary planning theory literature, however, it does not prescribe what those values should be; instead, it leaves to each planner the task of formulating her or his own set of professional values. If this adds up to political neutrality, so be it.

"Defeatism?" Hardly. The Feedback Strategy is intended to help planners become more effective, not less so. I suggest that a planner who has analyzed the political forces at work in a given situation has a better chance of succeeding than does the planner who charges ahead armed with little but ideological fervor. I am confident, in fact, that planners have the potential for significantly greater impacts on their communities than they generally assume; I am interested in expanding their scope of activity, not narrowing it.

"Anti-theoretical?" My focus has been on a particular subset of planning theories, those referred to in Chapter 2 as theories *for* planning rather than those *about* or *of* planning; that is, I have been concerned with theories that attempt to aid planners in the conduct of their professional roles, and I have assessed those theories through the lens of practice. Theories *about* and *of* planning have been addressed quite competently by many other authors; such theories were simply not the focus of this book. McDougall suggests that I am blaming planning theory for any planning that is found to be ineffective and uncreative. This is hardly the case. My concern about much planning theory is not that it has damaged planning practice, but rather that it has tended to be irrelevant; having affected practice so minimally, planning theory can hardly be held accountable for the profession's successes and failures.

The planner—whether practitioner or academic—whose connection to the planning profession is grounded primarily in the espousal of a particular ideology, and who has little or no concern for what might happen if practitioners were indeed to articulate and act upon that same ideology in their workplaces, will probably have little interest in the Feedback Strategy. The strategy is intended instead for those practitioners who, in addition to being introspective about their personal values, have a keen interest in maximizing the impact and effectiveness of their professional actions. This requires, in my opinion, a large measure of political savvy and a keen sense of vision—matters to which we shall turn in the next section.

NOTES

1. Kai N. Lee reflects much the same point in his "adaptive management" approach, which is based on the notion that policies are experiments from which we should learn. For an elaboration of this concept, as well as examples of its use in environmental policy, see *Compass and Gyroscope: Integrating Science and Politics for the Environment* (Washington, D.C.: Island Press, 1993). Also see Seymour Mandelbaum, "On Not Doing One's Best: The Uses and Problems of Experimentation in Planning," *Journal of the American Institute of Planners*, Vol. 41, No. 3 (May 1975), pp. 184–190.

2. The essence of planning, writes Howell Baum, is "acting with knowledgeable hypotheses about the consequences of alternative courses of action." See "Teaching Practice," *Journal of Planning Education and Research*, Vol. 17, No. 1 (Fall 1997), p. 21.

3. An excellent early example is found in Martin Meyerson's classic "Building the Middle-Range Bridge for Comprehensive Planning," *Journal of the American Institute of Planners*, Vol. 22, No. 2 (Spring 1956), pp. 127–139. More recently, evaluation has featured prominently in Melville C. Branch's approach to planning; see *Comprehensive Planning for the 21st Century: General Theory and Principles* (Westport, Conn.: Praeger, 1998), p. 124.

4. William H. Whyte, *City: Rediscovering the Center* (New York: Doubleday, 1988), p. 253.

5. Ibid.

6. For discussions of the ways in which we might evaluate comprehensive plans, see William C. Baer, "General Plan Evaluation Criteria," *Journal of the American Planning Association*, Vol. 63, No. 3 (Summer 1997), pp. 329–344; and Emily Talen, "After the Plans: Methods to Evaluate the Implementation Success of Plans," *Journal of Planning Education and Research*, Vol. 16, No. 2 (Winter 1996), pp. 79–91.

7. While writing this book I received a flyer from the City of Richmond's Department of Community Development announcing a series of neighborhood meetings. The flyer states, in part: "As we bring to a close a multi-year process of updating the City Master Plan, the City Planning Commission is hosting a series of information sessions to review a final draft of the document. These sessions are designed to provide city residents with the opportunity to ask questions *and provide feedback* regarding Master Plan recommendations for each of the City's eight... Planning Districts, prior to the Plan's projected approval by the Planning Commission and City Council this fall." (Emphasis added.) Assuming that citizen feedback is taken seriously in the process, Richmond's planners are indeed manifesting a major element of the Feedback Strategy. For another example—this time within the context of a seven-day charrette—see

Alexander Garvin, "A Mighty Turnout in Baton Rouge," *Planning*, Vol. 64, No. 10 (October 1998), pp. 18–20.

8. "The history of planning and policy analysis," writes R. Varkki George, "is replete with instances of solutions that targeted the wrong problem." See "Formulating the Right Planning Problem," *Journal of Planning Literature*, Vol. 8, No. 3 (February 1994), p. 241.

9. Glen McDougall, "The Latitude of Planners," in *Explorations in Planning Theory*, ed. Seymour J. Mandelbaum, Luigi Mazza, and Robert W. Burchell (New Brunswick, N.J.; Center for Urban Policy Research, Rutgers University, 1996), p. 191. *Agency*, in this quotation, refers to "the ability of individuals to intervene in social life through their action" (p. 189).

PART

5

Effective Planning
in a Political Milieu

CHAPTER

12

The Politically Savvy Planner

THE NATURE OF POLITICAL SAVVY

There are few immutable laws in planning, but here is one: *No strategy or model of planning—whether the Feedback Strategy or any of the others discussed in this book—will be effective if its user is politically inept.* Throughout this book I have stressed the fact that politics is an integral part of the planning process; it cannot be swept under the drafting table or the computer, or left in the hands of the politicians. A measure of political savvy is simply one of those characteristics that a planner must possess in order to be effective.[1]

John Levy asks why the planning arena is so highly politicized, and offers several answers: planning tends to involve issues that people care deeply about; these issues are often highly visible, and lend themselves to citizen action; and the financial stakes are often high, involving land values, housing costs, property taxes, and other factors that affect citizens' financial status.[2] To these must be added another, and perhaps even more fundamental, reason— namely, that almost any major planning decision or action has consequences that affect people differentially. (Recall the discussion of the public interest in Chapter 4.) Despite our understandable desire to describe the outcomes of proposed plans in win-win terms, an equitable distribution of costs and benefits almost never occurs in practice; careful examination usually reveals that a particular plan, policy, program, or action generates, to a greater or lesser degree, both winners and losers. Whether those wins and losses are genuine or merely perceived makes little difference; in either case, the planner cannot avoid becoming enmeshed in the web of politics.

The politically savvy planner knows how to survive in the political environment—and in fact commands a set of strategies for dealing effectively with it. Acknowledging the play of political power in the planning arena, then, need not distress the planner. The trick is in learning to use the political system to achieve planning ends. As one practitioner has noted, planners "need to have the political savvy to use the system and work with politicians, without violating our principles, to benefit the people we serve—a difficult task indeed."[3] Difficult, yes—but doable.

If planners are to use the political system effectively, they must be able to "read" the structure of power in a particular community. For example, what are the community's most powerful organizations and institutions, and who tends to control their decisions? Is power concentrated in a single pyramid, with one group of individuals or families controlling most major decisions,[4] or is it diffused across a number of functional areas (such as education, economic development, religion, labor, and so on), each with its own mini-pyramid?[5] (The power structure in some communities may combine both of these characteristics—with one group exerting considerable power in some, but not all, realms; other communities seem to have virtually no power structure whatsoever.) Is leadership in the community largely top-down, or have grass-roots organizations gained control over at least some functions of importance to them? Is the community highly conservative in its attitude toward planning and development, or have more progressive ideas managed to bear fruit now and then?[6] How much power does the local government have in relation to the community's major business institutions, and to other levels of government? Where does the planning department fit in the local scheme of things: is it respected and thus centrally involved in major community issues, or is it a barely tolerated afterthought, constantly battling for a seat at the table—and perhaps even for survival?

The answers to questions like these are critically important for the planner. Communities vary in their tolerance for change, and trying to achieve significant social progress in a community that is wedded to its past can pose major challenges. If a small number of people control most of a community's major decisions, a planner who is not in tune with those people is virtually guaranteed a frustrating professional experience. If, on the other hand, power is diffused, the politically astute planner has numerous opportunities to form alliances and coalitions around specific issues.[7] In short, political power tends to define the parameters within which the planner operates, and a planner should know a great deal about those parameters before accepting a position in a particular community. "If planners ignore those in power," John Forester has written, "they assure their own powerlessness. Alternatively, if planners understand how relations of power shape the planning process, they can improve the quality of their analyses and empower citizen and community action."[8]

To be effective in the "messy world of urban politics," Norman Krumholz and John Forester have written, planners must be "professionally able, organizationally astute, and most of all, politically articulate."[9] In Cleveland, where Krumholz served as planning director for a decade, having a politically articulate planning voice

> did not mean back-room deal making. It meant actively anticipating and counteracting threats to Cleveland's vulnerable populations. It meant articulating a vision of a better Cleveland, a city of more services and less poverty, a city of greater choice and less dependency, a city of adequate shelter not only downtown but all across town. Being politically articulate planners meant defining issues and setting agendas, working on problems before being invited to do so. It meant knowing ahead of time that politicians and city department staff would often be too busy, too uncertain, too self-interested, to get involved in some issues—and that this would produce opportunities for the planners to make a difference. Developing an articulate equity-oriented planning voice in Cleveland meant negotiating to serve the interests of the poor, but it meant much more than that, too: building trust and the planners' reputation, providing technical assistance, developing strong ties to the media to inform public opinion, at times leaking information to oppositional figures, drafting legislation, again and again bringing technical analysis to bear on issues of public costs, benefits, and well-being.[10]

Being politically articulate does not mean that planners must be politicians themselves. My point is simply that the ability to use the political system effectively, to operate in a politically savvy manner, is one of the several basic skills that any competent planner should possess. As Gene Boles puts it, political savvy "is synonymous with professional skill."[11]

THE ELEMENTS OF POLITICAL SAVVY

It is ironic that something so basic to the success of planning plays such a small part in the training we provide for future planners. While the nation's planning schools vary widely in this regard, most of them focus considerably more attention on methods of analysis, on the legal framework of planning, on ideology-based theories, on a variety of functional specializations (economic development, transportation, and so on), and on practicums (where the emphasis is on applying the skills and methodologies that have been taught) than on techniques for planning effectively within a political system. It is little wonder, then, that so many young planners enter the public arena with misgivings and trepidation.

Can political savvy be taught? "No," answers practitioner Linda L. Davis: "Surviving the political arena is not something you learn in planning school. You learn it on the job, sometimes through terrible mistakes but more often by watching others to see what works for them and by experimenting to see what works for you."[12] "Yes," answers educator Karen S. Christensen. To be sure, planning educators cannot ensure that their students have "savvy instincts," but they can certainly "teach components of savvy (such as meeting skills, adaptability, capability to invent options, and understanding organizational and political incentives and dynamics)."[13] While Davis's point about the importance of learning by experience is certainly well-taken, I am more sympathetic to Christensen's position. A planning education program that provides little or no exposure to the politics of planning must be considered woefully deficient.

What are the most important elements of political savvy for urban planners? Christensen lists several in the previous quotation. A longer list has been provided by Barry Checkoway, who discusses a number of skills involved in political strategy: setting goals, identifying issues, developing constituencies, selecting tactics, building organizational structures, finding and developing leaders, educating the public, establishing relationships with influentials, building coalitions, and advocating for political change.[14] Another author, Guy Benveniste, has written extensively on the politics of planning, with particular emphasis on the importance of skills in networking, coalition building, and negotiation.[15] He provides a number of useful insights on these matters (though the planners about whom he writes—for example, the heads of international teams invited to design new education systems for developing countries—tend to be rather distant cousins of most who will read this book).

My own list of the most important elements of political savvy for planners is as follows.

(1) A planner should be able to assess the possibilities and constraints of a particular situation in a reasonably accurate manner. The most common errors in this regard are those of rashness and timidity. Rashness means charging ahead (with an activity, project, plan, or policy) in a situation where one hopes to win but is clearly going to lose. To be sure, there are times when losing is strategically appropriate: it may be important, say, to get a particular idea on the table for later reconsideration, or to manifest support for a group whose backing may be needed later on; or the loss may be a preliminary step in a chain of events or decisions likely to lead to a desired outcome. Rashness, then, refers to those cases where one takes action before having laid the necessary groundwork, or is battling genuinely insurmountable odds, or is simply pigheadedly stubborn about the "right" thing to do—even though no good, and possibly even harm, will likely result.

Timidity is the opposite: being afraid to take action, out of fear of failure or of adverse consequences, in situations where success is a realistic possibility. Most of us can think of examples of both rash and overly timid behavior, often our own. The politically savvy planner, I suggest, is sufficiently perceptive to avoid these errors most of the time; he or she is adept at generating and analyzing feedback, and at using it effectively to assess the possibilities and constraints at hand. Linda Davis advises planners to

> know when you are fighting a losing battle. No matter what technical expertise you employ, no matter how strong and forthright your position, and no matter how actively citizens are involved, even "big guns," you may lose. Just as in poker, you have to know when to hold your hand and when to fold it. Otherwise, you will soon be out of the game entirely.[16]

(2) Closely related to an accurate assessment of a situation is a keen sense of timing. It may be that a particular program a planner wants to push will stand a better chance of success after the next city election; in the next budget year; after a lengthier and more ambitious citizen education process; after more time has been devoted to mobilizing political support; or after other, more pressing issues

have been dealt with. On the other hand, it is also possible to misread such factors and take no action when the prospects for success are actually quite good. The most common errors related to timing, then, are *impatience* and *missed opportunities*. Politically astute planners are able to avoid both; they are skilled at determining when to advance and when to bide their time.

(3) *A politically savvy planner must have outstanding communication skills.* On too many occasions I have seen otherwise compelling planning ideas fall flat because of avoidable flaws in the ways they were presented, whether orally or in writing. Graphic, computer-based, and other forms of communication are also important, of course; with regard to political savvy, however, my emphasis is on the basics of speaking and writing. When asked to assess the level of preparedness evidenced by recent graduates of the nation's planning schools, experienced practitioners have often complained about poor communication skills; to their credit, many schools have begun placing greater emphasis on this matter in recent years.[17] Needless to say, the Feedback Strategy presented in Chapter 11 requires frequent and competent communication between the planner and relevant others in the community; if that communication is insufficient or poorly carried out, the strategy (and, for that matter, any other approach) loses whatever utility it might otherwise possess.

Politically literate planners, according to Krumholz and Forester,

> know how to present focused analyses in language that others can understand. They know they must present those analyses on time, in whatever time is available, whenever they can get a hearing. Knowing they must present those accounts to audiences who will not always listen closely, those planners think carefully...about how to teach that audience about important issues at hand. Politically literate and articulate planners thus seek to be effective educators every bit as much as rigorous analysts or problem-solvers.[18]

Planners frequently make speeches or presentations in a variety of forums (public hearings, meetings of boards and commissions or neighborhood groups, civic clubs, and so on) and for a variety of purposes (to inform, persuade, describe alternatives, mobilize action, repair damage, provoke thought, even entertain). A planning agency's overall effectiveness is shaped in no small measure by the communication skills of those who regularly speak on its behalf.[19]

Common mistakes in the oral communication of planning ideas include the following:

- Misjudging the audience—giving the wrong talk to the wrong group, misunderstanding their interests or level of sophistication
- Failing to have clear goals for the talk—that is, not being sure what one is attempting to accomplish
- Using too much jargon (professional terms used frequently by planners may mean nothing to the average citizen—for example, the alphabet soup we use to designate various federal programs)
- Telling offensive, irrelevant, or just plain unnecessary jokes (well-timed humor can be very effective, but planned jokes often fall flat)
- Excessive verbal distractions (the ubiquitous "um" leading the way)
- Lengthy and detailed descriptions of data, which tend to lose the audience immediately
- Errors in technique—for example, reading the entire speech, making too little eye contact, jangling one's pocket change, fidgeting, pacing excessively, speaking in a monotone
- Dressing too formally or too casually for the particular occasion
- Poor use of graphic aids (overheads are useful for outlining major points but should not contain text that the speaker proceeds to read to the audience; nor should they contain large quantities of data, feature type too small to be read by all in the room, or be left on the screen after the speaker has finished referring to them).

Many other items could be added to this list; every planner who does much public speaking can easily generate a similar list of do's and don'ts. This should suffice, however, to illustrate the point that good communication cannot be taken for granted. Most planners become skilled speakers only through focused attention and practice.

Several of the above points (knowing one's audience, having clear goals, avoiding jargon and technical errors) apply to written communication as well.[20] It does indeed matter whether a planner is writing technical or legal documents, in-house memoranda, letters, reports (of a variety of types), and so on; each of these calls for a specific style, and the politically savvy planner should be able to handle all of them.

Bad writing is not a trivial matter. Excessive errors are, in effect, static in the communications system, and when the static becomes too loud it is difficult to hear the message. (E-mail seems to operate with a different, and considerably lower, set of standards; anything goes as long as the basic point gets across. I fear that some of this attitude may be spilling over to other forms of written communication as well.) Each planner should be realistic in assessing his or her level of writing skill. If this level is problematic, it is far better to rely on others for editing, final drafts, and so on, than to repeatedly issue badly written documents.

Working with the media is another important aspect of effective communication.[21] Preparing press releases in a manner that optimizes the likelihood of their being used, knowing how to translate important ideas into sound bites for television, maintaining good working relationships with reporters—these, too, are important aspects of political savvy.

(4) Planners should be effective negotiators. Nigel Taylor notes that planners must be able to identify, and establish communication with, the "actors" whose cooperation will be required if the planners' ideas are to be implemented. Since those actors generally have their own agendas, however, and since their agendas will not always coincide with those of the planners, negotiation is often necessary.[22] Moreover, as discussed in Chapter 9, planners may be called upon to mediate between two or more other groups with divergent agendas.

(5) Yet another element of political savvy is the ability to make effective use of a community's power relationships in striving for desired outcomes. This means, for example, knowing how to network, mobilize support, form coalitions with "friendly outsiders,"[23] and use appropriate organizations effectively. Every sizable community has a variety of public interest or "good government" groups whose objectives frequently coincide with those of the local planning department, yet planners rarely form alliances with these organizations. Planners may feel too politically vulnerable to form open partnerships with organizations outside of government, but I suspect that they have greater latitude in this regard than they think. I am inclined to agree with Peter Marris, who wrote in 1994: "In a time of impoverished governments, faltering urban economies, Federal neglect and political impotence, I suggest that planners, paradoxically, are freer to build alliances and propose their own solutions without worrying about their right to do so, because everyone is looking for workable proposals."[24]

This point also applies to the political relationships at work within any large planning agency or organization itself. Based on her case study of the Planning Agency for the Metropolitan Region of Rio de Janeiro, Brazil, Linda Gondim concluded that planning effectiveness "depends largely on ability to mobilize support from top-level officials, who control resources necessary for the performance of both 'technical' and 'political' roles."[25] Expertise alone, she wrote, is not enough; one must have "strategies for acquiring autonomy and influence over top-level officials within the planning agency in order to be heard by decision makers."[26] A majority of the planners in her study were—unfortunately, in her view—"oblivious to the importance of bureaucratic politics to the effectiveness of planning practice."[27] They perceived themselves as technocrats, viewed political power negatively (as an instrument of oppression), and resented those of their colleagues who did try to make use of the political system. "Refusal to deal with power in the daily reality of the planning organization," she concluded, "may be a major source of professional failure and personal frustration."[28]

(6) *The politically savvy planner must have a well-developed system of values that provides direction to his or her professional activities.* Political involvement devoid of values is frivolous at best, self-serving and potentially dangerous at worst. Those who engage the political system without the guidance of professional values tend to view power as an end in itself. The planner who seeks efficacy and power solely as a means of personal gratification is, in my view, the antithesis of the politically savvy planner.

(7) *Finally, the politically savvy planner should possess a compelling vision of what the community ought to be like in the future.* The entire concept of political savvy—of being efficacious in the local political system—makes little sense unless one has some sense of what is being sought. This topic is sufficiently important to merit its own chapter—the next one, in fact.

To summarize, I have suggested that the politically savvy planner (1) is able to make a reasonably accurate assessment of the possibilities and constraints of a particular situation; (2) has a keen sense of timing; (3) has outstanding communication skills; (4) is an effective negotiator; (5) knows how to make effective use of a community's power relationships; (6) is guided by a well-developed set of professional values; and (7) possesses a compelling vision of where the community should be headed.

NOTES

1. Useful overviews of the relationship between planning and politics are found in Anthony James Catanese, *The Politics of Planning and Development* (Beverly Hills: Sage Publications, 1984); Guy Benveniste, *Mastering the Politics of Planning* (San Francisco: Jossey-Bass Publishers, 1989); and William C. Johnson, *Urban Planning and Politics* (Chicago: Planners Press, 1997).

2. John M. Levy, *Contemporary Urban Planning*, 4th ed. (Upper Saddle River, N.J.: Prentice-Hall, 1997), pp. 80–81.

3. Sergio Rodriguez, "How to Become a Successful Planner," in *Planners on Planning: Leading Planners Offer Real-Life Lessons on What Works, What Doesn't, and Why*, ed. Bruce W. McClendon and Anthony James Catanese (San Francisco: Jossey-Bass Publishers, 1996), p. 33.

4. This formulation of "community power structure" was presented several decades ago in Floyd Hunter's *Community Power Structure: A Study of Decision-Makers* (Chapel Hill: University of North Carolina Press, 1953). Hunter's study, focused on Atlanta, Georgia, was subjected to considerable criticism on methodological grounds (he assumed the existence of a pyramid-shaped power structure, then set about trying to determine who occupied its peak, rather than beginning with more fundamental questions regarding the structure of power in Atlanta). It is still possible, however, to find communities whose power configurations can be described in this manner—as, for example, in small cities dominated by a single industry.

5. Writing less than a decade after Hunter's study, Robert Dahl described New Haven, Connecticut, in this manner in *Who Governs? Democracy and Power in the American City* (New Haven, Conn.: Yale University Press, 1961). So-called community power studies were in vogue for a number of years thereafter, with sociologists tending to follow Hunter's approach and political scientists preferring Dahl's; eventually, however, the topic faded from the scene, in part because this particular intellectual well had run dry, but also no doubt because of the emergence of more ideologically based conceptions of community power.

6. See Pierre Clavel, *The Progressive City* (New Brunswick, N.J.: Rutgers University Press, 1986).

7. An excellent treatment of this issue was Francine Rabinovitz's *City Politics and Planning* (New York: Atherton Press, 1969).

8. John Forester, *Planning in the Face of Power* (Berkeley: University of California Press, 1989), p. 27. Also see Norman Krumholz and John Forester, *Making Equity Planning Work: Leadership in the Public Sector* (Philadelphia: Temple University Press, 1990), p. 226.

9. Krumholz and Forester, *Making Equity Planning Work*, p. 225.

10. Ibid., pp. 225–226.

11. Gene Boles, "The Principles of Community Alignment and Empowerment," in McClendon and Catanese, *Planners on Planning*, p. 119.

12. Linda L. Davis, "Guidelines for Survival and Success," in McClendon and Catanese, *Planners on Planning*, p. 103.

13. Karen S. Christensen, "Teaching Savvy," *Journal of Planning Education and Research*, Vol. 12, No. 3 (Spring 1993), p. 203.

14. Barry Checkoway, "Political Strategy for Social Planning," in *Strategic Perspectives on Planning Practice*, ed. Barry Checkoway (Lexington, Mass.: Lexington Books, 1986), pp. 198–206.

15. Guy Benveniste, *Mastering the Politics of Planning: Crafting Credible Plans and Policies That Make a Difference* (San Francisco: Jossey-Bass Publishers, 1989). For a widely diverse set of commentaries (including my own) on this book, see the Summer 1993 issue of *Planning Theory*.

16. Davis, "Guidelines," pp. 114–115.

17. For a related discussion, see Connie P. Ozawa and Ethan P. Seltzer, "Taking Our Bearings: Mapping a Relationship among Planning Practice, Theory, and Education," *Journal of*

Planning Education and Research, Vol. 18, No. 3 (Spring 1999), pp. 257–266.

18. Krumholz and Forester, *Making Equity Planning Work*, p. 260.

19. For several useful "tips for better verbal presentations," see Pauline Graivier, "How to Speak So People Will Listen," *Planning*, Vol. 58, No. 12 (December 1992), pp. 15–18.

20. For some sound advice on this matter, see John Leach, "Seven Steps to Better Writing," *Planning*, Vol. 59, No. 6 (June 1993), pp. 26–27.

21. See Carol Brzozowski-Gardner, "Insiders' Edition," *Planning*, Vol. 62, No. 11 (November 1996), pp. 20–21.

22. Nigel Taylor, *Urban Planning Theory Since 1945* (London: Sage Publications, 1998), p. 117.

23. John Forester, *Critical Theory, Public Policy, and Planning Practice: Toward a Critical Pragmatism* (Albany: State University of New York Press, 1993), p. 59.

24. Peter Marris, "Advocacy Planning As a Bridge between the Professional and the Political," *Journal of the American Planning Association*, Vol. 60, No. 2 (Spring 1994), p. 145.

25. Linda M. Gondim, "Planning Practice within Public Bureaucracy: A New Perspective on Roles of Planners," *Journal of Planning Education and Research*, Vol. 7, No. 3 (Spring 1988), p. 171.

26. Ibid.

27. Ibid.

28. Ibid.

13

Vision

THE IMPORTANCE OF VISION

In 1988 I published an article in the *Journal of the American Planning Association* entitled "Four Critical Junctures in the History of the Urban Planning Profession: An Exercise in Hindsight."[1] It proved to be quite controversial; some readers considered it a perceptive overview of the state of the planning profession at that time, while others deemed it misguided and erroneous. The article was clearly an expression of my own professional values (it appeared, quite appropriately, in a section of the journal labeled "Interpretation"), and addressed my concern that the profession was in danger of losing the "reformist, visionary, future-oriented spirit" that had initially attracted so many of us to planning careers.

Contributing to this danger, I suggested, were choices that had been made collectively (largely by the accumulated impact of numerous small actions rather than by conscious decision) at four critical junctures or turning points in the profession's history. I noted that one could hardly identify the consequences—positive or negative—that might have resulted from alternative choices; the paths that had been selected, however, had in my view produced some dysfunctional outcomes for the profession. Those paths that the profession had pursued involved a collective quest for increased political power (not to be confused, by the way, with the possession of political savvy!), for sanction and financial support from the federal government, for academic respectability, and for validation by the private sector.

Given the problems that I believed those quests had created for the profession, I suggested that it was time to do some serious stocktaking. In the article I described this task as a matter of confronting and dealing with

> the soul of the profession. It is a soul enriched by the works of creative and dedicated figures in our history—Frederick Law Olmsted, Daniel Burnham, Henry Wright, Clarence Stein, Clarence Perry, Rexford Guy Tugwell, and many others. It is a soul influenced immeasurably by those—Paul Davidoff comes quickly to mind—who have reminded us of the critical responsibilities we bear for the well-being of all who reside in the communities we purport to serve. And fortunately, it is a soul that still receives nourishment from many planners who strive to serve the underlying values of the profession.[2]

I noted, in the article, that Donald Krueckeberg had recently cited two book reviews, one by Richard Bolan and the other by Allan Jacobs, in which "each praised the book he had reviewed for helping him to remember why he had chosen to become a planner: 'to pursue a humanistic vision' and 'a worthwhile utopia.'"[3] I contrasted that perspective with Norman Krumholz's less sanguine observation, at one point in his reflections, that most planners are "ordinary bureaucrats seeking a secure career, some status, and regular increases in salary."[4] Implicit in that contrast, I suggested, was "the field on which the battle for the profession's soul will take place."[5]

I concluded, then, with a call for a revitalization of the utopian tradition in urban planning. The profession, I argued,

> needs a new generation of visionaries, people who dream of a better world, and who are capable of designing the means to attain it. That, after all, is the essence of planning: to visualize the ideal future community, and to work toward its realization. It is a much-needed role in our cities, and young men and women continue to enter the profession because they want to perform that role. Let us nurture their instincts, and thereby restore the urban planning profession to its historic mission.[6]

As noted earlier, the article was controversial. I enjoyed the ensuing debates (both in print and on panels at several conferences), as well as the modest but impassioned collection of letters that arrived in my mailbox. Some of these letters were highly supportive, intended to assure me that the visionary spirit lives on in the hearts, if not the deeds, of many planners. Other letters took issue with the article. For example, a well-known planning director argued that a "new generation of visionaries" is hardly what we need; rather, "we need planners committed to making a difference. We need planners that can use planning skills and techniques to solve problems. We need planners who understand that ineffectiveness is failure and that there are proven strategies and tactics for becoming more effective."[7]

On several occasions I found myself on a conference panel with the author of that letter, giving us opportunities to discuss the matter further. My response was (and still is) to ask: effective toward what end? I too want planning to be effective, and to make a difference. I suggest, however, that the concept of effectiveness is meaningless unless it is integrated with a compelling vision of an improved urban society. It is not enough to settle for the politician's conception of effectiveness, or the developer's. Planners bear responsibility for increasing the level of public awareness about future possibilities, about what our communities are capable of becoming; we are responsible for helping communities define their desired future, and for helping them achieve it.[8] I reject, then, a dichotomy between the planner as visionary and the planner as a technician who gets things done. Each of these perspectives must inform the other, and we are an incomplete profession if we settle for only one of them. (I should add that once my fellow debater and I had fully expressed our views on this topic, we concluded that our positions were closer than we had thought.)

Another response to my article argued that, in reality, vision has *never* been a strong characteristic of the planning profession itself, that planners have historically been consumers and implementers of visions but have left to others the task of creating them. What, the author of this argument asked, did Ebenezer Howard, Patrick Geddes, Daniel Burnham, Benton MacKaye, Frederick Law Olmsted, Rexford Guy Tugwell, Lewis Mumford, and Robert Moses have in common? The answer was: all were visionaries, all had a significant impact on the planning of our cities and regions—and none were members of the planning profession. We have pursued their visions, indeed in a sense we have lived off of those visions—but they were the visions of architects, landscape architects, engineers, geographers, and so forth, rather than of planners.

Should this concern us? I don't think so. In one sense, of course, it is ultimately more fruitful to think of planning as a societal function than as a profession; hundreds of thousands of Americans have functioned as planners, and whether they have worn that label or belonged to professional planning organizations is ultimately inconsequential.[9] It is also true, however, that the list of names is incomplete; the profession has certainly had many visionaries of its own. Most important, however, is the fact that the source of visionary ideas is really irrelevant. What matters is how we as a profession interact with and use those ideas—the extent to which we join with other concerned groups and individuals in a collective effort to resolve our problems and create a better future. In short, being a visionary does not require that one be the *creator* of visions.

What, then, *does* it mean? One justifiable critique of my 1988 article was that I did not offer a definition of the term *vision*. I simply assumed (naively, as it turned out) that it was one of those concepts that everybody understands intuitively. Here, then, is what the term means to me when I use it.

In the most general sense, I use *vision* to denote *a system of interrelated goals*. For planners, goals describe the future state of affairs we would like to achieve in a number of functional areas— land use, transportation, the economy, the environment, aesthetics, social issues, and so on. Put all of these goals together, make sure they are compatible with one another at the margins, formulate some generalizations about the kind of community they would add up to, and you begin to have a vision of what the community should be like in the future. This vision serves, then, to focus one's thinking about individual issues as they arise. Indeed, the purpose of a community-wide vision is somewhat akin to that of a comprehensive plan for that community; one criterion for evaluating such plans, in fact, is to assess their effectiveness in communicating a compelling vision for the community's future.

To be infused with a keen sense of vision, however, suggests several general attitudes, orientations, and behavioral traits that go well beyond simply having a system of interrelated goals. Here are some dimensions of the term that have bearing, in my view, on the work of planners.

• Vision means having a long-range perspective. No other professional group is routinely looking more than a few years down the road; this is a gap that needs to be filled, and planners are the obvious people to do the job.

• Vision means being less interested in *forecasting* the future than in *creating* it. There is something almost antithetical to planning in our standard population and economic projections, for example. They make sense primarily as answers to the question, "What will likely occur here in the absence of any planned intervention?" Having received those answers, however, the visionary planner will ask: "What do we *want* to occur here?" Then: "How do we make it happen?"

• Vision means involving as many individuals and groups as possible in the process of dreaming about what might be, and of planning how to make it happen. Effective visionaries don't go it alone; they know how to involve the public in meaningful ways. Special efforts should be devoted to tapping creative talents wherever they can be found, and bringing those talents to bear on the process of building a better community.

• Vision means focusing on all dimensions of the quality of life in our communities, not just on economic bottom lines.

• Vision means dealing creatively and effectively with equity issues, making certain that all residents of a community have access to needed resources and to opportunities for personal fulfillment.

• And finally, to reiterate a point made earlier, vision means having a strong and compelling conception of the good community.

City- or region-wide visioning programs are a long-standing tradition in local planning, of course, and I suspect that hundreds (if not thousands) of such programs have been carried out.[10] These programs have varied widely in their methodologies, the commitment of local politicians and power figures, the extent of citizen involvement, and the nature and duration of their impact after the program's conclusion. In general, however, the long-term effects of such programs have tended to be minimal; they have usually been one-shot affairs, creating a brief stir but eminently forgettable a few years later. At one time in the recent past, my own city had three such programs under way simultaneously, sponsored respectively by the city government, the Chamber of Commerce, and a local "good government" organization. All three programs were competently run, but there was no coordination among them—and all three were dead and forgotten within six months of their completion. Not long afterward, the area's regional planning organization undertook a more ambitious visioning project; though initiated with high expectations and much publicity, it too eventually faded away without any lasting impact. I doubt that these experiences are unique to my area.

The lesson, I believe, is that visioning will have little impact if it is viewed as a special, one-time activity. Instead, it must be integrated into the local planning process on an ongoing basis. But is this really something that planners can do, given the many other demands on their time and energy?

HOW TO BE A VISIONARY—AND KEEP YOUR JOB

Urban planning (along with, I suspect, many other disciplines) underwent some major changes during the 1980s. The nation had shifted away from reliance on government to solve major societal problems; the American mood—characterized (but hardly caused) by the Reagan administration—was becoming less public-serving, more private- and self-serving. President Kennedy's "Ask what you can do for your country" had shifted to "What's in it for me?" Among its other effects, this paradigm shift made it more difficult for the planning profession to retain the visionary, idealistic, even utopian spirit that had once characterized it. The market for vision seemed to be in decline.

The growth of single-issue politics, an atmosphere of hostility to government in general (and taxes in particular), pressures for the privatization of key public services, growing hostility to land use controls and regulations, a general decline in respect for public service as a profession—these and other forces combined to create a climate that has not been highly supportive of a strong role for government-based planning. Certainly urban planning is not the only profession experiencing difficulties in this respect; I hear similar concerns from public administrators, social workers, public health professionals, public school educators, criminal justice officials, and others. In all likelihood, then, the last two decades of the twentieth century were not a particularly good time, in the sweep of this nation's history, to be a visionary in any profession. Whether the pendulum has begun to swing back in the other direction remains to be seen.

Given this situation, it has been tempting, for planners as well as others, to abandon the visionary perspective altogether. Whether employed by a city, county, or state government—or by a university—many of us have found ourselves preoccupied with damage control, dealing with daily pressures and crises and attempting to defend our shrinking resource base. There is a natural tendency under such circumstances—call it the survival instinct, if you will—

to dig in and focus on critical functions, those that we think will maintain what little political support we can cling to. Thus we lurch from project to project, devoting little or no attention to the overall vision that should be directing our efforts. (Yogi Berra is reputed to have said, "You got to be careful if you don't know where you're going, because you might not get there." It's a good tag line for visionless planning.) We should resist these temptations and tendencies. The visionary component of planning is too important to be ignored. Nor is it all that difficult to achieve.

A few years after my 1988 article, I found myself on a conference panel with a county planning director who expressed considerable skepticism about my emphasis on vision. "If I were to be perceived as a visionary," she said (and I am paraphrasing from memory here), "I would lose my job. My employers want me to be a hard-nosed realist, not a starry-eyed dreamer. I simply can't afford to do visionary planning." Fair enough. My response, however, was to ask her whether she had some notion of what her county should be like, say, ten years down the road. "Of course I do," was the answer. With that I rested my case; by my definition, she was a visionary. It is not necessary to wear a "V" on one's forehead, or to otherwise advertise oneself or one's activities as visionary; indeed, I agree that it would often be dysfunctional to do so. It is enough to have a sense, along with Yogi, of where one wants to be going; then, and only then, can one develop strategies for getting there.

Visionary planning does not need to be a grandiose process carried out on an epic or heroic scale. Instead, it is a spirit that should inspire all that a planner does. An article by Sylvia Lewis about Boulder, Colorado—"The Town That Said No to Sprawl"—offers an example. Bill Lamont, formerly Boulder's planning director, was interviewed about that city's successful (at that time) effort to control growth. "In Boulder," he is quoted as having said, "when we did 'growth management,' I just thought it was comprehensive planning 101. *You pull all the pieces together and move toward a vision for a particular city.*"[11] I can say it no better.

Kevin Kennedy, a student in one of my recent graduate planning classes, came close to doing so, however, in concluding his term paper as follows: "I see a planner as a guardian of ideals and dreams, entrusted with their safety. Almost anyone can administer regulations, but few can administer a vision."[12] The nation's urban planners are, I suggest, those few. This is our professional heritage, our reason for being. I am confident that we will continue to play this role with integrity, compassion, and distinction.

NOTES

1. Michael P. Brooks, "Four Critical Junctures in the History of the Urban Planning Profession: An Exercise in Hindsight," *Journal of the American Planning Association*, Vol. 54, No. 2 (Spring 1988), pp. 241–248.

2. Ibid., p. 246. It is worth noting that one critic took me to task for using the word *soul* in this passage, arguing that it sounded too "theological." I have since considered other terms—*ethos, culture,* and so forth—but have finally concluded that, in my view, professions do indeed "got soul"—or at least they should.

3. Donald A. Krueckeberg, ed., *The American Planner: Biographies and Recollections* (New York: Methuen, 1983), p. 1.

4. Norman Krumholz, "A Retrospective View of Equity Planning: Cleveland 1969–1979," *Journal of the American Planning Association*, Vol. 48, No. 2 (Spring 1982); reprinted in *Introduction to Planning History in the United States*, ed. Donald A. Krueckeberg (New Brunswick, N.J.: Center for Urban Policy Research, Rutgers University, 1983), p. 275.

5. Brooks, "Four Critical Junctures," p. 246.

6. Ibid.

7. Bruce W. McClendon, letter to author, April 13, 1988.

8. For a related discussion, see Richard C. Bernhardt, "The Ten Habits of Highly Effective Planners," in *Planners on Planning: Leading Planners Offer Real-Life Lessons on What Works, What Doesn't, and Why*, ed. Bruce W. McClendon and Anthony James Catanese (San Francisco: Jossey-Bass Publishers, 1996), p. 45.

9. "If the label 'planning' is attached to your office, you probably don't do much of it," wrote the public policy theorist Bertram Gross in 1967, tongue only partly in cheek. His point was simply that most of the important planning in our nation was being carried out not by professional planners but by the elected officials, bureaucrats, business and professional leaders, and others who occupied positions that enabled them to "get things done." See "The City of Man: A Social Systems Reckoning," in *Environment for Man: The Next Fifty Years*, ed. William R. Ewald Jr. (Bloomington: Indiana University Press, 1967), p. 154.

10. The literature about such programs is vast. A brief but useful guide to the planning and assessment of such programs is William R. Klein's "Visions of Things to Come," *Planning*, Vol. 60, No. 9 (May 1993), p. 10.

11. Sylvia Lewis, "The Town That Said No to Sprawl," *Planning*, Vol. 55, No. 4 (April 1990), p. 19. Emphasis added.

12. Kevin Kennedy, term paper, Internship Seminar, Department of Urban Studies and Planning, Virginia Commonwealth University, April 2000.

References

Alexander, Ernest R. "After Rationality, What? A Review of Responses to Paradigm Breakdown," *Journal of the American Planning Association*, Vol. 50, No. 1, Winter 1984.

———. *Approaches to Planning: Introducing Current Planning Theories, Concepts, and Issues*, 2nd ed., Philadelphia, Gordon and Breach, 1992.

———. "If Planning Isn't Everything, Maybe It's Something," *Town Planning Review*, Vol. 52, No. 2, April 1981.

Altshuler, Alan A. *The City Planning Process: A Political Analysis*, Ithaca, N.Y., Cornell University Press, 1965.

Arrow, Kenneth J. "Mathematical Models in the Social Sciences," in *The Policy Sciences*, edited by Daniel Lerner and Harold D. Lasswell, Stanford, Stanford University Press, 1951.

———. *Social Choice and Individual Values*, 2nd ed., New York, John Wiley & Sons, 1963.

Baer, William C. "General Plan Evaluation Criteria," *Journal of the American Planning Association*, Vol. 63, No. 3, Summer 1997.

Edward C. Banfield. "Ends and Means in Planning," *International Social Science Journal*, Vol. 11, 1959.

———. *Political Influence*, New York, The Free Press of Glencoe, 1961.

Barnard, Chester I. *Organization and Management*, Cambridge, Mass., Harvard University Press, 1948.

Barrett, Carol D. "Planners in Conflict," *Journal of the American Planning Association*, Vol. 55, No. 4, Autumn 1989.

Bassin, Arthur. "Does Capitalist Planning Need Some Glasnost?" *Journal of the American Planning Association*, Vol. 56, No. 2, Spring 1990.

Batty, Michael. "A Chronicle of Scientific Planning: The Anglo-American Modeling Experience," *Journal of the American Planning Association*, Vol. 60, No. 1, Winter 1994.

Baum, Howell, S. "Politics in Planners' Practice," in *Strategic Perspectives on Planning Practice*, edited by Barry Checkoway, Lexington, Mass., Lexington Books, 1986.

———. "Practicing Planning Theory in a Political World," in *Explorations in Planning Theory*, edited by Seymour J. Mandelbaum, Luigi Mazza, and Robert W. Burchell, New Brunswick, N.J., Center for Urban Policy Research, Rutgers University, 1996.

———. "Social Science, Social Work, and Surgery: Teaching What Students Need to Practice Planning," *Journal of the American Planning Association*, Vol. 63, No. 2, Spring 1997.

———. "Why the Rational Paradigm Persists: Tales from the Field," *Journal of Planning Education and Research*, Vol. 15, No. 2, Winter 1996.

———. "Teaching Practice," *Journal of Planning Education and Research*, Vol. 17, No. 1, Fall 1997.

Baumol, William J. *Economic Theory and Operations Analysis*, 2nd ed., Englewood Cliffs, N.J., Prentice-Hall, 1965.

Bayne, Patricia. "Generating Alternatives: A Neglected Dimension in Planning Theory," *Town Planning Review*, Vol. 66, No. 3, July 1995.

Beauregard, Robert A. "Between Modernity and Postmodernity: The Ambiguous Position of U.S. Planning," in *Readings in Planning Theory*, edited by Scott Campbell and Susan S. Fainstein, Cambridge, Mass., Blackwell Publishers, 1996.

———. "Bringing the City Back In," *Journal of the American Planning Association*, Vol. 56, No. 2, Spring 1990.

———. "Edge Critics," *Journal of Planning Education and Research*, Vol. 14, No. 3, Spring 1995.

Benveniste, Guy. *Mastering the Politics of Planning*, San Francisco, Jossey-Bass Publishers, 1989.

Bernhardt, Richard C. "The Ten Habits of Highly Effective Planners," in *Planners on Planning: Leading Planners Offer Real-Life Lessons on What Works, What Doesn't, and Why*, edited by Bruce W. McClendon and Anthony James Catanese, San Francisco, Jossey-Bass Publishers, 1996.

Black, Alan. "The Chicago Area Transportation Study: A Case Study of Rational Planning," *Journal of Planning Education and Research*, Vol. 10, No. 1, Fall 1990.

Blanco, Hilda. "Community and the Four Jewels of Planning," in *Planning Ethics: A Reader in Planning Theory, Practice, and Education*, edited by Sue Hendler, New Brunswick, N.J., Center for Urban Policy Research, Rutgers University, 1995.

———. *How to Think about Social Problems: American Pragmatism and the Idea of Planning*, Westport, Conn., Greenwood Press, 1994.

Bolan, Richard S. "Emerging Views of Planning," *Journal of the American Institute of Planners*, Vol. 33, July 1967.

———. "The Structure of Ethical Choice in Planning Practice," in *Ethics in Planning*, edited by Martin Wachs, New Brunswick, N.J., Center for Urban Policy Research, Rutgers University, 1985.

Boles, Gene. "The Principles of Community Alignment and Empowerment," in *Planners on Planning: Leading Planners Offer Real-Life Lessons on What Works, What Doesn't, and Why*, edited by Bruce W. McClendon and Anthony James Catanese, San Francisco, Jossey-Bass Publishers, 1996.

Branch, Melville C. *Comprehensive Planning for the 21st Century: General Theory and Principles*, Westport, Conn., Praeger, 1998.

Braybrooke, David, and Charles E. Lindblom. *A Strategy of Decision: Policy Evaluation as a Social Process*, New York, The Free Press, 1963.

Brooks, Michael P. "The City May Be Back In, But Where Is the Planner?" *Journal of the American Planning Association*, Vol. 56, No. 2, Spring 1990.

———. "Four Critical Junctures in the History of the Urban Planning Profession: An Exercise in Hindsight," *Journal of the American Planning Association*, Vol. 54, No. 2, Spring 1988.

———. "Getting Goofy in Virginia: The Politics of Disneyfication," *Planning 1997: Contrasts and Transitions*, Proceedings of the American Planning Association National Planning Conference, edited by Bill Pable and Bruce McClendon, pp. 691–722. San Diego, Calif., April 5–9, 1997.

———. "Planning and Political Power: Toward a Strategy for Coping," in *Explorations in Planning Theory*, edited by Seymour J. Mandelbaum, Luigi Mazza, and Robert W. Burchell, New Brunswick, N.J., Center for Urban Policy Research, Rutgers University, 1996.

———. "A Plethora of Paradigms?" *Journal of the American Planning Association*, Vol. 59, No. 2, Spring 1993.

———. *Social Planning and City Planning*, Chicago, American Society of Planning Officials, Planning Advisory Service Report No. 261, September 1970.

Bryson, John M. *Strategic Planning for Public and Nonprofit Organizations: A Guide to Strengthening and Sustaining Organizational Achievement*, rev. ed., San Francisco, Jossey-Bass Publishers, 1995.

Bryson, John M., and William D. Roering. "Applying Private-Sector Strategic Planning in the Public Sector," *Journal of the American Planning Association*, Vol. 53, No. 1, Winter 1987.

Brzozowski-Gardner, Carol. "Insiders' Edition," *Planning*, Vol. 62, No. 11, November 1996.

Campbell, Scott, and Susan S. Fainstein. "Introduction: The Structure and Debates of Planning Theory," in *Readings in Planning Theory*, edited by Scott Campbell and Susan S. Fainstein, Cambridge, Mass., Blackwell Publishers, 1996.

Campbell, Scott, and Susan S. Fainstein, eds. *Readings in Planning Theory*, Cambridge, Mass., Blackwell Publishers, 1996.

Catanese, Anthony James. *Planners and Local Politics: Impossible Dreams*, Beverly Hills, Sage Publications, 1974.

———. *The Politics of Planning and Development*, Beverly Hills, Sage Publications, 1984.

Checkoway, Barry. "Paul Davidoff and Advocacy Planning in Retrospect," *Journal of the American Planning Association*, Vol. 60, No. 2, Spring 1994.

————. "Political Strategy for Social Planning," in *Strategic Perspectives on Planning Practice*, edited by Barry Checkoway, Lexington, Mass., Lexington Books, 1986.

Christensen, Karen S. "Teaching Savvy," *Journal of Planning Education and Research*, Vol. 12, No. 3, Spring 1993.

Clavel, Pierre. *The Progressive City*, New Brunswick, N.J., Rutgers University Press, 1986.

Dahl, Robert. *Who Governs? Democracy and Power in the American City*, New Haven, Conn., Yale University Press, 1961.

Dahl, Robert A., and Charles E. Lindblom. *Politics, Economics, and Welfare: Planning and Politico-Economic Systems Resolved into Basic Social Processes*, New York, Harper & Row, 1953.

Dalton, Linda C. "Why the Rational Paradigm Persists: The Resistance of Professional Education and Practice to Alternative Forms of Planning," *Journal of Planning Education and Research*, Vol. 5, No. 3, Spring 1986.

Davidoff, Paul. "Advocacy and Pluralism in Planning," *Journal of the American Institute of Planners*, Vol. 31, No. 4, November 1965.

Davidoff, Paul, and Thomas A. Reiner. "A Choice Theory of Planning," *Journal of the American Institute of Planners*, Vol. 28, May 1962.

Davis, Linda L. "Guidelines for Survival and Success," in *Planners on Planning: Leading Planners Offer Real-Life Lessons on What Works, What Doesn't, and Why*, edited by Bruce W. McClendon and Anthony James Catanese, San Francisco, Jossey-Bass Publishers, 1996.

de Neufville, Judith Innes. "Planning Theory and Practice: Bridging the Gap," *Journal of Planning Education and Research*, Vol. 3, No. 1, Summer 1983.

Dror, Yehezkel. *Public Policymaking Reexamined*, San Francisco, Chandler Publishing Company, 1968.

Echeverria, John, and Sharon Dennis. "Takings Policy: Property Rights and Wrongs," *Issues in Science and Technology*, Fall 1993.

Etzioni, Amitai. *The Active Society: A Theory of Societal and Political Processes*, New York, The Free Press, 1968.

————. "Mixed Scanning: A 'Third' Approach to Decision-Making," *Public Administration Review*, Vol. 27, December 1967.

————. *The Spirit of Community: Rights, Responsibilities, and the Communitarian Agenda*, New York, Crown Publishers, 1993.

Fainstein, Norman I., and Susan S. Fainstein. "New Debates in Urban Planning: the Impact of Marxist Theory within the United States," in *Critical Readings in Planning Theory*, edited by Chris Paris, Oxford, Pergamon Press, 1982.

Fainstein, Susan S. "The Politics of Criteria: Planning for the Redevelopment of Times Square," in *Confronting Values in Policy Analysis: The Politics of Criteria*, edited by Frank Fischer and John Forester, Newbury Park, Calif., Sage Publications, 1987.

Ferraro, Giovanni. "Planning As Creative Interpretation," in *Explorations in Planning Theory*, edited by Seymour J. Mandelbaum, Luigi Mazza, and Robert W. Burchell, New Brunswick, N.J., Center for Urban Policy Research, Rutgers University, 1996.

Flyvbjerg, Bent. *Rationality and Power: Democracy in Practice*, Chicago, University of Chicago Press, 1998.

Foglesong, Richard. "Planning for Social Democracy," *Journal of the American Planning Association*, Vol. 56, No. 2, Spring 1990.

Foley, John, and Mickey Lauria. "Plans, Planning and Tragic Choices," Working Paper Number 62, College of Urban and Public Affairs, University of New Orleans, n.d.

Forester, John. "Bridging Interests and Community: Advocacy Planning and the Challenges of Deliberative Democracy," *Journal of the American Planning Association*, Vol. 60, No. 2, Spring 1994.

————. "Critical Theory and Planning Practice," *Journal of the American Planning Association*, Vol. 46, No. 3, July 1980.

————. *Critical Theory, Public Policy, and Planning Practice: Toward a Critical Pragmatism*, Albany, State University of New York Press, 1993.

————. *Planning in the Face of Power*, Berkeley, University of California Press, 1989.

Friedmann, John. "The Public Interest and Community Participation: Toward a Reconstruction of Public Philosophy," *Journal of the American Institute of Planners*, Vol. 39, No. 1, January 1973.

———. "Teaching Planning Theory," *Journal of Planning Education and Research*, Vol. 14, No. 3, Spring 1995.

———. "Toward a Non-Euclidian Mode of Planning," *Journal of the American Planning Association*, Vol. 59, No. 4, Autumn 1993.

Gans, Herbert J. *People and Plans: Essays on Urban Problems and Solutions*, New York, Basic Books, 1968.

Garvin, Alexander. *The American City: What Works, What Doesn't*, New York, McGraw-Hill, 1996.

———. "A Mighty Turnout in Baton Rouge," *Planning*, Vol. 64, No. 10, October 1998.

George, R. Varkki. "Formulating the Right Planning Problem," *Journal of Planning Literature*, Vol. 8, No. 3, February 1994.

Godschalk, David R., and William E. Mills. "A Collaborative Approach to Planning through Urban Activities," *Journal of the American Institute of Planners*, Vol. 32, March 1966.

Gondim, Linda. "Planning Practice within Public Bureaucracy: A New Perspective on Roles of Planners," *Journal of Planning Education and Research*, Vol. 7, No. 3, Spring 1988.

Graivier, Pauline. "How to Speak So People Will Listen," *Planning*, Vol. 58, No. 12, December 1992.

Grant, Jill. *The Drama of Democracy: Contention and Dispute in Community Planning*, Toronto, University of Toronto Press, 1994.

Gross, Bertram M. "The City of Man: A Social Systems Reckoning," in *Environment for Man: The Next Fifty Years*, edited by William R. Ewald Jr., Bloomington, Indiana University Press, 1967.

Hall, Peter. "The Turbulent Eighth Decade: Challenges to American City Planning," *Journal of the American Planning Association*, Vol. 55, No. 3, Summer 1989.

Harper, Thomas L., and Stanley M. Stein. "A Classical Liberal (Libertarian) Approach to Planning Theory," in *Planning Ethics: A Reader in Planning Theory, Practice, and Education*, edited by Sue Hendler, New Brunswick, N.J., Center for Urban Policy Research, Rutgers University, 1995.

Harvey, David. "On Planning the Ideology of Planning," in *Planning Theory in the 1980s: A Search for Future Directions*, edited by Robert W. Burchell and George Sternlieb, New Brunswick, N.J., Center for Urban Policy Research, Rutgers University, 1978.

Hatch, C. Richard. "Some Thoughts on Advocacy Planning," *The Architectural Forum*, Vol. 128, June 1968.

Hayek, F. A. *The Counter-Revolution of Science: Studies on the Abuse of Reason*, New York, The Free Press of Glencoe, 1955.

Hayes, Michael T. *Incrementalism and Public Policy*, New York, Longman, 1992.

Healey, Patsy. "A Planner's Day: Knowledge and Action in Communicative Practice," *Journal of the American Planning Association*, Vol. 58, No. 1, Winter 1992.

Helling, Amy. "Collaborative Visioning: Proceed with Caution! Results from Evaluating Atlanta's Vision 2020 Project," *Journal of the American Planning Association*, Vol. 64, No. 3, Summer 1998.

Hemmens, George. "The Postmodernists Are Coming, the Postmodernists Are Coming," *Planning*, Vol. 58, No. 7, July 1992.

Hendler, Sue. "Feminist Planning Ethics," *Journal of Planning Literature*, Vol. 9, No. 2, November 1994.

Hoch, Charles. *What Planners Do: Power, Politics, and Persuasion*, Chicago, Planners Press, 1994.

Howe, Elizabeth. *Acting on Ethics in City Planning*, New Brunswick, N.J., Center for Urban Policy Research, Rutgers University, 1994.

———. "Normative Ethics in Planning," *Journal of Planning Literature*," Vol. 5, No. 2, November 1990.

———. "Professional Roles and the Public Interest in Planning," *Journal of Planning Literature*, Vol. 6, No. 3, February 1992.

————. "Role Choices for Planners," *Journal of the American Planning Association*, Vol. 46, No. 4, October 1980.

Howe, Elizabeth, and Jerry Kaufman. "The Ethics of Contemporary American Planners," *Journal of the American Planning Association*, Vol. 45, No. 3, July 1979.

Hunter, Floyd. *Community Power Structure: A Study of Decision-Makers*, Chapel Hill, University of North Carolina Press, 1953.

Innes, Judith E. "Challenge and Creativity in Postmodern Planning," *Town Planning Review*, Vol. 69, No. 2, April 1998.

————. "Information in Communicative Planning," *Journal of the American Planning Association*, Vol. 64, No. 1, Winter 1998.

————. "The Planners' Century," *Journal of Planning Education and Research*, Vol. 16, No. 3, Spring 1997.

————. "Planning Theory's Emerging Paradigm: Communicative Action and Interactive Practice," *Journal of Planning Education and Research*, Vol. 14, No. 3, Spring 1995.

————. "Planning through Consensus Building: A New View of the Comprehensive Planning Ideal," *Journal of the American Planning Association*, Vol. 62, No. 4, Autumn 1996.

Innes, Judith E., and David E. Booher. "Consensus Building and Complex Adaptive Systems: A Framework for Evaluating Collaborative Planning," *Journal of the American Planning Association*, Vol. 65, No. 4, Autumn 1999.

Irving, Allan. "The Modern/Postmodern Divide and Urban Planning," *University of Toronto Quarterly*, Vol. 62, No. 4, Summer 1993.

Jacobs, Harvey M. "Contemporary Environmental Philosophy and Its Challenge to Planning Theory," in *Planning Ethics: A Reader in Planning Theory, Practice, and Education*, edited by Sue Hendler, New Brunswick, N.J., Center for Urban Policy Research, Rutgers University, 1995.

Johnson, William C. *Urban Planning and Politics*, Chicago, Planners Press, 1997.

Kaiser, Edward J., and David R. Godschalk. "Twentieth Century Land Use Planning: A Stalwart Family Tree," *Journal of the American Planning Association*, Vol. 61, No. 3, Summer 1995.

Kaplan, Abraham. "Some Limitations on Rationality," in *Nomos VII: Rational Decision*, edited by Carl J. Friedrich, New York, Atherton Press, 1964.

Kaplan, Marshall. "Advocacy and the Urban Poor," *Journal of the American Institute of Planners*, Vol. 35, No. 1, March 1969.

Kaufman, Jerome L. "Making Planners More Effective Strategists," in *Strategic Perspectives on Planning Practice*, edited by Barry Checkoway, Lexington, Mass., Lexington Books, 1986.

Kaufman, Jerome L., and Harvey M. Jacobs. "A Public Planning Perspective on Strategic Planning," *Journal of the American Planning Association*, Vol. 53, No. 1, Winter 1987.

Kennedy, Kevin. Term Paper, Internship Seminar, Department of Urban Studies and Planning, Virginia Commonwealth University, April 2000.

Klein, William R. "Visions of Things to Come," *Planning*, Vol. 60, No. 9, May 1993.

Klosterman, Richard E. "A Public Interest Criterion," *Journal of the American Planning Association*, Vol. 46, No. 3, July 1980.

————. "Arguments for and Against Planning," in *Readings in Planning Theory*, edited by Scott Campbell and Susan S. Fainstein, Cambridge, Mass., Blackwell Publishers, 1996.

Kraushaar, Robert. "Outside the Whale: Progressive Planning and the Dilemmas of Radical Reform," *Journal of the American Planning Association*, Vol. 54, No. 1, Winter 1988.

Krueckeberg, Donald A., ed. *The American Planner: Biographies and Recollections*, New York, Methuen, 1983.

———. *The American Planner: Biographies and Recollections*, 2nd ed., New Brunswick, N.J., Center for Urban Policy Research, Rutgers University, 1994.

———. *Introduction to Planning History in the United States*, New Brunswick, N.J., Center for Urban Policy Research, Rutgers University, 1983.

Krumholz, Norman. "Advocacy Planning: Can It Move the Center?" *Journal of the American Planning Association*, Vol. 60, No. 2, Spring 1994.

———. "A Retrospective View of Equity Planning: Cleveland 1969–1979," *Journal of the American Planning Association*, Vol. 48, No. 2, Spring 1982. Reprinted in *Introduction to Planning History in the United States*, edited by Donald A. Krueckeberg, New Brunswick, N.J., Center for Urban Policy Research, Rutgers University, 1983.

Krumholz, Norman, and John Forester. *Making Equity Planning Work: Leadership in the Public Sector*, Philadelphia, Temple University Press, 1990.

Leach, John. "Seven Steps to Better Writing," *Planning*, Vol. 59, No. 6, June 1993.

Leavitt, Jacqueline. "Feminist Advocacy Planning in the 1980s," in *Strategic Perspectives on Planning Practice*, edited by Barry Checkoway, Lexington, Mass., Lexington Books, 1986.

Lee, Kai N. *Compass and Gyroscope: Integrating Science and Politics for the Environment*, Washington, D.C., Island Press, 1993.

Levy, John M. *Contemporary Urban Planning*, 4th ed., Upper Saddle River, N.J., Prentice-Hall, 1997.

Lewis, Sylvia. "The Town That Said No to Sprawl," *Planning*, Vol. 55, No. 4, April 1990.

Lindblom, Charles E. *The Intelligence of Democracy: Decision Making through Mutual Adjustment*, New York, The Free Press, 1965.

———. "The Science of 'Muddling Through,'" *Public Administration Review*, Vol. 19, Spring 1959.

Lowry, Kem, Peter Adler, and Neal Milner. "Participating the Public: Group Process, Politics, and Planning," *Journal of Planning Education and Research*, Vol. 16, No. 3, Spring 1997.

Lucy, William H. "APA's Ethical Principles Include Simplistic Planning Theories," *Journal of the American Planning Association*, Vol. 54, No. 2, Spring 1988.

Mandelbaum, Seymour. "On Not Doing One's Best: The Uses and Problems of Experimentation in Planning," *Journal of the American Institute of Planners*, Vol. 41, No. 3, May 1975.

Marcuse, Peter. "Professional Ethics and Beyond: Values in Planning," in *Ethics in Planning*, edited by Martin Wachs, New Brunswick, N.J., Center for Urban Policy Research, Rutgers University, 1985.

Marris, Peter. "Advocacy Planning As a Bridge Between the Professional and the Political," *Journal of the American Planning Association*, Vol. 60, No. 2, Spring 1994.

McConnell, Shean. "Rawlsian Planning Theory," in *Planning Ethics: A Reader in Planning Theory, Practice, and Education*, edited by Sue Hendler, New Brunswick, N.J., Center for Urban Policy Research, Rutgers University, 1995.

McDougall, Glen. "The Latitude of Planners," in *Explorations in Planning Theory*, edited by Seymour J. Mandelbaum, Luigi Mazza, and Robert W. Burchell, New Brunswick, N.J., Center for Urban Policy Research, Rutgers University, 1996.

———. "Theory and Practice: A Critique of the Political Economy Approach to Planning," in *Planning Theory: Prospects for the 1980s*, edited by Patsy Healey, Glen McDougall, and Michael J. Thomas, Oxford, Pergamon Press, 1982.

Metzger, John T. "The Theory and Practice of Equity Planning: An Annotated Bibliography," *Journal of Planning Literature*, Vol. 11, No. 1, August 1996.

Meyerson, Martin. "Building the Middle-Range Bridge for Comprehensive Planning," *Journal of the American Institute of Planners*, Vol. 22, No. 2, Spring 1956.

Meyerson, Martin, and Edward G. Banfield. *Politics, Planning and the Public Interest*, Glencoe, Ill., The Free Press, 1955.

Milroy, Beth Moore. "Into Postmodern Weightlessness," *Journal of Planning Education and Research*, Vol. 10, No. 3, Summer 1991.

Moore, Terry. "Planning without Preliminaries," *Journal of the American Planning Association*, Vol. 54, No. 4, Autumn 1988.

———. "Why Allow Planners to Do What They Do? A Justification from Economic Theory," *Journal of the American Institute of Planners*, Vol. 44, No. 4, October 1978.

Myers, Dowell, et al. "Anchor Points for Planning's Identification," *Journal of Planning Education and Research*, Vol. 16, No. 3, Spring 1997.

Neuman, Michael. "Planning, Governing, and the Image of the City," *Journal of Planning Education and Research*, Vol. 18, No. 1, Fall 1998.

Ozawa, Connie P., and Ethan P. Seltzer. "Taking Our Bearings: Mapping a Relationship among Planning Practice, Theory, and Education," *Journal of Planning Education and Research*, Vol. 18, No. 3, Spring 1999.

Patton, Carl. "Citizen Input and Professional Responsibility," *Journal of Planning Education and Research*, Vol. 3, No. 1, Summer 1983.

Rabinovitz, Francine. *City Politics and Planning*, New York, Atherton Press, 1969.

Rawls, John. *A Theory of Justice*, Cambridge, Mass., Harvard University Press, 1971.

Rittel, Horst W. J., and Melvin M. Webber. "Dilemmas in a General Theory of Planning," *Policy Sciences*, Vol. 4, 1973.

Rodriguez, Sergio. "How to Become a Successful Planner," in *Planners on Planning: Leading Planners Offer Real-Life Lessons on What Works, What Doesn't, and Why*, edited by Bruce W.

McClendon and Anthony James Catanese, San Francisco, Jossey-Bass Publishers, 1996.

Rondinelli, Dennis A. "Urban Planning as Policy Analysis: Management of Urban Change," *Journal of the American Institute of Planners*, Vol. 39, No. 1, January 1973.

Sandercock, Leonie. "Voices from the Borderlands: A Meditation on a Metaphor," *Journal of Planning Education and Research*, Vol. 14, No. 2, Winter 1995.

Sandercock, Leonie, and Ann Forsyth. "A Gender Agenda: New Directions for Planning Theory," *Journal of the American Planning Association*, Vol. 58, No. 1, Winter 1992.

Scott, A. J., and S. T. Roweis. "Urban Planning in Theory and Practice: A Reappraisal," *Environment and Planning A*, Vol. 9, No. 10, October 1977.

Scott, Mel. *American City Planning Since 1890*, Berkeley, University of California Press, 1971.

Simon, Herbert A. *Administrative Behavior*, 2nd ed., New York, The Macmillan Company, 1957.

———. *Models of Man*, New York, John Wiley & Sons, 1957.

Skjei, Stephen S. "Urban Problems and the Theoretical Justification of Urban Planning," *Urban Affairs Quarterly*, Vol. 11, No. 3, March 1976.

Starr, Roger. "Advocators or Planners?" *ASPO Newsletter*, Vol. 33, December 1967.

———. "Pomeroy Memorial Lecture: The People Are Not the City," *Planning 1966*, Selected Papers from the ASPO National Planning Conference, Philadelphia, Pennsylvania, April 17–21, 1966, Chicago, American Society of Planning Officials, 1966.

Stollman, Israel. "The Values of the City Planner," in *The Practice of Local Government Planning*, edited by Frank So, Israel Stollman, and Frank Beal, Washington D.C., International City Management Association, 1979.

Strong, Ann Louise, Daniel R. Mandelker, and Eric Damian Kelly. "Property Rights and Takings," *Journal of the*

American Planning Association, Vol. 62, No. 1, Winter 1996.

Susskind, Lawrence, and Connie Ozawa. "Mediated Negotiation in the Public Sector: The Planner As Mediator," *Journal of Planning Education and Research*, Vol. 4, No. 1, August 1984.

Susskind, Lawrence E., Sarah McKearnan, and Jennifer Thomas-Larmer, eds. *The Consensus Building Handbook: A Comprehensive Guide to Reaching Agreement*, Thousand Oaks, Calif., Sage Publications, 1999.

Talen, Emily. "After the Plans: Methods to Evaluate the Implementation Success of Plans," *Journal of Planning Education and Research*, Vol. 16, No. 2, Winter 1996.

Taylor, Nigel. "Mistaken Interests and the Discourse Model of Planning," *Journal of the American Planning Association*, Vol. 64, No. 1, Winter 1998.

———. *Urban Planning Theory Since 1945*, London, Sage Publications, 1998.

Tennenbaum, Robert. "Hail, Columbia," *Planning*, Vol. 56, No. 5, May 1990.

Throgmorton, James. "Learning through Conflict at Oxford," *Journal of Planning Education and Research*, Vol. 18, No. 3, Spring 1999.

Tibbetts, John. "Everybody's Taking the Fifth," *Planning*, Vol. 61, No. 1, January 1995.

Turow, Scott. "Law School v. Reality," *New York Times Magazine*, September 18, 1988.

Verma, Niraj. "Pragmatic Rationality and Planning Theory," *Journal of Planning Education and Research*, Vol. 16, No. 1, Fall 1996.

von Mises, Ludwig. *Omnipotent Government*, New Haven, Conn., Yale University Press, 1944.

Wachs, Martin, ed. *Ethics in Planning*, New Brunswick, N.J., Center for Urban Policy Research, Rutgers University, 1985.

———. "When Planners Lie with Numbers," *Journal of the American Planning Association*, Vol. 55, No. 4, Autumn 1989.

Wegener, Michael. "Operational Urban Models: State of the Art," *Journal of the American Planning Association*, Vol. 60, No. 1, Winter 1994.

Weiss, Andrew, and Edward Woodhouse. "Reframing Incrementalism: A Constructive Response to the Critics," *Policy Sciences*, Vol. 25, No. 3, August 1992.

Whyte, William H. *City: Rediscovering the Center*, New York, Doubleday, 1988.

Wildavsky, Aaron. "If Planning Is Everything, Maybe It's Nothing," *Policy Sciences*, Vol. 4, 1973.

Yiftachel, Oren. "Planning and Social Control: Exploring the Dark Side," *Journal of Planning Literature*, Vol. 12, No. 4, May 1998.

———. "Planning Theory at a Crossroad: The Third Oxford Conference," *Journal of Planning Education and Research*, Vol. 18, No. 3, Spring 1999.

Young, Robert. "Goals and Goal-Setting," *Journal of the American Institute of Planners*, Vol. 2, March 1966.

Zeckhauser, Richard, and Elmer Schaefer. "Public Policy and Normative Economic Theory," in *The Study of Policy Formation*, edited by Raymond A. Bauer and Kenneth J. Gergen, New York, The Free Press, 1968.

Zotti, Ed. "New Angles on Citizen Participation," *Planning*, Vol. 57, No. 1, January 1991.

Index

A

Advocacy, 177
Advocacy planner, 141
Advocacy planning, 107–14, 137
    central themes of, 107–8
    current status of, 114–17
Advocate Planners' National
    Advisory Committee, 112–13
Alexander, Ernest, 83–84, 92
American Institute of Certified
    Planners (AICP), 68
        Code of Ethics and
        Professional Conduct,
        72, 74–75
American Institute of Planners
    (AIP), 27, 68
American Planning Association
    (APA), 27
American Society of Planning
    Officials, 70
Anti-rationality argument, 91
Arrow, Kenneth, 56–57, 85
Association of Collegiate Schools of
    Planning (ACSP), 11, 26–27
Attitude evaluation, 159
Attitude surveys, 151

B

Banfield, Edward C., 83, 86, 143
Baum, Howell, 18, 92
Baumol, William, 54–55
Bayne, Patricia, 140
Beauregard, Robert, 21, 26
Bentham, Jeremy, 64–65
Benveniste, Guy, 188–89
Bergson, Abram, 55–56, 58
Berra, Yogi, 202

Black, Alan, 88
Bolan, Richard, 76, 113, 197
Boles, Gene, 187
Bounded rationality, 84–85, 97
Braybrooke, David, 99
Bryson, John, 87
Budgeting, zero–based, 87
Burnham, Daniel, 198

C

Capitalist democracy, 12
Centralized non-rationality, 97–105
Centralized rationality, 81–95
Checkoway, Barry, 108, 188
Choice theory, 110–11
Christensen, Karen S., 188
Citizen participation, 13, 146–47
Classical economics, 82, 97–99
Collaborative planning, 150–51
Communication skills, 190–92
Communicative action theory,
    121–23, 137
        current status of, 125–31
        implications for practice,
        123–25
Communitarianism, 65
Conflict, 72
Consensus building, 124–25, 128,
    129, 131
Cost-benefit analysis, 66, 87
Creative trial ballooning, benefits
    of, 153–55
Cultural dimension of planning, 42

D

Dahl, Robert, 84–85, 99
Dalton, Linda, 92–93

Davidoff, Paul, 108–17, 137
Davis, Linda, 58, 188–89
Decentralized non-rationality, 119–31
Decentralized rationality, 107–17
Dennis, Sharon, 46
Dimensions of planning control, 42–43
Disjointed incrementalism, 99
Dror, Yehezkel, 103
Duany, Andres, 121

E
Echeverria, John, 46
Eminent domain, 44
Equity planning, 53, 115–16
Ethical dilemma, 68
  typology of, in planning practice, 70–72
Ethical normative theory, 22, 23–24
Ethics, 67–72
  macro, 69
  micro, 68
  situational, 69–70
Etzioni, Amitai, 65, 104–5, 140–41
Evaluation, 178–79
  attitude, 159
  impact, 159

F
Facilitation skills, 125
Facilitator, role of, 125
Fainstein, Norman, 40
Fainstein, Susan, 40
Feedback, critical role of, 144–45
Feedback strategy
  considering alternatives, 166–68
  defining problem operationally, 161–66
  designing and implementing experiment, 170–71
  evaluating, 171–72
  making disposing decision, 172–75
  making preliminary choice,

168–70
  potential shortcomings of, 178–81
  of public planning, 158–81
  relationship to other paradigms, 176–78
Flyvbjerg, Bent, 91–94, 125
Focus groups, 151–52
Foglesong, Richard, 41
Forester, John, 21, 122–24, 136, 187, 190
Fourteenth Amendment, 44
Friedmann, John, 41, 63–64, 66
Functional normative theory, 22, 24

G
Garvin, Alexander, 15
Geddes, Patrick, 198
Goal formulation, 145–53
Godschalk, David, 150–51
Gondim, Linda, 193
Grant, Jill, 30
Grass-roots activism, 147

H
Habermas, Jurgen, 122
Harper, Thomas, 64–65
Harvey, David, 40
Hemmens, George, 119–20
Hoch, Charles, 16
Howard, Ebenezer, 198
Howe, Elizabeth, 16, 53–54, 58

I
Idea generation, 139–44
Impact evaluation, 159
Impossibility theorem, 56–57
Incrementalism, 99–101, 137, 177
  current status of, 101–5
  disjointed, 99
Information
  accuracy and integrity of, 71
  control and release of, 71
Innes, Judith, 29, 120, 124–26, 129–30
Issue advocacy, 116

J

Jacobs, Allan, 197

*Journal of Planning Education and
    Research*, 27–28

Journal of Planning Literature, 27–28

*Journal of the American Planning
    Association* (JAPA), 28

Justice, 65

K

Kaldor, Nicholas, 55

Kaplan, Marshall, 110

Kaufman, Jerome, 16

Kennedy, Kevin, 202

Klosterman, Richard, 50–53, 57–58

Krueckeberg, Donald, 197

Krumholz, Norman, 53, 65, 115,
    187, 190, 197

L

Lamont, Bill, 202

Levy, John, 45, 185

Lewis, Sylvia, 202

Libertarianism, 65

Lindblom, Charles, 84–85, 99–104,
    137, 139–40

Loyalty, 70–71

M

MacKaye, Benton, 198

Macro ethical issues, 69

Management by objectives, 87

Marcuse, Peter, 69

Market behavior, analysis of,
    152–53

Marris, Peter, 116, 192

McDougall, Glen, 179–80

Mediated negotiation, 123–24, 128,
    129, 131

Metzger, John T., 115–16

Meyerson, Martin, 83

Micro ethical issues, 68

Mills, William, 150–51

Mission statement, 89

Mixed scanning, 104–5

Moore, Terry, 51–52, 154

Moses, Robert, 198

Mumford, Lewis, 198

N

Negotiation, 192

    mediated, 123–24, 129

Neuman, Michael, 129

Normative theory, 22

    ethical, 22, 23–24

    functional, 22, 24

O

Olmsted, Frederick Law, 198

Opinion surveys, 151

Ozawa, Connie, 122

P

Pareto, Vilfredo, 54–55

Patton, Carl, 146

People advocacy, 116

Planners

    as applied scientist, 81–95

    habits of effective, 160–61

Planning, 27

    as alive and well, 47

    defined, 9

    dilemmas in, 73

    dimensions of control in,
        42–43

    generic themes character-
        izing, 11

    as impossible, 37–39

    as impotent, 39–42

    as malevolent, 42–43

    as perilous, 36–37

    political power and, 13–19

    "pooper scooper" theory of,
        52–53

    as profession, 10

    rational, 87–89, 137–38, 176

    relationship between politics
        and, 5

research on, 23
as social experimentation, 158–60
source of ideas, 139–44
as unconstitutional, 43–47
uses of theory in, 21–25
Planning practice
gap between planning theory and, 25–28, 41, 129–30
relationship between planning theory and, 5
typology of ethical dilemmas in, 70–72
Planning–programming-budgeting systems, 87
Planning theory, 21–25
current, 28–31
gap between planning practice and, 25–28, 41, 129–30, 130
postmodern, 29–30
relationship between planning practice and, 5
Political power, planning and, 13–19
Political processes, 153
Political savvy, 185–87
elements of, 188–93
Politics, relationship between planning and, 5
Positive theory-building, 22–23
Postmodernism, 29–30, 119–21
Power relationships, 91, 192–93
Pragmatic rationality, 82–84
Private planning, 36
Private property rights, balance between public interests and, 46–47
Procedural dimension of planning, 42
Property-rights movement, 46–47
Public goods, characteristics of, 51–52
Public interests, 53–59, 185

balance between private property rights and, 46–47
Public planning, 9–13, 36
feedback strategy of, 158–81
normative foundation of, 64
rationales for, 50–60
Pure rationality, 82

R
Rabinovitz, Francine, 12
Radical reform, distinguishing between social reform and, 41–42
Rationality, 111, 137
bounded, 84–85
impossibility of pure, 97
nature of, 81–87
pragmatic, 82–84
pure, 82
Rationality-based planning, 137–38, 176
strategies in, 87–89
Rationality concept, current status of, 91–95
Rational model of planning, 24, 28–29
Rational planning, 88
Rawls, John, 65, 109
Reengineering, 87
Referenda, 153
Reiner, Thomas A., 110
Reinvention, 87
Rittel, Horst, 12

S
Satisficing, 97–99, 139–40
Seltzer, Ethan, 122
Shortcuts, 72
Simon, Herbert, 84, 97–99, 103, 139
Single-issue politics, growth of, 201
Situational ethics, 69–70
Social experimentation, planning as, 158–60, 176
Social planning movement, 111

Social reform, distinguishing
between radical reform and,
41–42
Socioeconomic dimension of
planning, 42
Starr, Roger, 113
Stein, Stanley, 64–65
Stollman, Israel, 57, 63, 66
Strategic planning, 89–91
SWOT analysis, 89, 90

T
Takings clause of Fifth
Amendment, 44
Taylor, Nigel, 15, 25–26, 66, 74, 91,
100, 122, 192
Territorial dimension of
planning, 42
Theory-practice gap, 41, 129–30
existence of, 25–28
Throgmorton, James, 126
Tibbetts, John, 46
Timing, sense of, 189–90
Total quality management, 87
Trial ballooning, benefits of, 153–55
Tugwell, Rexford Guy, 198
Turow, Scott, 26

U
Utilitarianism, 64–65

V
Value judgments, 55–56

Values, 60, 62–67, 117, 193
defined, 62
professional, 63–64
Verma, Niraj, 82
Village of Euclid v. Ambler Realty Co.
case, 45–46
Vision, 193
importance of, 196–201
Visionary, skills of, 201–2

W
Wachs, Martin, 71
Webber, Melvin, 12
Wegener, Michael, 87–88
Whyte, William H., 103, 159
Wicked problems, 12
Wildavsky, Aaron, 37–38
Wise use movement, 46
Workable goals, formulating,
145–53

Y
Yiftachel, Oren, 42–43, 126
Young, Robert, 147

Z
Zero-base budgeting, 87
Zoning
constitutionality of, 45–46
legitimacy of, 45–46
Zotti, Ed, 151–52